Gospel Light's

CHILDREN'S MINISTRY
SMART PAGES

First Aid Kit

Young Explorer's Bible

GLUE

Gospel Light

HOW TO MAKE CLEAN COPIES FROM THIS BOOK

You may make copies of portions of this book with a clean conscience if

- you (or someone in your organization) are the original purchaser;

- you are using the copies you make for a noncommercial purpose (such as teaching or promoting your ministry) within your church or organization;

- you follow the instructions provided in this book.

However, it is ILLEGAL for you to make copies if

- you are using the material to promote, advertise or sell a product or service other than for ministry fund-raising;

- you are using the material in or on a product for sale; or

- you or your organization are not the original purchaser of this book.

By following these guidelines you help us keep our products affordable.

Thank you,

Gospel Light

NOTE

Editorial Staff

Founder, Dr. Henrietta Mears • **Publisher Emeritus,** William T. Greig • **Publisher, Children's Curriculum and Resources,** Bill Greig III • **Senior Consulting Publisher,** Dr. Elmer L. Towns • **Product Line Manager,** Cary Maxon • **Senior Managing Editor,** Sheryl Haystead • **Senior Consulting Editor,** Wesley Haystead, M.S.Ed. • **Senior Editor, Biblical and Theological Issues,** Bayard Taylor, M.Div. • **Editorial Team,** Sally Carpenter, M.Div., Mary Davis • **Contributing Editors,** Michelle Anthony, Debbie Barber, Suzanne Bass, Debbie and Mike Broyles, Joe Cox, Richard Lukas, Arlonne Monroe • **Art Director,** Lenndy McCullough, • **Designer,** Zelle Olson

Contents

OPEN UP YOUR HEART TO A CHILD'S LOVE!

Ready or not, the class begins when the first child arrives.

A Place Where God Is at Work

Organizing Your Children's Ministry

Whether you are ready to frame a new ministry or reframe and refurbish an existing one, here are ideas to get you excited and help you get off the ground! This is your opportunity to dream, pray and plan for a ministry in which things are so well organized that time and energy are still available for you to focus on the work God wants to do in young lives!

This practical information includes considering the reasons you minister to children, the reasons to write a mission statement and ways to reach your stated goals, how to assess what your children are learning, how to recruit and publicize your ministry and how to best understand the people you recruit so that they can be trained to fill the place God has planned for each one.

Organization may not seem like the most enjoyable part of ministry! But to face it with zeal, remember the benefits of the process: Good organization encourages efficient administration. Efficient administration provides you and your teachers with more time and energy to give to the most important parts of children's ministry! Every moment you gain can be spent praying for, learning, loving, teaching, encouraging, helping and mentoring individual children. These moments are what God uses to build a ministry that is effective in leading children to become wholehearted followers of Jesus Christ!

WHY DO WE NEED CHILDREN'S MINISTRY?

If you are reading these words, it is probably because you are involved in children's ministry at your church, either as a paid staff member or as a volunteer. That probably means you care about children, about their families, about your church and about God's purposes here on Earth. Hurray! We're off to a great start. Even if you don't fit the above profile, keep reading anyway: You may discover that you, too, were meant for children's ministry!

We need children's ministry because children matter to God.

Jesus made it quite clear that children—even little children who are not yet articulate—matter to God. He values them not only for what they will become in the future but also for who they are today! Jesus even recommended to His grown-up, self-important disciples that to understand God's kingdom, they needed to observe, learn from and imitate young children! (For further study, read Mark 10:13-16.)

We need children's ministry because children need to learn about God.

We all agree that children need to learn about God: That's the stated purpose of children's ministry! However, for children to learn about God effectively, they may not necessarily need more information or newer programs. The most effective way for any child to learn about God is through the attitudes and actions of a person who is willing to live out the Christian life before him or her. For every child—from an infant to the oldest child in your ministry—a relationship with a living, breathing Christian who cares about him or her is the cornerstone of learning about God.

Even in the best children's ministries, there may be an unspoken agreement that the main purpose of a children's program is to keep children happy, quiet and far from the adults so that adults can do the truly important things like worship and Bible study. But this view of both children and of ministry to them yields a manager's mind-set rather than a minister's mind-set. As managers, we see a group to be managed through entertainment ("As long as they're having fun!") or pacification ("At least they're quiet!"). With a manager's mind-set, a session is considered successful if no one got hurt, if all the adults were left undistracted and if the children went away reasonably happy. This is child care, not children's ministry. While good child care is a fine thing, it is only a small part of ministry to children!

When we (and those who teach) choose a minister's mind-set, we ask God to help us see each child as an individual with whom to build a relationship. As we take time to build loving relationships, children (and their parents) come to see, hear and experience how the love of God through Jesus Christ looks, sounds and behaves! A minister's mind-set causes us to truly hear,

see and love each child with the purpose of building a relationship that shows that child who Jesus is.

We need children's ministry because it's biblical.

Consider these words from Psalms: "We will tell the next generation the praiseworthy deeds of the Lord, his power, and the wonders he has done" (Psalm 78:4). The very foundation for our ministry to children is girded with declarations such as these from God's Word. Best of all, Psalm 78 goes on to describe the amazing result we can expect from teaching children about the Lord: "Then they would put their trust in God and would not forget his deeds but would keep his commands" (Psalm 78:7). When we give our utmost attention and best effort to children's ministry, we are fulfilling the vision set forth in the Bible for teaching the faith.

We need children's ministry because it provides for the future.

Imagine your church's future if for the next 10 years, a group of adults would commit themselves to fostering the *spiritual* growth and well-being of the children in your congregation? What would your church be like if reaching children in your community became one of its major priorities? The future is as bright as God's power and as sure as His promises. To most effectively reshape society, children are the ones with whom to begin.

We need children's ministry because it's the best investment we can make.

Between the ages of 5 and 12, there is a 32 percent probability that a person will embrace Jesus as his or her Savior—and the percentage drops off dramatically thereafter. Researcher George Barna remarks, "In other words, if people do not embrace Jesus Christ as their Savior before they reach their teenage years, the chance of their doing so at all is slim."[1] Thus, in terms of financial and time investment, children's ministry creates the highest spiritual yield of any age group! The lifetime impact of children's ministry is immeasurable. A strong children's ministry not only gives a great return today, fueling and strengthening the entire church body but also yields a brighter future for every area of a church's ministry.

A strong children's program also grows a church from the outside, bringing in new families who did not previously attend church. The majority of families who become part of the church from outside it say they connected mainly because of the way their children were loved and cared for by the leaders and teachers in children's ministry. Beyond that, children who are growing and learning are the most effective means of inviting other children who then come to know Christ and take the good news back to their own families!

Note

1. George Barna, *Transforming Children into Spiritual Champions* (Ventura, CA: Regal Books, 2003), p. 34.

HOW CAN WE CONCISELY COMMUNICATE OUR IDENTITY AND GOALS?

WHY WRITE A MISSION STATEMENT?

In the every-week flurry of any children's ministry, there are needs to be met, supplies to be bought, problems to be solved and children to be loved. It may not seem as if there is any time to actually *think* about the big picture of the purpose for which your children's ministry exists! However, creating a mission statement can help to build and keep a ministry in top form.

A mission statement provides direction. This old adage is a wise one: "If you aim at nothing, you're likely to hit it." Without a destination, we don't know where we are going; without a goal, we won't even be able to tell if we have lost our way! To help a ministry understand its goals and think about ways to become more intentional, a mission statement is a valuable tool.

A mission statement is a survival tool. A mission statement can help with individual survival for the children's leader who may feel overwhelmed and overworked. To increase hope and mental health during tough times, a stated mission can be a lifesaver!

HOW TO WRITE A MISSION STATEMENT?

Set aside a time first for yourself and then for key members of your team to consider the big picture of your children's ministry. The process requires time and a willingness to focus. Begin with prayer. Invite God to direct your thoughts as you brainstorm answers to the following:

★ What are the reasons we want to minister to children?

★ What could God do through this ministry?

★ What is our overall goal?

★ What steps do we need to take to reach this goal?

★ What priorities will help us stay focused on reaching our goal?

Write down any and all ideas. After a time of prayer, refine the ideas into words that clearly and concisely convey what you mean. If your church has its own mission statement, craft your ministry's statement to line up under the mission of the church. The development of your statement should be an outgrowth in support of the overall direction of your church body.

Write your statement in a few clearly-stated sentences. They (like road signs) will help you stay informed and focused as you keep moving down the path toward the goal. (Avoid Christian jargon. Express your mission statement in words any unchurched person can understand!)

When you ask God for a view of what He could do in the future with your ministry, you get a sense of His destination for you. As you formulate a mission statement, you gain clearer understanding of what it will take to press on toward that future.

WHAT WILL A MISSION STATEMENT DO FOR US?

The exercise of formulating a mission statement will produce far more than a nicely worded catchphrase or even a well-constructed theological document: These words will become tools by which to evaluate your motives, your programs, and even your disasters, so that you don't lose focus on what is most important! This process will also help you discover the characteristics that make your children's ministry unique. Incorporate those characteristics into your thinking to consider unusual ways God could use your ministry. As each person contributes to the process, you'll find team unity increasing. This statement is a clear expression of what your children's ministry is, made unique by the gifts of each member of your team!

Here are samples of mission statements from a variety of children's ministries:

★ To be a Bible-based, functioning community of believers who actively teach and model for children how to become committed followers of Christ.

★ To partner with families as they lead children to know God personally through Jesus Christ, to mature in the character and likeness of Christ and to put their faith into practice for all of their lives.

★ To lead children into knowing Christ and then to help them mature in following Christ.

★ To reach and teach children and their families in ways that will give them the greatest possible opportunity to become wholehearted followers of Jesus Christ.

★ To change the lives of children by connecting them to Christ through worship, fellowship, discipleship and outreach.

★ To express Christ's compassion for children and families by loving them and nurturing them in their journey to follow Him.

★ To help families and children to KNOW Jesus Christ as Savior and Lord, to GROW in their faith as followers of Jesus and to GO out into the world to represent Him.

Use your mission statement when meeting with your church board and your pastor to help clarify your purpose and the plans to accomplish it. Post the mission statement where you and your staff see it often, so that it may be used as a tool to evaluate what goes on. Help everyone recognize that the mission statement is designed to clarify God's mandate for your children's ministry. (For more on uses of mission statements, see the article on recruiting and publicity on p. 11.)

HOW DOES THE MISSION GET ACCOMPLISHED?

Once your mission statement is in place, help your staff begin to list measurable ways to know if the mission is being fulfilled. (To help teachers think about how to determine if your mission is being accomplished, encourage them to notice the way in which the purpose of a lesson in curriculum is accomplished through measurable goals.)

For instance, your mission statement may refer to equipping families to lead their children to Christ. Teachers might then measure their accomplishment of the mission by evaluating themselves by the following standards: knowing every child's family, having family contact information at hand, sending home family growth ideas once a month and helping with two informal parenting classes yearly.

When teachers and helpers catch the vision of what God can do and then take responsibility for accomplishing some part of that mission in a way unique to the skills God has given each person, the mission of your children's ministry will skyrocket toward accomplishment!

HOW DO YOU GET THEM? HOW DO YOU KEEP THEM?

Keeping a positive attitude about recruiting and publicity can be a challenge! Children's ministry may not seem to be a top priority in the congregation. Adults may feel that they are too busy or have already done their time in teaching children. Potential recruits can seem scarce. However, it is essential to think of recruiting and publicity not as the incessant beating of the drum of desperation but rather as a chance to trumpet the great accomplishments of God in your community! (After all, when our attitudes change, so change the attitudes of others!)

Here are seven suggested strategies:

Strategy 1: Formulate an identity. Create a simple mission statement for your children's ministry (see pp. 9-10). Give your children's ministry a name (Kids' Connection, The Ark, etc.). Make a logo. (If you are not the creative type, assign logo creation to an able volunteer—or have a contest!) A logo need not be fancy or expensive. The art may come from the kids themselves. But it needs to be something you are eager to use. Put the name, logo and mission statement of your ministry on every pillar and post, on the walls of the building, on every piece of paper you send out, on T-shirts . . . you get the idea. Creating an identity and stating a mission tells the children they are important and tells the adults that you are serious about what you are doing, which in turn creates awareness and excitement! When your church members are aware of and excited about what God is doing through your church's children's ministry, their eagerness to join ranks will increase as you sound the trumpet for volunteers who want to be part of God's great accomplishments. (It works far better in the long run than being dragged in by the pounding drums of desperation!)

Strategy 2: Keep publicity ongoing. Publicize the accomplishments and joys of your church's children's ministry throughout the year. On a regular basis, enthusiastically present to your congregation information about the goals and benefits of and opportunities for ministry with children. This keeps familiarity high; people rarely commit to work in a program with which they are not familiar. Consider scheduling one of these publicity ideas every month or two throughout the year:

★ Display photos of children and teachers from a recent event in newsletters or on bulletin boards. (Use close-ups so that people can actually see the children's faces without coming nose to nose with the bulletin board!)

★ Solicit short articles from teachers or parents about their recent experiences in a children's program. (Funny, to-the-point articles stick in people's memories!) Publish the articles in church newsletters or on the church website.

★ Invite a teacher from a children's ministry program to be interviewed in adult Bible study groups or Sunday School classes. If possible, look for ways to connect this teacher's experience to the current topic of study in the class (i.e., talk about the importance of children to a class that is focusing on the Body of Christ).

★ Attractively display children's art in well-traveled areas of your facility. Enlist children to help create bulletin board displays about their learning.

★ Interview several children about aspects of their experience in children's ministry programs. Ask open-ended questions such as, "What would you tell people is best about (name of children's program)?" or "Who do you look forward to seeing when you come to (program name)?" Place children's quotations in a newsletter article or display them on a bulletin board.

★ Put brief articles in newsletters about the value of one aspect of Christian education. Add several specific prayer requests for the children's ministry and an invitation to pray.

The major benefit of these publicity ideas comes when you use them all year long—not just during times when you are actively recruiting people to serve.

Strategy 3: Keep the potential staff list updated. Continually work to identify potential staff for your programs with the major goal being to help people find fulfilling places of ministry. Avoid the trap of recruiting volunteers only when you face a vacancy! Consistently seeking to discover people with the potential for ministry gives you the chance to focus on finding the position that fits the person and his or her gifts, rather than desperately grabbing any live body that might be willing to fill a vacant spot. The ultimate goal is to recruit people to the position to which God has called them.

Consider everyone in your congregation as potential participants in children's ministry. Don't look only to the parents of children in your programs. Use the church membership list, new members' classes, adult class lists, suggestions from adult teachers or leaders, lists of previous teachers and survey forms. Consider men, singles, seniors and collegians. Get recommendations from present teachers. Look for people whom you have observed interacting in positive ways with children. Work with your church's youth leadership to plan ways to involve teens in ministry without isolating them from youth programs and leaders. (You may want to limit your use of teens to class times when teen groups are not meeting.)

Consider also how you might involve what might seem like unlikely groups in children's ministry. The men's sports ministry group or the senior's sewing group can be challenged to do some short-term missions to your church's own children or to children in the neighborhood! The men might sponsor and staff a one-day sports camp while the senior's sewing group might help an elementary choir program by teaching and helping children sew simple costumes for productions. Short-term assignments like these help people know the children as individuals, grow their excitement about children's ministry and use their unique gifts and skills.

OPEN UP YOUR HEART TO A CHILD'S LOVE!

Strategy 4: Keep others involved in recruiting. Ask others to help you in your recruiting effort. The total church staff needs to share the concern for recruitment. The pastor, Christian education board, children's ministry coordinators, teachers and helpers must support, encourage and, above all, pray for potential teachers. If recruiting is the responsibility of only two or three people, those people will become overworked and discouraged—and recruitment prospects become limited to the friends and acquaintances of these few people. (Often, the friends and acquaintances of these few then try to avoid them as well!)

Involving many people in recruiting does not mean everyone is trying to sign up new teachers. Rather, everyone on the staff must be informed of recruiting needs and praying regularly that the needs will be met. The goal for involvement in recruiting is to be intentional about mentioning children's ministry opportunities, to be aware of others' potential and to be willing to help where appropriate in the recruiting process. Also ask several people to join you on a prayer team that specifically prays for your recruiting efforts and potential volunteers.

In a large church, it is often helpful to have a committee that is responsible for the various steps in effective recruiting. Form a new committee at least once a year. Invite to the committee people who know a wide variety of members in the congregation and who also have skills in different areas: teacher appreciation, new teacher orientation, personal contact, etc.

Strategy 5: Keep contacting potential staff. After your list is made, prayerfully prioritize it. Of all the people who could possibly be contacted, who should be approached first? Determine any requirements a person must meet in order to be considered. Involve responsible leaders in your church when evaluating or approving those to be contacted. Your church may have established guidelines for volunteers (length of church attendance or membership, etc.).

Then personally contact each prospective teacher or helper by phone or by mail. People who are recruited in the halls or parking lots of a church may feel as though desperation was the motivation. Both they and the job will seem to be of less-than-crucial importance. If you choose to send a form letter to prospects, add a personal note to the letter. Do not depend on recruiting announcements in church bulletins or newsletters—they are often the least effective means of recruiting! It's best to personally recruit from a pool of people who have been recommended to you or who have demonstrated the characteristics you're looking for in teachers and helpers.

Next schedule a personal meeting that allows an unhurried period of time in which you and the prospect can get better acquainted, answer each other's questions and clarify information as needed. If the initial contact is by mail, follow up the letter with a phone call. Never underestimate the importance of personal contact or expect that people will join your staff simply because they received a letter in the mail. Make a job description available to each prospect for the position you are asking that person to fill (see sample job descriptions on pp. 47-55).

When a large number of teaching positions need to be filled, consider setting up a recruiting station! Place in a well-traveled area of your church a display with a large, attractive poster, a video, a PowerPoint presentation or photographic display that will bring attention to the program for which you are recruiting. If you want to display a list of jobs to be filled, be sure to show that some positions are already filled. (No one wants to be the first to sign up!)

Strategy 6: Keep potential volunteers on your side. When you have talked with a prospective teacher or helper and answered questions, offer a time of observation in the appropriate program. Then encourage him or her to prayerfully consider this opportunity. Agree on a date by which the decision will be made, usually about a week. If the answer is yes, be ready to offer orientation and training to help the new staff member make a good beginning. If the answer is no, thank the prospect for taking the time to consider the ministry. Invite that person to please pray for the children's ministry since he or she is now more familiar with its programs. Don't pressure; avoid guilt and that person will likely become an enthusiastic volunteer when the time is right!

Strategy 7: Place a high value on commitment. When a volunteer has applied and been screened, be sure he or she receives both a job description (see pp. 47-55 for job descriptions) and a commitment form (see p. 63). This will help each volunteer know what is expected and will invest each one with a sense of the importance and value of the commitment he or she is making. Communicate with volunteers how the church will support them in their ministry to children (resources, facilities, curriculum, etc.). Consider inviting new teachers to stand during a worship service so that the pastor may pray and commission them in their new ministry. As your church family shows they value children's ministry, volunteers will increase and flourish!

Learning for Life Be a Teacher

Many church websites highlight the ministries and activities of the congregation. Often, there is a page available for the children's ministry. This page can be one of your biggest allies in publicity, recruiting and community outreach! Whether your web designer is a 15-year-old or a paid professional, consider the following before you get started:

● The people you want to reach (church family, prospective families, potential volunteers, grandparents, current volunteers, families of the church's preschool, etc.).

● The mission statement and goals of your ministry. (Include the logo!)

● The programs you offer. Include every weekend, midweek and weekday programs that new families might not realize are available. Include programs such as sign language classes or classes especially designed for children with disabilities as well. Regularly update information about availability and openings for camps or special events, registration deadlines, application forms, etc.

● The curriculum you use. For every age level, link a page containing the scope and sequence for the course. (If you use several curricula for one age level, be sure to list which curriculum is used during which service time.)

● A volunteer link to a page that provides application forms for prospective volunteers and that outlines general requirements, the process for volunteer application and current job descriptions (include recruiter contact information for each program or job description). To increase volunteer interest, invite potential volunteers to subscribe to a free children's ministry e-newsletter.

● A new child enrollment link that provides class times, program schedules, enrollment procedures and downloadable forms to enroll a child in a program (include family information forms, medical alert forms, activity permissions forms, etc.).

Include a link and encourage new families to sign up for the ministry e-newsletter.

● A map of the site and the church campus.

● The policies and procedures (both for new parents and for volunteers); some churches may make the volunteer handbook available online.

● The staff (current paid staff with photos, interns, volunteers, updated contact information, etc.).

● A timely news feature on the site that changes weekly. Keep this news in a regular spot on the website. Incorporate this information, along with other items of interest, in a weekly e-newsletter.

● Links for parents (women's ministry, men's ministry, child care provided by church members, family support groups, childbirth or parenting classes, etc.).

● Links for children (Christian children's magazines or curriculum suppliers may have child-friendly activities on their websites).

● Consistent navigation symbols and working links.

● Ways to interact with the site and ways to encourage revisits.

● Frequently asked questions (FAQ) page.

● Uncluttered appearance, easy to navigate and easy to read.

● Children's artwork gallery or photo gallery (be sure parental permission is secured before posting photos of children).

● Downloadable forms (permission and medical forms for upcoming events), desktop pictures, games for children, etc.

A truly functional website will not only advertise your ministry and its programs, but also it can reduce telephone calls, provide materials and create interaction with new families that will make them want to come to church for the live experience!

HOW CAN WE RECOGNIZE THE MILESTONES OF A CHILD'S SPIRITUAL GROWTH?

Every so often, parents, teachers or children's pastors suddenly realize that although the children in their care are graduating to the next grade, they have passed no test that confirms a certain amount of spiritual growth or Bible knowledge. Sometimes panic ensues and a flurry of testing measures are tried. (Can the children repeat the Lord's Prayer? Psalm 23? John 3:16? Can they find verses in the Bible? Can they pray aloud? Can they recite the catechism?)

It is admirable to be intentional when it comes to teaching our children. When we have clear objectives in mind, we are better able to think about the bigger picture of their spiritual growth. We can ask ourselves, *What kind of spiritual growth would I hope to see in these kids 10 years from now?* and *What can I do today to help make that happen?* This kind of thinking keeps us on point as teachers, parents or children's pastors.

However, when we try to test kids for spiritual growth, we often work from a school model of testing, grades and scores. Many of us have taken a test when we were not at our best and discovered that the test was not a highly accurate reflection of our knowledge or ability! Also, within school systems, such testing forays are not only related to measuring intellectual achievement, but also they more usually are related to gaining greater funding. That isn't our purpose for children's ministry. It's not likely that we can show our church boards our children's test scores ("Look! Thirty-six kids can say the Lord's Prayer!") and expect to gain a higher percentage of the church budget! Instead, let's consider a biblical model.

Jesus said, "What shall I compare the kingdom of God to? It is like yeast that a woman took and mixed into

a large amount of flour until it worked all through the dough" (Luke 13:20-21). If you have ever tried to make bread without first having seen it done, you know how difficult it was to understand what the recipe meant by the words "sponge" or "elastic." However, once you had seen, smelled and touched bread dough in those stages, the terms became quite clear. Since it was Jesus Himself who compared the growth of God's kingdom (societal change growing out of spiritual maturity and understanding) to microscopic yeast, perhaps we need to look beyond the school system's method and consider Jesus' methods for ways to most accurately assess the children we love.

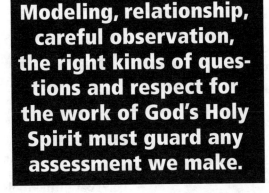

Modeling, relationship, careful observation, the right kinds of questions and respect for the work of God's Holy Spirit must guard any assessment we make.

We recognize that Jesus had far more insight than any of us will ever have. He is the master teacher of all time! First notice that Jesus preached to thousands yet selected only a small group to be trained. How did He train them? He walked with, ate with and spent time with His disciples. In this way, He modeled in everyday life the behavior He wanted them to imitate! He taught them by His words, but more than that, He modeled those words by His actions.

Second, Jesus built a close relationship with each one. There were three with whom He spent the most time—Peter, James and John. Then there were nine more with whom He had very close relationships. (Does that tell us how important it is to have good teacher-to-child ratios?) He knew these men well. They were not once-a-month, casual acquaintances. He carefully observed each one in every situation so that He would know his strengths and weaknesses.

Third, He asked masterful questions. As He and His disciples walked to Caesarea Philippi, He asked them, "Who do people say I am?" (Mark 8:27)—a nonthreatening, open-ended question that revealed both what they had heard and what they understood.

They responded freely. Then Jesus moved to a personal question of the same kind: "'But what about you?' he asked. 'Who do you say I am?'" (Mark 8:29). In the context of a well-established loving relationship, He asked open-ended questions (questions that have no right answer but are an effective way to find out what people do or do not understand). He asked and answered many other kinds of questions, too; but moving from open-ended questions that revealed His friends' hearts and minds to questions that made them personally respond to the truth were far more effective than parroting right answers or memorized facts.

Fourth, Jesus the creator already knew something we are just now learning about the brain: Most learning takes place not while people are taking in information; rather, the most learning actually happens during the quiet times—those pauses and moments of silence. He often told His disciples not to tell anyone what He had told them. Could it be that He wanted them to process and understand the truth He had spoken before they told it to others? For a child, more learning may happen while walking to school on Monday, thinking about something that happened on Sunday. How can that be measured?

Only with these ideas in mind is it then appropriate to offer an assessment tool.

Modeling, relationship, careful observation, the right kinds of questions and respect for the work of God's Holy Spirit must guard any assessment we make.

The rate at which the kingdom of God works through a life cannot be measured in any standard way. We cannot gauge the numerous factors that affect any child's life outside of our relationship with him or her.

In the same way, we must realize not only that high marks on any kind of assessment are subject to the mind-set of the assessor but also that high marks cannot guarantee a child has reached some level of complete (or even moderate) spiritual maturity or understanding. But even as we keep these things in mind, we can use an assessment tool as an effective part of our relationship building and our loving observation. (Note: Some parents may prefer that teachers not be involved in the assessment process. Provide parents with the parent assessment tool on pp. 23-25.)

These assessment tools are merely tools. Because these tools are not modeled on a school test, there is no pass-fail connotation. The concepts included are basic core truths about God, Jesus, the Bible, prayer, the Church and Christian living. The tools are designed to evaluate a child's current place along a spectrum of understanding these core truths that ranges from some awareness to the ability to put that core truth into action. The tools may be adapted to meet the needs of a particular church. Other concepts to consider when evaluating a child's spiritual understanding can be found in the age-level characteristics article on pages 155-159. You may also suggest that, instead of using the assessment tools to measure a child's progress, teachers and parents use the tools as lists of goals for their teaching and put into practice the suggested action steps.

The goal of the tools is to help us focus our desire to be intentional in the ways we teach the children we love. However, if you have experienced seeing the yeast work through the dough, you know how it feels to knead it. You know how it feels, smells and looks when it is ready. In the same way, the most important

thing you can do for each child is to lovingly encourage him or her on toward maturity—that will always be "kneaded"!

ACTION STEPS FOR THE CHILDREN'S MINISTRY COORDINATOR/DIRECTOR

From Jesus' model of assessment and action, we can see the imperatives:

1. Provide programs that allow for large amounts of small-group and relationship-building time as a norm, not an occasional focus. (Regardless of the entertainment-type ministry programs advertising that they require fewer adults, such programs cannot by themselves provide for close relationships that nurture spiritual growth.)

2. Communicate to teachers and helpers the vision of your children's ministry and the mission of what you want to accomplish and how you plan to get there. Take good care of these fellow visionaries by providing the training that will give them the skills they need (how to ask questions, how to talk and listen to children, how to weave God's Word into conversations, etc.). Provide support that helps them know that they are doing vitally important work in the church.

3. Distribute the assessment tools to parents and/or teachers, taking care to review the information presented in this article.

Teacher Assessment Tool

ACTION STEPS FOR TEACHERS

1. Focus on building relationships! During the time you are teaching, stop to recognize the importance of simply listening to children. Prayerfully consider whether God would direct you to invest more time with these children through occasional or regular times to talk and pray together.

2. Children will imitate what you do. Children learn more by what they see you do than by your words alone. Modeling kindness, patience, gentleness, self-control and a sense of humor will teach them far more than words alone.

3. Understand that because you see children on such a limited basis, you cannot expect even your best evaluation or assessment to be completely accurate. Don't make any final conclusions or take too much personal responsibility. Rather, use this assessment to understand the best ways you can pray for and help children. Remember, the church's goal is to support parents in nurturing spiritual growth in their own children.

4. Taking time to assess children's spiritual growth provides a wonderful reason to connect with parents or other family members. Talk about ways you and they can work together to help the children grow spiritually.

CHILD INFORMATION

Child's Name _____

Child's Address _____

Child's Phone Number _____

Child's E-Mail Address _____

Child's School _____

Mom's Name _____

Mom's Address _____

Mom's Phone Number _____

Mom's E-Mail Address _____

Mom's Church Involvement

High   Medium   Low

Dad's Name _____

Dad's Address _____

Dad's Phone Number _____

Dad's E-Mail Address _____

Dad's Church Involvement

High   Medium   Low

Who brings child?

Mom   Dad   Grandparent   Child's Friend

Other _____

Child's Attendance Pattern

Regular   Two Times a Month   Irregular

Comments _____

EVALUATION

1. How well do you know child's parents?

Not at all   Acquaintances   Friends   Close Friends

Comments _____

Action Ideas

- Introduce yourself to parents at all-church events
- Greet parents at classroom door
- Visit child at home
- Invite parents to observe in class

2. How would you evaluate the child's desire to be at church?

High   Medium   Low

Comments _____

Action Ideas

- Call, e-mail or write to child at home
- Plan fun relationship-building event during the week

3. Does the child bring a Bible to class?

Yes   No

Comments _____

Action Ideas

- Provide Bible for child
- Provide classroom Bibles

4. How comfortable is the child in locating Bible references?

_____

Action Ideas

- Put up a Bible book poster
- Provide bookmarks
- Play games to learn books of the Bible and develop Bible skills

5. How would you evaluate the child's understanding and demonstration of the following core Bible truths?

Core Bible Truth	Awareness/Recognition (can state the core truth)	Understanding/Verbalization (can restate the core truth in his or her own words)	Demonstration (puts the core truth into action)	Incorporate Action Ideas into your small-group time.
God • God created the world and He loves and cares for all people. • We can praise God for His power and love.	No 1 2 3 4 5 Yes 1 2 3 4 5	No 1 2 3 4 5 Yes 1 2 3 4 5	No 1 2 3 4 5 Yes 1 2 3 4 5	**Action Ideas** • Give examples of ways you see God's power shown in the world today. • Invite students to describe things for which they wish to thank God.
Jesus • Jesus is God's Son and was sent by God to be our Savior. • When we choose to follow Jesus, believing that He died to take the punishment for our sins and is alive today, we become members of God's family.	1 2 3 4 5 1 2 3 4 5	1 2 3 4 5 1 2 3 4 5	1 2 3 4 5 1 2 3 4 5	**Action Ideas** • Tell students when and how you became a Christian. • Describe one or two reasons you continue to follow Jesus. • Invite students to become members of God's family.
Bible • The Bible is true and is God's Word to us. • We can read the Bible to discover ways to love and obey God.	1 2 3 4 5 1 2 3 4 5	1 2 3 4 5 1 2 3 4 5	1 2 3 4 5 1 2 3 4 5	**Action Ideas** • Tell students about ways that knowing God's Word has helped you in everyday life. • Connect Bible verses to current news stories and situations in students' lives.
Prayer • Prayer is talking to God. • We can talk to God anytime, praising Him and asking His help for others and ourselves.	1 2 3 4 5 1 2 3 4 5	1 2 3 4 5 1 2 3 4 5	1 2 3 4 5 1 2 3 4 5	**Action Ideas** • Invite students to share prayer requests. • Help students form prayer partners. • Pray individually with student who shares a concern. • Keep a prayer journal, listing prayer requests and answered prayers.
Church • The Church is made up of everyone who believes in Jesus as Savior. • Everyone who believes in Jesus as Savior is part of the Church and can worship and serve God together.	1 2 3 4 5 1 2 3 4 5	1 2 3 4 5 1 2 3 4 5	1 2 3 4 5 1 2 3 4 5	**Action Ideas** • Share examples of ways your church family helps and encourages others. • Lead students in completing a service project to help others in your church family or your community.
Christian Living • God's followers respond to God's love by loving Him and others. • We can show our love for God through attitudes and actions (kindness, honesty, patience, etc.) that please Him.	1 2 3 4 5 1 2 3 4 5	1 2 3 4 5 1 2 3 4 5	1 2 3 4 5 1 2 3 4 5	**Action Ideas** • Recognize and thank students for loving actions you observe. • Regularly invite students to tell situations in which they find making right choices difficult and brainstorm ways to obey God in these situations.

Parent Assessment Tool
ACTION STEPS FOR PARENTS

1. Don't be overwhelmed by anyone's expectation that you must rear children to be spiritual superstars. Rearing your children is your responsibility, but it ultimately rests in God's hands—and He loves them more than you do! So pray diligently for your children as you set the tone for your family by loving and worshiping God and putting Christ first in your everyday life.

2. Always remember that your children will do more of what they see in your life than of what you say. Your words must match your actions.

3. Consider ways to support your child's learning at church: Get to know his or her teacher, help in the classroom or invite the teacher to your home. Make sure your child attends often enough to make friends and then help your child cultivate those friendships through play dates, social times with other families and invitations to your home. Talk with your child regularly about what he or she enjoys about programs at church. Talk also about parts he or she dislikes and brainstorm ways to help your child adjust; share that information with teachers as appropriate.

4. Think of one action you can take every week to help your child grow spiritually. Repeat that action at least three times during the week.

INFORMATION ABOUT YOUR CHILD   Child's Name _____   Age _____

How would you evaluate the child's understanding and demonstration of the following core Bible truths?

	Awareness/ Recognition (can state the core truth)	Understanding/ Verbalization (can restate the core truth in his or her own words)	Demonstration (puts the core truth into action)	Incorporate Action Ideas into family discussion time.
	No Yes	No Yes	No Yes	
God				**Action Ideas**
• God created the world and He loves and cares for all people.	1 2 3 4 5	1 2 3 4 5	1 2 3 4 5	• In everyday situations, look for "teachable moments" when you can talk about ways you see God's power shown in the world today.
• We can praise God for His power and love.	1 2 3 4 5	1 2 3 4 5	1 2 3 4 5	• In a family prayer time, invite your child to describe things for which to thank God. Tell characteristics of God for which you are grateful. • Memorize a verse together about God's power and love (e.g., Psalm 106:1).
Jesus				**Action Ideas**
• Jesus is God's Son and was sent by God to be our Savior.	1 2 3 4 5	1 2 3 4 5	1 2 3 4 5	• Talk with your child, asking questions such as What questions do you have about who Jesus is? Why do you think it's important to know about Jesus' death and resurrection? What are some things you really like about Jesus?
• When we choose to follow Jesus, believing that He died to take the punishment for our sins and is alive today, we become members of God's family.	1 2 3 4 5	1 2 3 4 5	1 2 3 4 5	• Share with your child how you became a Christian. • Purchase (or obtain from your church) an age-appropriate booklet on how to become a Christian. Read it with your child and then talk together about it. • As the Holy Spirit leads, ask your child if he or she would like to become a member of God's family. Help him or her pray, asking for God's forgiveness, declaring faith in Jesus' death and resurrection and asking to become part of God's family. • Encourage your child to tell the pastor or a teacher at your church about having joined God's family. • Memorize a verse together about Jesus and salvation (e.g., Romans 5:8).
Bible				**Action Ideas**
• The Bible is true and is God's Word to us.	1 2 3 4 5	1 2 3 4 5	1 2 3 4 5	• Provide a Bible and/or a Bible storybook for your child.
• We can read the Bible to discover ways to love and obey God.	1 2 3 4 5	1 2 3 4 5	1 2 3 4 5	• Regularly read Bible stories with your child. • Regularly read the Bible yourself. Briefly share with your child what you have learned from your reading. • Tell your child stories of everyday situations in which knowing God's Word has helped you. • Connect Bible verses to current news stories and situations in your child's life. • Memorize a verse together about the benefits of reading and knowing God's Word (e.g., Psalm 119:105) and keep a journal of Bible verses memorized together.

How would you evaluate the child's understanding and demonstration of the following core Bible truths?

Core Bible Truth	Awareness/Recognition (can state the core truth)		Understanding/Verbalization (can restate the core truth in his or her own words)		Demonstration (puts the core truth into action)		Incorporate Action Ideas into family discussion time.
	No ___ Yes		No ___ Yes		No ___ Yes		
Prayer • Prayer is talking to God. • We can talk to God anytime, praising Him and asking His help for others and ourselves.	1 2 3 4 5 1 2 3 4 5		1 2 3 4 5 1 2 3 4 5		1 2 3 4 5 1 2 3 4 5		**Action Ideas** • Invite your child to pray with you daily or weekly, focusing on issues of interest to your child. • Share with your child ways you have seen God answer prayer. • Keep a family prayer journal: List prayer requests and then note the dates and answers as they come. • Memorize a verse together about prayer (e.g., Philippians 4:6).
Church • The Church is made up of everyone who believes in Jesus as Savior. • Everyone who believes in Jesus as Savior is part of the Church and can worship and serve God together.	1 2 3 4 5 1 2 3 4 5		1 2 3 4 5 1 2 3 4 5		1 2 3 4 5 1 2 3 4 5		**Action Ideas** • Share examples of ways people in your church family help and encourage each other. • Plan and complete a family service project to help others in your church family or your community. Consider making such projects a regular family activity. • Demonstrate ways to care for others by your own actions; invite your child to offer his or her help to others as well. • Memorize a verse together about ways God's family helps each other (e.g., Galatians 6:10).
Christian Living • God's followers respond to God's love by loving Him and others. • We can show our love for God through attitudes and actions (kindness, honesty, patience, etc.) that please Him.	1 2 3 4 5 1 2 3 4 5		1 2 3 4 5 1 2 3 4 5		1 2 3 4 5 1 2 3 4 5		**Action Ideas** • Recognize your child for loving actions you observe. • Invite your child to tell situations in which making right choices is difficult. Brainstorm ways to obey God in these situations. • Model right actions, occasionally connecting your actions with a Bible verse that describes the reason you acted as you did. • Pray with and for your child, asking God's help for him or her to make right choices. • Memorize a verse together about Christian living (e.g., Ephesians 5:1-2).

CAN'T WE ALL JUST GET ALONG?

Overseeing the children's ministry of a church is always a joy. It never resembles walking through a battlefield; the church agrees that children are important and that children's programs are vital—right? Legions of present (and former) directors might wearily attest to just the opposite! Due to a church's history and a ministry's lack of clarity or accountability, a church board and a children's ministries staff may live under a cloud of misunderstanding that threatens to suffocate communication, cooperation and shared vision in ministry. It need not be so!

To get along, a director of children's ministries (professional or volunteer) needs to constantly build positive relationships with his or her church leaders. A first step is to understand the church's oversight structure. Who runs what? To whom are you responsible for curriculum decisions, staffing decisions, financial decisions? (If this chain of command is not already clear, help the board set a policy that keeps accountability high.)

The next step is to write out both a clear mission statement for your ministry and an understandable philosophy of children's ministry. Post them. Pass out copies to your church's decision makers. Then remain faithful to the mission statement and the philosophy; keep these tools before you so that you can consistently evaluate what you are doing by your stated purposes. When you and your church board understand the purpose and goals of your children's ministry in clear and specific terms, there will be far less of the wrangling that develops so easily when things aren't clear. This may require new discipline on your part, but it will create accountability and clarity that will open wide the door to communicating your vision, eliminating personality issues and gaining greater cooperation! (For more information on mission statements, see pp. 9-10.)

HOW CAN I GET MY PASTOR AND CHURCH BOARD ON MY TEAM?

A children's ministry director may feel that the programs of the ministry are not valued and that the people involved remain unheard by the church leadership. Although pastors are technically teachers, teaching children doesn't always seem to be an enthusiastically pursued common goal. Some pastors have had negative experiences in which children's ministry was more a hindrance than a help to the overall church goals. Some simply are overwhelmed with other crises and so assume they have no responsibility for the children—that's why you are there! However, it's not impossible to get your pastor and church board to care actively about the importance of children's ministry in your church. Here are some suggestions:

1. Pray. Pray for your pastor and board, not that they will see things your way, but that you will have a servant's heart for them. Ask God to show you creative ways to share your vision of children's ministry as well as effective ways to express your love and appreciation for them as people.

2. Share the positives with your pastor and board in tangible ways. Send out e-mails about specific things God is doing in "*our* children's ministry." Take photos of the children's classes. Leave one on the board table or pastor's desk, with a note attached that tells what a child said about the class or a way children gained from the class. Do this often, so the pastor and board members may grow in recognizing the value of children's ministry.

From time to time ask a family whose children are involved in children's ministry to attend a board meeting to briefly share how children's ministry benefits their lives and to invite the board to pray for families in the church.

3. Invite the pastor and individual board members to participate in children's classes in ways that reflect their skills and experience. Invite them to be briefly interviewed about their lives and Christian experiences; ask one to lead a game or tell a story. These experiences give adults a chance to build relationships with children. When they see the children as real people and spend time in children's classrooms, their perspectives about programs and facilities can change radically!

4. Ask their advice. Don't put on a happy face and always tell the leadership that things are fine. Rather, ask for their insights when dealing with challenges. Respect their wisdom and consider their advice when planning responses.

5. Build trust. Support the ministry goals and needs of other staff members and program areas. Be faithful in following overall church guidelines. In your own decision making, consider what is best for the total church ministry, not just children's ministry.

WHAT CAN I DO WHEN OTHERS HAVE UNREALISTIC EXPECTATIONS?

Perhaps your board or pastor wants children's ministries to organize and staff a program regardless of a lack of interest from families or a lack of volunteers to staff it. Perhaps there is a lack of interest in supporting the budget over which you have worked long hours. Unrealistic expectations are often a by-product of lack of communication. When the pastor and board are on your team, when they understand the mission and philosophy of the ministry (see above), your greatest need then is to communicate clearly.

Here are some tips to keep confrontation from becoming conflagration!

★ Use simple "I" statements to express your specific points of concern (such as "I feel that the goals for this program are not realistic because they duplicate the goals of an existing program"). Your goal is to make clear your point of view, not to win an argument or look smarter than the person questioning you.

★ It's OK not to know all the answers. It's OK to take time to assess and think about issues. But be accountable to make decisions or respond in agreed-upon ways by a given date.

★ Don't panic. As you help the church board understand the parameters of a situation, invite them to tell you how they would handle it within those parameters. Take notes on their ideas and answers. They might know something you don't or have a perspective that hadn't occurred to you.

★ Remember that God uses conflict! It can clarify direction and cause growth, even when we have to sacrifice something or might feel that the process is too difficult. Confrontation usually gives us reason to practice forgiving others or asking to be forgiven!

WHAT CAN I DO WHEN OTHERS MAKE DECISIONS THAT AFFECT CHILDREN'S PROGRAMS?

When the pastor preaches long, when someone cancels Sunday School or when someone expects your department to handle child care for a special event—all without asking you first—you might want to run screaming into the night! But if you've chosen to hang in there, try these tips:

★ Understand that God is still in control. Remember that He loves you *and* those people who have driven you to the edge.

★ Don't wait. Go immediately to the person with whom you need to communicate before the situation grows more confused. Maintain a nonadversarial position by asking information-gathering questions.

(Amazingly enough, we aren't always told the whole story by the first person who reports to us!) Once the situation is clear, ask that person for his or her recommendation. (After all, the person who set the chain of events in motion certainly thought about these things!) You may or may not be able to do what this person thinks is the right thing to do. But you can listen and be grateful that this person cares enough to speak up.

★ Talk with others about how to reduce similar miscommunication in the future. Ask yourself, *Were children's ministry policies not clearly communicated to other leaders?*

WHAT CAN I DO WHEN I AM SWAMPED BY ADMINISTRATIVE DETAIL?

You got into children's ministry because you love children and because you are passionate about bringing children to Jesus. So what are you doing working on the computer for hours or spending most of your time with adults and isolated from children? The answer for you may be that it goes with the territory. However, you're wise to take stock of what it is you are doing with your time.

★ Keep a journal in which you keep track of your time for several weeks to help you clarify how your energy is actually being spent.

★ Identify jobs for which you feel responsible that could actually be done by another person. Some jobs you may need to keep for yourself, because if they are not done effectively the consequences are significant. (Sometimes delegating tasks to others is difficult because it requires a willingness to accept or seek help. "It's easier to do it myself" is a common declaration that contributes to a pattern of the leader's doing too much work instead of leading.)

★ Pray and inquire for one or two people who love children but who really don't want to work with them directly. To these blessed saints you may pass some administrative detail work, curriculum preparation, etc., to free up your time.

★ Intentionally schedule this newfound free time as "kid time." Spend it with children (perhaps your own!) or use it to prepare to teach a class that fits your schedule. (Taking time to teach puts you in a position not only to see firsthand how programs are going but also to give you the chance to create a master teacher program so that you can help to better train your teachers. It's a win-win situation—work with kids, have no guilt!)

TOP 10

TIME-SAVERS FOR CHILDREN'S MINISTRY DIRECTORS!

1. Carry a small notebook (or electronic personal data assistant) with you whenever you are supervising (or perhaps anytime you are at church). Take notes as people talk to you. Questions asked or ideas given won't get lost. Review and address these items weekly!

2. Every Monday, while weekend events are still fresh in staff members' minds, send an e-mail to each age-level coordinator or team leader similar to this: "Please respond in one or two sentences for each category below.

I've made progress in . . .

I'm having difficulty with . . .

I need a decision from you concerning . . .

I'm thankful for . . .

Please reply to me by noon on Wednesday. Thank you for all you do!" Communication will flow freely and problems can be handled early on.

3. Place an in basket and individual or age-level out baskets at a designated (and well-publicized) spot so that teachers can leave items for you and can check for items left for them.

4. Develop a comprehensive calendar every year. Include all events (teacher recruiting events, training events, holiday events, registration, children's events, etc.), quarter beginnings and endings, curriculum ordering deadlines, major maintenance items (paint a room, etc.), staff vacations, and so on.

5. From that calendar, work backward to create a standard to-do list for each month. For instance, if you expect to hold a Family Advent Night in early December, add securing the appropriate facility to your June list. Add recruiting activity leaders and a coordinator to your September list. Add publicity and requests for donations to your October and November lists.

TIP: Remember, the larger the church, the earlier you need to begin planning and recruiting!

6. Handle incoming mail only once. Open mail with a trash can and Post-it Notes at hand. Mark with a note anything that needs to go to another person. Then throw out what is not needed. Be very selective about what you keep!

7. Build a binder of essential policies and procedures that is updated each year and passed on to new leaders as needed. Purge your files once a year to eliminate what is not current. Or purge a file whenever you are preparing to add to it!

8. Refer often to your mission statement and use it to evaluate what you plan to do. Otherwise, you may get sidetracked and lose focus, causing your volunteers to become stressed.

9. Learn to say no or "We could look at this idea for another time (next quarter, etc.)." Affirm the one who gave the idea but remain focused on the plans you have already made.

10. When planning a major event or activity, select a point person for that event. Let everyone know that this person is the one to contact. This eliminates your having to field questions and dispense information for every activity that comes along.

BE ONE WHO
SURVIVES
IN CHILDREN'S MINISTRY!

Say yes only to a workload that honors God. (If you are feeling pressured to give up spending a chunk of daily time alone with God, you need to look for ways to trim your workload.)

Understand that you can't do it all. (You are not the Savior; Jesus is. Trust and obey Him in peace instead of responding in panic to the crisis *du jour*.)

Respect the abilities of others around you. (Another person may not do it your way—but to go beyond mere delegation to duplication of ministry, give another the chance to grow and be used by God!)

Value and share the vision for his or her ministry position with each volunteer. (When everyone shares the value of and the vision for his or her own ministry, you will have surrounded yourself with people who understand and care about children's ministry. Unity will be promoted—and volunteers will return!)

Identify the core programs that work best and the reasons they do. (Invest only in new programs that help you accomplish your mission.)

Verify the ideas that come to you through prayer, God's Word and the wise counsel of experienced people. (Not every idea needs to be implemented; however, every person does need to be heard!)

Expect God to do HIS job. (He is fully able to take care of what you cannot do and also able to do *through* you both what seems easy and what seems impossible!)

Surround yourself with people who are both committed to your ministry vision and who care about you as a person. (These gifted people will keep your accountability high, help you be creative and will carry you during hard times.)

A Place Where Truth Is Taught

Programs and Curriculum

What does it take not only to make children happy, safe and loved but also to teach them the truth of God's Word and ways to make it real in their lives? Time to consider the programs you offer and the teaching materials you use!

Here is an overview of the kinds of programs your church may choose to provide and tips on choosing the programs that will most greatly benefit the children and families of your church and community.

Includes guidelines for choosing curriculum and ways to group children to make programs and curriculum their most effective.

WHAT WILL HELP YOU TEACH CHILDREN EFFECTIVELY?

The children's ministry of a church may offer a wide variety of programs or only one or two. Those programs may be simple or elaborate. But whatever ministry is available to your church's children, it needs to be rooted firmly in God's Word. We do children a disservice when we merely entertain them or only teach them moral lessons. Christian education means that we teach what the Bible says and then help the students apply it to their lives every day.

So is the best answer to simply open a Bible and read it aloud to children? Not usually, although that certainly has value in some circumstances. For effective teaching, children need to learn what God's Word says in ways that have real meaning for them, here and now! Otherwise, a child's mind has no mental hooks upon which to hang the information learned.

Because children are active and curious, teaching them God's Word needs to be done in a way that enables each one to understand and then live out Bible truth. This is where the value of good curriculum shines—it is designed to make Bible teaching effective! But by which points should you measure a curriculum?

★ Knowledge of God's Word (Is the material consistently biblical? How does it prepare the teacher spiritually to teach? What does it teach the children?)

★ Knowledge of children (How does the curriculum make Bible truth understandable to children? Are concepts clearly and appropriately presented to the age group for which it is written?)

★ Knowledge of effective teaching techniques (How does the curriculum help the teacher understand the children and their abilities? How does it help teachers

learn ways to talk to children, how to discipline without distracting, etc.?

Good curriculum should help the teacher gain the goal: children who better understand what God's Word says and know ways to live out what was learned.

An important part of that kind of teaching comes through fostering relationship with a teacher who models the love of God in his or her life. (Unfortunately, such relationship is not available on DVD!) Relational teaching involves children in the learning, so they can discover for themselves. Rather than entertaining children, relational teaching excites them about learning and understanding God's Word for themselves and then helps them know how to live what they now understand. Relational teaching also encourages teachers in effective ways to build relationship—which then challenges teachers to live in a way that is consistent with their words!

While it may be tempting to write your own curriculum, there are several points to consider: First, it often becomes time-consuming and frustrating to reinvent the wheel. Second, it is harder to recruit volunteers when they are not sure if materials they will be using are age-appropriate, attractive to children and complete. Such curriculum usually lacks appropriate visuals and student materials that help keep children's interest high and reinforce the information given in the lesson. Third, self-published curriculum may not provide an in-depth approach to Bible coverage. Children may be exposed only to parts of the Bible that have appeal to the writers. Published curriculum follows a set scope and sequence so that over time, children learn foundational theological concepts through solid Bible teaching presented in age-appropriate ways. It is usually said that the benefit of writing one's own curriculum is that a church can address specific needs that God has brought to their attention. However, the best course is still usually to find an appropriate curriculum resource and then customize it for particular needs.

In choosing curriculum for more than one program, try to keep material consistent in both its teaching philosophy (see pp. 7-8 for more on philosophy) and its doctrine. While there may be more than one valid approach to learning, training teachers is easier when your church's educational philosophy is consistent and well understood. Teachers will teach more effectively by gaining proficiency with one particular curriculum rather than adapting often to a variety of materials with differing or even conflicting educational and biblical principles. Use the curriculum checklist on page 35 for further help in determining the best curriculum for your programs.

Compare Your Curriculum Options

Curriculum _____   Age Level _____

Use the following rating scale and questions to rate your curriculum options:

   5 = Superior   4 = Excellent   3 = Good   2 = Fair   1 = Poor

Bible Content and Usage

____ Is the curriculum designed to teach the Bible as God's inspired and authoritative Word?

____ Is there balanced coverage of the Old and New Testaments?

____ Does the overall plan of the curriculum point students to faith in Christ as Savior and Lord, and also nurture and guide them to "grow up in Christ"?

____ Does the material present Bible truths in a manner appropriate to the abilities and development of the students' age levels?

____ Are hands-on Bible usage and skill development encouraged at appropriate age levels?

Teacher

____ Does the curriculum challenge the teacher to prepare spiritually for the task of teaching?

____ Is the material clearly arranged to show the teacher an understandable and logical lesson plan?

____ Are the Bible-learning and life-response aims specifically and clearly stated for each lesson?

____ Does the material provide the teacher with a variety of Bible learning activities?

____ Are the materials clearly presented, enabling the teacher to be prepared with a reasonable amount of effort?

____ Are there enough ideas and suggestions to adapt the material for longer or shorter sessions, larger or smaller groups, or limited equipment?

____ Does the curriculum give teaching tips to improve teachers' skills?

Student

____ Is the vocabulary appropriate for the age and abilities of the students?

____ Does the curriculum provide a variety of ways for students to participate actively in the learning process?

____ Are the student materials attractive and do they encourage involvement?

____ Do the teacher resources provide a variety of attractive aids to stimulate student interest and involvement?

____ Are the Bible-learning activities appropriate to the mental, spiritual, social and physical development of the students?

Beyond the Classroom

____ Does the material provide ideas for making and sustaining meaningful contact with both students and families outside the classroom?

____ Does the take-home paper contain activities that assist the family in relating the student's learning to everyday life?

____ Does the curriculum speak to issues relevant to the students' everyday life?

____ Does the curriculum provide materials and suggestions for ways students may understand the privilege and joy of sharing Christ?

____ Does the curriculum encourage outreach and church growth?

WHAT DO THE CHILDREN AND FAMILIES IN YOUR CHURCH REALLY NEED?

Children's ministry catalogs, websites and publications brim with bright advertisements for programs and products! As you survey the programs available not only in your church but also in your community, it's important to ask, "How can we as a church determine what programs are best to offer? What's the best use of our time and our volunteers to make our children's ministry most effective?" Here are suggestions to help you determine the best programs for your church to offer. Pray that God will help you think creatively and wisely as you move through the planning process.

STEPS TO CONSIDER

First, do some detective work! Check the listings of local schools and colleges, parks and recreation departments, youth clubs, service organizations and churches to find out what both your church and your community offer to children and families. As you research, categorize by the times offered: weekend, weekday, evening, after-school programs. Categorize by kind: child care/Mother's Day Out, Vacation Bible School, special events, parenting classes, music, dance, art, drama, sports camps, craft classes, Bible study, etc.

Second, consider the programs offered by your church. To fine-tune your focus, write a one-sentence definition of each program. For instance, "Midweek program: Evening, Bible study time with games and crafts, aimed at helping our most regular attendees grow as followers of Jesus." Then look at each program through the lens of your ministry's mission statement. How does a program support the overall mission of your children's ministry? How could it be changed to help fulfill the mission statement? (See pp. 9-10 for more information about writing a mission statement.)

Third, once you have defined your church's current programs and their purposes, evaluate them according to these questions:

What programs allow for children and families to build relationships with each other?

What programs build bridges to children and families in our community? What programs meet the needs of children whose parents are not involved in our church?

What programs help parents develop biblical parenting skills?

What programs meet the needs of single parents? Working parents? Parents of preschoolers? Parents of preadolescents? Children who have no family at church?

What programs focus primarily on the child? On the entire family?

What community programs compete with church programs because of times they are held? (Consider the schedules of sports programs offered in your community.) What can we change to increase effectiveness?

What programs promote Bible learning? Scripture memorization? How and where could we increase these components in other programs?

Fourth, determine several short-term goals (one to two years) and some long-term goals (three to five years) for your children's ministry. Base the goals on the following questions:

What are the needs of the parents, children and families in our church? (To get accurate information, consider distributing a written survey [see sample on p. 39]. Or invite parents to a brainstorming meeting and poll them by using these questions.)

What programs already work well? What are the benefits, both spiritual and relational, of those programs?

What programs might need to be replaced due to low attendance, lack of resources or volunteers?

What programs can you realistically provide, based on your current resources?

What programs could you add to your existing programs? (It's OK to dream!) What might be the spiritual benefits? What resources would be needed?

To begin a new program, it might be best to start with a short-term program (six to eight weeks, meeting once a week) to see how it works. If it does not work as well as you had hoped, you are not committed to it for a year!

Recognize, too, that a program which has been in place for years may not necessarily be effective. As you take stock, plan ways to update or change the program. It's even OK to discontinue a program. When you plan to discontinue a program, be sure to communicate to parents and leaders the reasons for ending the program and get support from the leadership of the church and the program leaders who will be affected. Give several months notice and expect that some leaders, teachers and parents will need more information as the final day of the program approaches.

TYPICAL PROGRAMS TO OFFER

Sunday School: A program, sometimes called by different names, offered for all ages, usually all year long, often on Sunday morning. Classes run 45-90 minutes. Groups are made up of peers and at least one teacher and a helper, with at least one adult for every six to eight children for building personal relationships. Sunday School runs either before, after or during a weekend service.

Second Hour: A supplement to Sunday School that usually runs concurrently with the main worship service. A mixed-age group of children participates in large-group experiences such as singing, a Bible story and small-group times of making a craft, eating a snack or having a discussion. Some churches attempt to pattern this time after adult worship services. However, this is effective only if the pattern is adapted to make worship time meaningful to children. Expect to shorten times for all service elements, use nonsymbolic vocabulary that children can understand, and provide for plenty of physical movement. (The goal here is to involve children in worship and help them understand the elements of worship. It's wise not to make this an experience that causes them to equate boredom with worship!)

Midweek: A program that runs concurrently with an adult midweek Bible study, choir practice, teachers' meetings, etc. It can include a variety of activities, from recreational games to Bible study, Scripture memory programs, crafts, service projects and snacks.

Saturday Evening: More and more churches hold Saturday-evening services. Because the children attending these programs are usually coming from a long day of active sports or other pastimes, their needs may be quite different from the needs of those who attend on Sunday morning or even on Sunday evening. Depending on the time of the service, children may not have had dinner. A program that is too high energy may overload children who are already tired or hungry at the end of a busy day. Consider incorporating low-key activities (board games, puzzles, etc.) and possibly serving a snack at the beginning or middle of the session to help tired, hungry kids relax and unwind before teaching time begins.

Sunday Evening: Sunday-evening programs can vary widely from a classroom time with a format similar to a Sunday School format to a mixed-age group using a club format that includes Bible study, Scripture memorization, skits, snacks, games, etc.

After School: Effective after-school programs are more than school-aged child care. They may include a Bible club component, tutoring time (with teens or seniors as tutors), recreational games, snacks and crafts as well as unstructured recreational time. Some churches also offer computer literacy and technology classes to children in this program as well as to adults.

Focus Classes: These classes are open only to those who register in advance and often meet on weeknights. They may include a Bible club format but focus primarily on one area: discipleship, drama, service projects, puppets, music, sports, care groups (divorce, abuse or grief issues), etc.

Special Events: These range from one day or evening to one or two weeks and include such events as Vacation Bible School, sports or drama camps, family retreats, family fun nights, seasonal programs such as Family Advent Nights, etc.

Choirs: Programs that teach some rudiments of music and drama by involving children in a production that is then performed for the church family or the community. Because of the dearth of arts programs in many public schools, a choir program can be a church's most effective outreach. (People who would never come to a church service eagerly attend to see family or friends perform!)

Whatever programs you choose, improve or discontinue, begin with prayer. Pray through each idea, each decision. Ask God to open your eyes to see with fresh perception, to open your mind to the truth into which Jesus promised the Holy Spirit would lead us. Trust His leading and refuse to be stressed!

Know that there will always be someone who is unhappy with changes. Remain calm and loving. Ask those people "what do you think?" kinds of questions to determine exactly what they feel. (Often the biggest need with an unhappy person is to be heard!) Then, if it is appropriate, invite that person to volunteer and help in just the way he or she suggested. You may discover a valuable ally and helper!

Parent Questionnaire

1. What programs at our church have your children participated in during the last six months?

2. Which of these programs would you like your children to attend again? What did you like about them?

3. How could these programs be improved?

4. In what specific ways have our church ministries helped improve your child's life? Your family life?

5. Our mission statement is _____. How effective have we been in fulfilling that mission in your child's life?

6. In what ways would you like further help for your child and/or family?

HOW DO WE GROUP CHILDREN FOR MAXIMUM LEARNING?

Grouping children is a significant part of planning and organizing children's ministry programs. Every church needs a well-thought-out policy about grouping children for effective learning as well as to determine room sizes, teacher ratios and times to promote children from one class to the next.

Here are some basic guidelines for grouping children. As with all generalizations, other factors (facilities, staff, etc.) may influence how these statements apply.

1. Generally, children do best in a group of others about the same age. Also most teachers find it easier to guide groups when the children are at similar stages of development. Even in a group in which all children are in the same grade, there could easily be a four-year range of abilities.

2. Teachers and children benefit when classes are maintained at similar sizes. If you have a room full of fourth graders while your third-grade class is nearly empty, teaching will be less effective. Evaluate your promotion policies to determine the best dividing line between the classes. Just because the current age-level divisions worked well last year does not mean they will be appropriate this year! Rearrange classes based on nearest birthdates or alphabetically by last name to make the sizes of the classes even.

3. Generally, grade level is the safest criteria to use in dividing classes. In large churches in which there are multiple classes of the same grade level, children may be grouped by age. The same dividing date, however, does not need to be used in all groups. In order to maintain a balanced class size, it is fine to have one class include a 14-month span while the class next door has a 9-month span. Simply post at the door the specific age range of the group (for example, "Children whose birthdays fall between May 1, 2004, and July 1, 2005").

4. Generally, children benefit more by being in a small group rather than in a large group. Being a member of a small group means more personal attention, better building of relationships and more effective learning. The younger the children, the more difficult it is for them to be in large groups.

PROMOTION

Promotion—the moving of students from one class to the next as a group—may be done at the end of a school year coinciding with graduation to the next grade, or it may be done at the beginning of a school year coinciding with entry into the next grade. When you are planning your promotion policy, keep in mind that the primary goal should be to minimize the number of transitions children experience.

After you determine your plan, publicize promotion so that it is understood, expected and enjoyed! Unless the promotion policy is clear to parents, some will automatically take a child to another class as soon as a birthday occurs. Others will bring the child (who was absent on promotion day) to their old class for several weeks! Here are steps to making promotion day flow smoothly.

★ Publicize the date of promotion in the bulletin. Post promotion information clearly in classroom halls, etc., several weeks ahead of time. ("Beginning on September 10, all children whose birthdays fall between January 1 and June 30, 2005, will move to room 23 with Janis and Ben Lee.")

★ Send out postcards or flyers a week or two in advance of promotion day. Include information about class locations and teachers' names. Outline the procedure your children will follow.

★ For a week or two before promotion, have a representative of each older group visit the younger group to briefly describe typical activities and what he or she enjoys about the group.

★ If your church is large, recruit for the day additional greeters who will help parents find their children's new classrooms. Provide greeters with a list of classrooms and age groups along with additional copies to give to parents as reminders. Don't forget to provide this information to ushers and information booths in other areas of the church campus as well.

★ On promotion day, students may begin class with their current teacher and at an announced time be escorted to their new classes for a get-acquainted time with the new teachers. Or students may simply arrive at the new classroom on promotion day.

PRETEEN AND EARLY TEEN GROUPINGS

Public schools vary in the way they group preteens and young teens. Some school districts group sixth, seventh and eighth graders together in middle school, while others group seventh, eighth and ninth graders in junior high schools. The patterns of grouping may not even be consistent among the schools around your church. What to do?

It's easiest to follow the same plan as the majority of schools in your area simply to minimize the confusion! If sixth graders are attending middle school in your area but the church youth group is not geared to them, consider forming a special class just for sixth graders (a "top dogs" concept) in which they are part of the children's division but are treated differently from the rest of the upper elementary grades. (This can become a very enjoyable milestone class experience for both children and teachers, with a separate logo, activities, etc.) Wherever you decide to make the division, plan to give your oldest group a lot of extra attention. The final year before moving to the youth department is vital to a child's spiritual growth.

WHAT IS BEST WITHIN A MIXED-AGE CLASS SETTING?

Many small churches find it necessary to combine ages of children in a class due to limited numbers of children or a shortage of classrooms. Mixed-age classes can benefit younger children as they learn from older ones and can give older ones responsibility that helps them feel important.

Before mixing ages, take time to consider the safety factors, the curriculum and the absolute need for adequate staffing.

Safety will be a prime concern, especially for the youngest members of this class. How developmentally mature and how big is the youngest one? Will this classroom be safe for that child as it is? What supplies and equipment need to be removed?

Curriculum should be appropriate to the age level of the greatest number of children. Then consider ways to adapt the material for younger and older children. (Or look for programs that provide options for both younger and older children.)

Teachers are even more important in a mixed-age setting. There should be more teachers than the recommended numbers (see chart on p. 45 so that the youngest are adequately cared for and the oldest are challenged and taught. (Relying on the older ones to be "helpers" is fine, but don't count them as adults in your ratios and don't assume that they no longer need appropriate teaching to gain an understanding of God's Word!) When mixed-age classes are understaffed, the result is often a significant amount of negative learning instead of positive learning!

GROUPING CHILDREN BY GENDER

There are many pros and cons of grouping children (especially upper elementary ages) into single-gender groups. Bolstered by the success of all-female math classes, some people believe that girls achieve more when not challenged by the distractions of coeducation. Girls-only or boys-only classes can be a good option in some cases, especially if there are personality issues that need a fresh approach or if the nature of specific topics to be discussed would cause frozen, embarrassed silence in a coed group. But overall, children benefit from the variety of relationships offered in a coed group and are familiar with coed grouping in school.

A Place Where People Are Primary

Staff

A church may find its children's ministry well staffed with a surplus of adult helpers, understaffed with a surplus of children, or somewhere in between!

Wherever you find yourselves, this section describes what you need to know about staffing your programs. Whether you are new at this or an old hand, there is information that will benefit you, help your volunteers and bless the children you serve in order to show them the love of Jesus.

This section includes information about application and screening to make the ministry safe, information about ratios and terms of service to make the ministry effective and job descriptions and training ideas to make the ministry the best it can be.

Ratios

WHAT'S THE BEST RATIO FOR EFFECTIVE LEARNING?

Serious consideration needs to be given when planning for the teachers and helpers needed in your children's ministry. Often, the planning process goes like this: "Wow. We have X number of kids in X age group. So-and-so likes kids that age. Maybe we can get him or her to take the class!" This is not the kind of planning that yields a quality program. Rather, it bespeaks a cycle of desperation/pressure/guilt/resentment that results in blowups, burnout and discouraged volunteers!

As a rule of thumb, there should always be at least two adults in every classroom in case of emergency. (For more safety precautions to prevent legal liability, see pp. 58-60.) While a teen helper might be substituted for an adult, it is always best to have a teen helper in addition to the two adults.

The chart below gives the recommended teacher-to-child ratio. But it is important to remember that both for physical safety and for spiritual growth, the ratio should always tend toward more, not fewer, teachers. More teachers to children mean an increase in personal attention, an improvement in safety and more effective learning. Children need as many loving adults around them as they can get!

In addition, teachers who have small classes are more able to build relationships with individual children, follow up on absentees and extend outreach to families. When a class is too large, it becomes a mass of humanity instead of a group of individuals, and as a result, a teacher is unable to build relationships. He or she generally feels overwhelmed. This is a good way to discourage volunteers!

IF PUBLIC SCHOOLS TEACH FORTY AT A TIME, WHY CAN'T WE?

People sometimes question the recommended ratio. Obviously, schools consistently operate with much larger numbers of children in one class and with only one teacher. But there are very significant reasons why this larger ratio is not appropriate for a church ministry program.

★ First, large child-to-teacher ratios in weekday programs are imposed for economic reasons, not educational reasons. Teachers in these programs clearly realize that children in such large groups do not receive the quality care of instruction they really need. For this reason, these programs often use part-time or volunteer aides to reduce the ratios and provide some personal attention.

Grades	Teacher to student ratio	Maximum number of students per room
1 to 5 or 6	1 to 6 or 8	24 to 30

★ Second, these programs have the same children several days a week in preschools and every day in elementary schools. Children are in the program for the majority of the day. The many hours of contact provide the teacher with time to give personal attention during the week. This luxury of time does not exist in a church program in which a child may be present only for an hour or two and then may be absent the next week. If relationships are to be built, if attention is going to be given, if teaching is going to be effective, then a structure must be in place to allow the teacher to interact personally with each child during each session. This rarely happens if the recommended ratios are exceeded. In addition, studies have shown that classes with just enough teachers per students did not grow as fast as classes that started with lower-than-needed ratios.

★ Third, most children's ministry programs are staffed by volunteers, not paid professionals. Often, these volunteers have minimal training and take minimal time for preparation. Expecting them to work with the same group size as a professional who is with the same children daily is unreasonable, discouraging and damaging to both the children and the volunteers.

★ Fourth, relationships between teachers and children are the most powerful dimension in the church's ministry! While it may be possible to entertain or manage a large group of children (with videos, entertainers, or the like), we have a higher calling as ministers to children: to love each child in a personal, individual way that gives that child a glimpse of God's everlasting love for them! The goal of children's ministry is not just to keep children occupied or safely involved, it is to introduce children to Christ and help them be lifelong followers of Him. This eternal goal requires that we do what is best for children, not just what is adequate.

Job Descriptions

WHAT POSITIONS DO YOU NEED TO REALLY SUCCEED?

On a sports team, every player has a position. In the army, every soldier has an assignment and a specialty. In business, a written description is given for every position. Why? In order for people to be accountable to the work assigned to them, they need to know what the job entails! When we expect volunteers (who have perhaps no training) to do a job well, it's perhaps even more important to have a written job description! To create an excellent program, volunteers need to know what to do and then how to do it (for more on training, see pp. 64-70). The goal is to have a person for every job and a (clearly defined) job for every person so that an effective and mutually supportive team can be built.

Here are a series of basic sample job descriptions. Customize and use them to help organize the positions that need to be filled in your ministry.

CHILDREN'S MINISTRY COORDINATOR/DIRECTOR

Task: To guide planning and development of a program of Bible learning for all age levels in Children's Ministry

Term: One year, beginning in September

Supervisor_____

Responsibilities

- Pray regularly for each member of the Children's Ministry staff.

- Recruit leaders, teachers and helpers for all Children's Ministry positions.

- Plan and coordinate a regular program of training for all Children's Ministry staff.

- Give practical tips for solving problems.

- Observe, evaluate and affirm leaders, teachers and helpers in order to help them understand their strengths and to encourage them in areas where improvement is possible.

- Coordinate regular planning meetings for team members that include both teacher training and opportunities for spiritual growth.

- Oversee the purchase, distribution and use of all equipment and supplies (curriculum, snacks, art supplies, etc.).

- Communicate the church's approved safety policy to all Children's Ministry staff, regularly evaluate its use and take necessary steps to put the policy into practice.

- Lead in planning a Children's Ministry staff get-together at least twice a year in order to build a sense of teamwork among all team members.

- Express appreciation to the Children's Ministry staff, including an end-of-the-year event.

- Communicate with church leaders and the congregation regarding the purpose, value and procedures of Children's Ministry.

Note: This position may be held by a volunteer or paid staff person. In a small church, one or more of these tasks may be the responsibility of the pastor, Christian education committee member, children's ministries elder, etc. A church with one or more age-level coordinators may assign some of these responsibilities to those leaders. This leadership role then becomes a role of coordination, encouragement and support.

CHILDREN'S MINISTRY ELEMENTARY COORDINATOR

Task: To plan and develop a program of Bible learning through loving adult care, Bible stories and learning activities for elementary children each Sunday morning

Term: One year, beginning in September

Supervisor _____

Responsibilities

- Recruit leaders, teachers and helpers for all elementary program classes.

- Plan and lead a regular program of training for all staff.

- Observe, evaluate and affirm teachers in order to note strengths to encourage and areas where improvement is possible.

- Pray regularly for elementary leaders, teachers and helpers.

- Lead regular planning meetings for teachers that include training and opportunities for spiritual growth.

- Oversee the purchase, distribution and use of all equipment and supplies (curriculum, snacks, art supplies, etc.).

- Communicate the church's approved safety policy to all elementary staff, regularly evaluate its use and take necessary steps to put the policy into practice.

- Plan a staff get-together at least twice a year in order to build a sense of teamwork among all teachers.

- Express appreciation to the elementary staff, including an end-of-the-year event.

- Communicate with parents regarding the purpose, value and procedures of elementary programs.

- Communicate regularly with supervisor and leaders of related programs (weekday school, second-hour coordinator, etc.).

Note: This position may be held by a volunteer or paid staff person. In a small church, one or more of these tasks may be the responsibility of the supervisor (Christian education committee member, children's ministries elder, etc.).

CHILDREN'S MINISTRY TEAM LEADER

Task: To prayerfully support and build relationships with both teachers and children in order to ensure effective Bible learning

Term: One year, beginning in September

Supervisor _____

Responsibilities

- Coordinate teacher tasks, including use of supplies and room setup.

- Greet children as they arrive and guide them to an activity.

- Assist teachers as needed (discipline, activity completion, etc.), maintaining the time schedule for the session.

- Observe, evaluate and affirm teachers in order to note strengths to encourage and areas where improvement is possible.

- Lead the large group time (Bible study and/or worship), involving other teachers as appropriate.

- Pray regularly for others on the teaching team.

- Work with your supervisor to identify and enlist qualified people to join your teaching team.

- Lead regular session planning meetings, including training and opportunities for spiritual growth.

- Plan a team get-together in order to build friendships among the team once a quarter.

- Communicate regularly with supervisor.

Note: In a class with just two teachers, the leader responsibilities may be informally shared. When three or more people are on the team, one person should be designated as the Team Leader.

CHILDREN'S MINISTRY TEACHER

Task: To prayerfully build relationships with children and guide them in life-changing Bible learning

Term: One year, beginning in September

Supervisor _____

Individual Responsibilities

- Maintain a personal relationship with Jesus Christ.
- Desire to grow in faith and commitment to God and participate in personal Bible study and prayer.
- Worship regularly with the church family.

Team Responsibilities

- Pray regularly for each child and others on your teaching team.
- Participate in scheduled teachers' meetings.
- Participate in at least one training event during the year to improve teaching skills.
- Express needs as a teacher to your supervisor.

Teaching Session Responsibilities

- Arrive at least 15 minutes before session begins.
- Arrange materials and room to create an effective learning environment.
- Greet each child upon arrival and involve him or her in conversation and meaningful activity.
- Model the love of Christ by getting to know children and sharing their concerns, needs and joys.
- Guide Bible learning by
    1. Being well prepared to use Bible stories, verses/passages, questions and comments appropriate to the age level in order to accomplish the lesson aims;
    2. Selecting a variety of Bible learning activities and encouraging each student to actively participate in each lesson;
    3. Participating with children in learning activities and in large-group times.

Student Follow-Up Responsibilities

- Follow up on visitors and absentees with mailings, phone calls and/or personal visits.
- Care for each class member with prayer, telephone calls, birthday cards, etc.
- Communicate individual student needs to parents.

CHILDREN'S MINISTRY GREETER

Task: To greet families and check in children as they arrive

Term: Six months, September through February or March through August

Supervisor _____

Responsibilities

- Be present in the classroom from 9:30 A.M. until 10:00 A.M. each Sunday morning.

- Put out a new check-in form each teaching session. Place previous check-in form into the Attendance Form box in the reception office.

- Assist parent(s) as needed to check in.

- Offer a friendly greeting to each family, alerting families to any special announcements or procedural changes.

- Pay special attention to visitors. Get names and addresses, give name tags, direct children and parents to appropriate rooms, etc.

- Communicate regularly with supervisor.

SUPPLY ROOM COORDINATOR

Task: To keep the supply room organized and ready for teacher use

Term: Six months, September through February or March through August

Supervisor _____

Responsibilities

- Once a week, check the supply room to clean up and sort donated materials and pick up supply requests from teachers.

- Purchase supplies as needed. Consult with Children's Ministry Coordinator as needed. Turn in receipts to (name).

- Place supply requests for donated items in newsletter and/or bulletin as needed.

- Keep a current copy of appropriate supply and equipment catalogs.

- Update supply list twice a year, post list in supply room and distribute to teachers.

- At least twice a year, thoroughly clean and reorganize the supply room.

- Communicate regularly with supervisor.

CHILDREN'S MINISTRY PUBLICITY COORDINATOR

Task: To communicate all children's programs and events

Term: One year, beginning in September

Supervisor _____

Responsibilities

- Determine the ongoing publicity needs for children's programs, including mailed publicity, displays at church, bulletin and/or newsletter inserts.

- Oversee the production and distribution of all children and parent letters, flyers, posters, etc., working with others as needed (office staff, children's leaders, etc.).

CHILDREN'S MINISTRY FOOD COORDINATOR

Task: To be aware of food-related medical concerns of attending children and to oversee the provision of food—snacks or meals—as needed at children's ministry programs

Term: One year, beginning in September

Supervisor _____

Responsibilities

- Determine the food needs for all children's programs, working with children's ministry teachers.

- Provide food through purchases and donations of money or food. If parents are asked to provide food, set up and oversee a schedule of donations.

- Keep an up-to-date file of all food-related medical concerns (allergies, diabetes, etc.) of attending children and keep teachers aware of these concerns as needed.

- Store unused food properly or discard.

- Follow safe food-handling practices.

CHILDREN'S MINISTRY CAMP COORDINATOR

Task: To plan and reserve summer and/or winter camp reservations, publicize the camp program and oversee all details (counselors, registration, transportation, etc.)

Supervisor _____

Responsibilities

- In coordination with supervisor, reserve date and number of campers at (name of camp). Coordinate camp dates with school schedules.

- Request and display camp brochures in the appropriate classrooms and in other well-traveled areas of the church facility.

- Write bulletin notices for camps and send publicity materials with parent letters well in advance of registration due dates.

- Set up and oversee procedures for accepting registrations and fees.

- Mail all checks and registration to the camp registrar.

- Plan and coordinate scholarships and fund-raisers as needed.

- Two weeks prior to camp, send an information letter to each camper. Include information about final payment of all camp fees, transportation arrangements, luggage, address at camp, medical release forms, etc.

- After camp, ask several campers to write an article for church newsletter and/or arrange for several campers to be interviewed in church service.

- Communicate regularly with supervisor.

FAMILY OUTREACH COORDINATOR

Task: To plan, organize and direct the family ministry efforts of the Children's Ministry

Term: One year, beginning in September

Supervisor _____

Responsibilities

- Provide up-to-date student/family rosters for all teachers.

- Encourage leaders to get to know, pray for and communicate with family members of students.

- Coordinate family education efforts of the Children's Ministry.

- Evaluate the manner in which families are cared for through the Children's Ministry.

- Plan special events or programs for families.

- Recruit, meet with and supervise age-level family ministry coordinators as needed.

- Communicate regularly with supervisor.

CHILDREN'S MINISTRY SECURITY COORDINATOR

Task: To provide security for children and teachers during the times programs are meeting

Term: One year, beginning in September

Supervisor _____

Responsibilities

- Check children in and out of classroom and/or facility if greeter is not available to do so.

- Help to keep attendance records complete and up to date.

- Prevent unauthorized people (adults or children) from entering a classroom and/or facility.

- Oversee "restroom return" for elementary children who go to and return from the restroom.

- Communicate immediate security concerns to supervisor.

- Consider ways to improve children's and/or classroom security and communicate these ideas to appropriate personnel.

CHILDREN'S MINISTRY WEEKNIGHT PROGRAM COORDINATOR

Task: To oversee planning and development of a program of Bible learning for weeknight (mid-week, Saturday night) children's ministries

Term: One year, beginning in September

Supervisor _____

Responsibilities

- Recruit teachers and helpers for weeknight-program positions.

- Pray regularly for each member of weeknight-program staff.

- Answer questions and give practical tips for solving problems.

- Observe, evaluate and affirm teachers and helpers to help them understand their strengths and to encourage them in areas where improvement is possible.

- Coordinate regular planning and training meetings for team members that include both teacher training and opportunities for spiritual growth.

- Oversee the purchase, distribution and use of all equipment and supplies (curriculum, snacks, art supplies, etc.).

- Communicate the church's approved safety policy to weeknight-program staff, regularly evaluate its use and take necessary steps to put the policy into practice.

- Lead in planning a weeknight-program staff get-together at least twice a year in order to build a sense of teamwork.

- Express appreciation to weeknight-program staff with an end-of-the-year event.

- Communicate with church leaders and the congregation regarding the purpose, value and procedures of weeknight ministries.

Note: This position may be held by a volunteer or paid staff person. In a small church, one or more of these tasks may be the responsibility of the pastor, Christian education committee member, children's ministries elder, etc.

WHAT DO WE TEACH BY SIMPLY BEING THERE?

As even the most devoted followers of Jesus seem to grow busier and busier, churches continually struggle to recruit teachers who will serve continually and regularly. Although people serving in support tasks such as record keeping or preparing curriculum may easily commit to a year of service, it can be difficult to obtain year-long commitments from people to serve as teachers.

However, continuity should be a goal for which your church strives! All children in your programs will benefit significantly from the security of seeing familiar faces every time they come. (The behavior of the youngest ones will immediately make the importance of continuity clear to you!) Children who know the people in their classrooms feel secure. They create fewer discipline problems so that the teacher has more time and attention to give to each child, creating the ideal climate for positive learning.

Children aren't the only ones who benefit from consistent teachers! Adults who spend time consistently teaching the same group of children will also find their experience much more enjoyable. Relationships that

are built will benefit and inspire both children and adults. Teachers have time to get to know the children in their classes, learn about each one and appreciate their growth and development. This kind of relationship-building yields positive interaction and powerfully encourages volunteers to continue!

The ideal plan is to schedule teachers to teach every session for 12 months at a time with allowance for vacations and other occasional absences. Some churches recruit teachers for 9 months (concurrent with the traditional school year) and then recruit a different staff for the summer months. However, with a church's children on several different school schedules (year-around, tracks, traditional, etc.) you may find that summer is no longer easy to define! This is another reason to recruit for a 12-month period. Make it clear to volunteers, however, that this does not mean they can never be absent. They may still take vacations, stay home when they are sick or plan a few weekends off throughout the year!

Helpers or aides may be asked to commit for terms of one or more consecutive months. (If helpers serve a

class for one month at a time, schedule two helpers' terms of service so that they overlap. This will result in both some new and some familiar faces in a class each week.)

Recruiting teachers or helpers into a one-Sunday-a-month rotation system may seem like the easiest method. However, this kind of rotation does not do a satisfactory job of meeting children's educational and emotional needs. With many children already absent every other weekend, children whose teachers rotate may rarely see a familiar face, let alone build any kind of meaningful relationship! (This greatly increases potential discipline challenges!) For children already suffering from a lack of consistent relationship, a rotation system again reinforces the idea that adults can't be expected to care very much or to be very trustworthy. This only contributes to the already-tenuous quality of many children's lives. Simply by showing up consistently, a teacher gives children tremendous lessons in faithfulness, love and security! Publicly honor those teachers who continue over one year to highlight the value of such a commitment.

In addition, a constantly rotating staff of volunteers also puts the coordinator at risk of becoming overwhelmed by the logistics of scheduling, training and distributing materials on a weekly basis.

Take time to ask God for the kinds of volunteers you are seeking. To find consistent and committed volunteers, it may be best to look beyond frazzled parents who feel duty-bound because their child is in a class. Are there retired schoolteachers, grandparents or college students who express through attitudes and actions care and concern for children? Who in your congregation might be willing to let children count on them? Remember, the actions of the teachers in your programs will teach far more than their words alone! God has the resources. He loves these children far more than you do. Ask Him to surprise you!

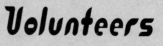

WHO IS WORKING IN YOUR CHILDREN'S MINISTRY?

An important step in the recruiting process is establishing a set of procedures for screening and approving volunteers. Determine with others in your church the procedures your church will follow to protect both children and volunteers. Consider consulting a legal expert in church-liability issues who is familiar with the applicable laws in your state.

Application Forms: Every person who is a volunteer or paid member of your staff should be asked to fill out an application form (see sample on pp. 59-60). Carefully evaluate the information on the form, and if needed, contact the references listed. (Note: It is best to have your pastor or someone designated by the pastor review applicant names in case confidential information is known by the pastor that would prevent the applicant from serving in children's ministries.) All applications and reference checks should be kept confidential.

Church Policies: In addition to evaluating the information on the application, the church must also apply its own policies when evaluating volunteers who are applying to work with children. Some sample policies: a volunteer must have been attending the church for more than 6 months; volunteers under 18 years of age may not work during a time when a youth event in which they could take part is scheduled. Other policies might include excluding youth volunteers from helping in a class in which children are fewer than five years younger than the volunteer. Some potential applicants will not meet church policies. When letting an applicant know his or her application process was not completed, be sure to state the church's policy so that the volunteer understands the reason.

Personal Interview: If you are in a large church and are contacting potential volunteers who are not well known to your staff, set up an interviewing team of two people to meet with those who have agreed to accept a teaching position. In the interview, review the information on the application form. Talk informally about the person's background and interest in ministry. The purpose of the interview is to get acquainted with the potential teacher so that you are able to assess the person's skills and abilities in a more personal way than in a written statement.

Fingerprinting and Background Checks: Some churches require fingerprinting and police background checks for all staff who work with children. Resources for these services are available on the Internet. (Check with your local law-enforcement department or state Department of Justice for information on how such checks are handled in your area.) If a cost is involved, plan your departmental budget to include that cost. It is a worthwhile expense.

Volunteer Application Form

IMPORTANT: *This is a sample form, not intended to be reproduced.*
Adapt to your specific needs.

First Church has a child/youth safety policy founded on respect and love for the children and youth of our church and community. This safety policy gives children, youth, parents and all Children's Ministry staff a sense of confidence and peace. We ask your cooperation in completing and returning this application.

Personal Information

Name_____

Address_____

Phone_____ Cell phone _____ E-mail _____

Best time to call: Morning _____ Afternoon _____ Evening _____

Day and month of birth_____

Occupation_____

Where employed_____

Phone_____

Can you receive calls at work? ❑ Yes ❑ No

Do you have a current driver's license? ❑ Yes ❑ No

License number _____

Children ❑ Yes ❑ No

Name(s) and age(s)_____

Spouse ❑ Yes ❑ No

Name_____

Are you currently a member of First Church? ❑ Yes ❑ No

If yes, how long? _____

Please list other churches and locations where you have regularly attended over the past five years.

_____

1. Are you currently under a charge or have you ever been convicted of any crime?

2. Are you currently under a charge or have you ever been accused or convicted of child abuse or of any crime involving actual or attempted sexual misconduct or sexual molestation of a minor?

❑ Yes ❑ No

If yes, please explain_____

_____

Are you currently under a charge or have you ever been accused or convicted of possession/sale of controlled substances or of driving under the influence of drugs or alcohol?

❑ Yes ❑ No

If yes, please explain_____

_____

Is there any other information that we should know?_____

_____

Church Activity

1. Please write a brief statement of how you became a Christian.

   _____
   _____
   _____

2. In what activities/ministries of our church are you presently involved?

   _____
   _____

3. Experience:

   a. What volunteer or career experiences with children/youth have you had in the church or the community?

   _____

   b. List any gifts, calling, training, education or other factors that have prepared you for ministry to children/youth.

   _____

4. Preferences: In what capacity and with what age group would you like to minister? Explain your choice.

   _____
   _____

5. Concerns: What causes the greatest feelings of apprehension as you contemplate this ministry?

   _____

Personal References

(Not a relative)

Name _____ Phone _____

Address _____

Name _____ Phone _____

Address _____

Applicant's Statement

The information contained in this application is true and correct to the best of my knowledge. I authorize any of the above references or churches to give you any information that they may have regarding my character and fitness to work with youth or children.

I hereby certify that I have read and that I understand the attached provisions of (insert title of your state's penal code regarding the reporting of child abuse and neglect).

Signature _____ Date _____

WHAT DO I DO WITH THEM NOW THAT I HAVE THEM?

When a new volunteer commits to serve on your staff, the training phase of your recruitment program begins. You can't separate recruiting and training! The beginning is the most important—and probably the most risky—time for a new recruit. A well-prepared new teacher is likely to succeed and be willing to teach again. However, a new teacher left to flounder will likely become discouraged and give up after a few weeks. Give every possible help to assure that your new teachers are a smashing success!

Prepare Every Teacher

Always meet with a new teacher or helper before that person steps into a classroom. Explain the goals, methods, curriculum and organization of your children's ministry program. An orientation class is the simplest way to do this if a group of new staff members begin at a given time. Provide child care and refreshments or a light meal to make the event festive and user-friendly!

Provide each one with a new-teacher packet that includes the following:

★ A copy of the current curriculum materials for that class.

★ A copy of classroom policies and procedures (arrival and dismissal procedures, map of campus, resource room information, health and safety policies, child-safety policies, etc.).

★ A copy of names and phone numbers of other teachers.

★ A copy of the class schedule.

★ A copy of the training calendar.

★ A class roster.

Distribute an overview of a teacher's role (see pp. 223-224) for teachers to read. Use the information in that article to lead a discussion of helpful information that every teacher needs to know. Invite several veteran teachers to this event to answer questions and share tips with new teachers.

Create a Handbook

Many churches develop a teacher handbook that is distributed to new teachers when they join the staff. Handbooks can be brief, providing the most basic information (as outlined in the new-teacher packet above), or they can be extensive, providing information about teaching philosophy, age-level characteristics and teaching skills. Some churches find it most effective to schedule new-teacher orientation after each new teacher has been given the handbook to read. This way, directors can ask open-ended questions based on handbook information to find out what areas they most need to address with the new teachers. (See pp. 69-70 for more information on handbooks.)

Use the Job Descriptions

When meeting with new teachers, use the job descriptions for each position to guide you in listing the specific tasks expected. Try to fully answer the question, What are the basic things a person should do in order to succeed in this ministry? Explain why each action is important and how it will benefit the teacher. (For example, "It is important to get each session off to a good start by allowing time for friendly, informal conversations as children arrive. In order to allow for this relaxed beginning, teachers need to be in their rooms, ready to welcome and guide children, at least 15 minutes before the announced starting time of the session.") Take advantage of any orientation resources that correlate with the curriculum (curriculum walk-through CDs, explanatory videos, etc.).

Some churches find it helpful to have teachers sign the commitment form (see p. 63) as part of a new teacher's orientation. Signing this form highlights the importance of each teacher's ministry and helps him or her to feel he or she has made a firm commitment.

Pair with Experienced Teachers

If a new volunteer is joining the staff for a class already in progress, arrange for the new person to observe and assist an experienced teacher several times. If the teachers in the class are meeting to plan lessons, invite the new volunteer to attend. Give the new volunteer one or two simple assignments for the next session. Increase responsibility each week as the new worker shows ability and confidence. Ideally, all new teachers and helpers should be paired with a mentor teacher for three to six weeks. Even if the new teacher does not teach with the mentor, the mentor should be available to answer questions and help guide the new teacher through phone calls or e-mail. (You may wish to recruit a retired professional teacher whose skills you admire to be an on-call mentor in this way. It's a great way to use the wisdom of seniors who no longer teach but love and understand kids.)

Be a Great Trainer

When a pro sports team recruits a college player, a tremendous amount of training takes place before that player ever steps onto the field. In the same way, great teachers may have natural talent but must have training to be able to advance and grow. Reading the handbook and attending an orientation class are only the beginning!

Plan a basic orientation course that presents key topics for teachers: how children learn, age-level characteristics and needs of children, discipline tips, storytelling hints, etc. Large churches may have enough new teachers that they can conduct orientation courses as part of their adult education program. Some churches have even found that by inviting the entire congregation to attend training classes, three benefits emerge: Class participants determine if they are gifted in the area of teaching, training helps them as parents with their own skills, and everyone gains an improved understanding of the children's ministry programs!

CHILDREN'S MINISTRY COMMITMENT

I, _____, because I feel called by God, commit to the following guidelines as a Children's Ministry teacher for the period of _____ to _____. This commitment is reviewable and renewable.

I will

• Serve on the teaching team for the _____ class/department.

I am committed to Our Lord

• I have a personal relationship with Jesus Christ which I desire to model for children.

• I enjoy studying God's Word regularly and desire to grow in my faith and commitment to Him (through personal study, adult classes or home Bible study groups).

Our Church

• I worship regularly with our church family.

• I support the doctrinal statement and leadership of our church.

My Students

• I enjoy children and desire for them to know of God's love and concern for their lives.

• I will take the necessary time to prepare my lessons during the week, incorporating my own God-given gifts into each lesson.

• I will care for my students individually (through prayer, telephone calls, birthday cards, etc.).

• I will be faithful in attendance, arriving at least 15 minutes before the session begins. If I must be absent, I will contact an approved substitute and alert my team leader.

• I will follow up with mailing or visits to absentee class members.

• I will participate in at least one training event during the year to improve my teaching skills.

• I will pray regularly for the children in my class.

My Teaching Team

• I will communicate regularly with my team teachers.

• I will participate in scheduled teachers' meetings.

• I will care for and return all equipment and curriculum provided.

• I will express my needs as a teacher to the Christian Education Committee.

_____

Teacher

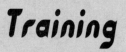

HOW DO WE DO THIS JOB ANYWAY?

Sometimes children's ministry leaders are so glad to have someone (anyone!) willing to teach a group that they are tempted to forego the essential steps that turn the willing volunteer into an effective teacher. (Sending in an untrained volunteer sends this message: "We're glad you're babysitting, but at the core, we don't believe teaching children is all that important." Ouch!)

Training is like watering a garden: Water a garden only once a year and it is unlikely to produce fruit. In the same way, a teacher needs more than one "watering" of training to be equipped for fruitful ministry. In order for training to truly make a difference, it must be ongoing. Building the skills of teachers is an important process that creates effective children's ministry—because teachers are made, not born! Your volunteers deserve to know the skills they need to effectively guide children in Bible learning!

Consistent planning creates solid, ongoing training. When leaders and teachers meet regularly, they can encourage and support one another in trying new ideas, evaluating progress, finding solutions to problems and sharing successes. When taking one step of learning at a time, new teachers get thorough training instead of a quick, haphazard orientation. When they can absorb information about teaching methods and program procedures slowly, they gain confidence. With ongoing training, a plan is already in place to communicate and discuss the changes that will take place during the year. Veteran teachers benefit, too: They can enhance their skills, help train new teachers and gain fresh enthusiasm!

It's easy to tell volunteers we appreciate them. But as the old saying goes, talk is cheap. However, a well-run training event says loudly to every teacher, "You are important. We value you and our kids. We want you to grow and want them to gain all they can from your ministry." That's affirmation in actions that speak louder than words!

A good ongoing training program:

Relates to the age level taught. Many principles of learning are similar for all age groups, but teachers need to know specific ways to apply these principles with the children they teach.

Is practical. Training should always focus on practical ways to use the information being taught in upcoming sessions or programs.

Is related to the curriculum. Training should help teachers see how their teacher's manual can help them continue to use the information learned at a training event. For this reason, a training event should provide teachers with time to plan together, using their curriculum resources.

Can be practiced. Unless a teacher practices a new skill or method, he or she will probably not feel confident enough to use it in class. Every training event should involve practice or role-play so participants both observe and practice the skills they are being trained to use.

Is regularly scheduled. When people are recruited to teach, they should clearly understand when, where and how they will regularly be equipped to succeed in their jobs.

Is consistent. The training should always reflect the same teaching and learning philosophy (see pp. 7-8 for more on teaching philosophy). Teachers then understand how and why they teach and how best to teach, regardless of the age level. Choose topics that reinforce each other so that over time, teachers can "put the pieces of the puzzle together." (Presenting conflicting educational philosophies and methods leaves teachers feeling they received pieces from different puzzles: The ideas don't fit together, leaving teachers puzzled indeed!)

KINDS OF TRAINING

Workshops and conferences. All teachers will benefit by attending training conferences or workshops that enrich their total teaching ministry. Teachers need opportunities to learn new skills, find solutions to problems, correct mistakes and expand their vision. Many churches plan at least two special training events each year, approximately four to six months apart. More than one such event is recommended because not all teachers are able to attend any one event.

After any training event, evaluate what learning occurred. Were your objectives for the event met? Have teachers acquired or improved the needed skills? If the answer is yes, concentrate on the next area of need. If the answer is no, consider how you can address the need in a different manner.

Class or age-level training. Teachers who meet together to plan upcoming lessons can include a time of training in their meetings so that during the next class session, they can immediately put into practice what they have learned.

If training sessions gain a reputation for being well worth a teacher's time, well organized and informative, they are more likely to be well attended. (Offering really good food is always a plus as well!)

Individual training. In addition to participating in special training events or planning meetings with other teachers, individual teachers can improve their skills in a variety of ways. Provide ways for teachers to improve skills on their own:

★ Observing a Sunday School class or other program that is functioning well. (Give guideline questions: How did the teacher involve students? How did the teacher achieve the lesson aim? How did the teacher communicate interest and caring for students?) It is not necessary that the observed class be perfect. People learn as much from weaknesses as from strengths.

★ Providing books, DVDs, videos, etc., that offer training on a particular skill (discipline, discovery learning, communication skills, etc.). Keep a supply of such materials to loan to teachers on a regular basis. Suggest that teachers use these resources to build their skills during times such as a car commute.

★ Distributing a teacher memo every weekend. Include an encouraging note, a teaching tip or two and necessary announcements. Memos can be sent in e-mail form or even posted on your church's website. In a monthly newsletter, include articles that highlight a particular skill and list specific ways to put the skill into practice. Ask an experienced teacher to describe how he or she applies the skill in specific situations.

★ Surveying teachers to discover specific training needs. Ask each teacher to indicate topics and skills he or she would like to learn more about.

★ Provide forms (see pp. 66-68) for teachers to use in evaluating their skills.

Teacher training meetings that are worthwhile can create tremendous teamwork, encouragement and learning. Don't deprive your teachers of the chance to be their best for Christ!

EVALUATING AND IMPROVING YOUR ROLE AS A TEACHER

Check each statement as it applies to you.

1 = Always   **2 = Often**   **3 = Sometimes**   **4 = Seldom**   **5 = Never**

	1	2	3	4	5
The Teacher Is One Who Guides					
I ask the Holy Spirit to help me guide my students.					
I study the Bible content and pray to apply it to my own life.					
I pay attention to the individual growth needs of each student.					
I set specific learning objectives for my class.					
I plan sessions that emphasize active learning experiences.					
I assist learning by creating a positive classroom environment.					
I plan and ask appropriate questions to guide learning.					
I am excited when students discover Bible truths for themselves.					
I evaluate each student's learning after each class session.					
I contact students outside of class to learn about their needs.					
The Teacher Is One Who Stimulates and Motivates					
I select activities that interest and challenge my class.					
I encourage students to explore and discover God's truth themselves.					
I invite students to honestly express ideas and feelings.					
I help students make plans to apply truths in life situations.					
I affirm students for evidence of positive changes.					
The Teacher Is One Who Models					
I practice specific ways for my class to put truth into action.					
I set a positive Christian example for students both in and out of class.					
I tell my students of both my victories and struggles in following Christ.					
I show students how I confess and repent when I fall short.					
The Teacher Is One Who Cares					
I know each student's name and family.					
I accept my students as they are, even when they are wrong.					
I show interest in each student by carefully listening.					
I clearly communicate the God-given value of each person.					
I pray for each of my students by name.					
I give time to each student outside of class.					
I provide practical help and friendship to my students.					
I foster a climate of positive discipline in my classroom.					
I contact absentees to show that I missed them.					

FOCUS ON LIFE NEEDS

Check the box that most closely answers the following questions:

1 = Always   2 = Often   3 = Sometimes   4 = Seldom   5 = Never

Teaching is too often focused only on what a teacher does, rather than on what a student does in response.

Physical How often do you . . .	1	2	3	4	5
Monitor the room's lighting, temperature and air flow to ensure students' comfort?					
Equip rooms with appropriate furniture arranged to encourage interaction?					
Provide access for those with physical limitations?					
Social **How often do you . . .**					
Encourage positive relationships, avoiding put-downs of others?					
Maintain group sizes and teacher ratios that make personal attention possible?					
Seek out ways to include people besides the regular attenders?					
Plan ways for group members to interact and work together?					
Emotional **How often do you . . .**					
Really listen when a student is talking?					
Actively seek to make your class an emotionally safe place?					
Show respect and acceptance for a student who is upset or bored or fearful?					
Honestly share your own feelings, including times when they have not been positive?					

FOCUS ON LIFE NEEDS
(continued)

Intellectual How often do you . . .	1	2	3	4	5
Allow students the freedom to disagree without making them feel rejected?					
Guide students to discover Bible truth, not just listen to it being presented?					
Limit the use of questions that elicit one-word (yes, no, etc.) or straight factual answers?					
Encourage students to compare their opinions with what the Bible says?					
Give personal guidance to students who lack the Bible knowledge of others in the group?					
Spiritual **How often do you . . .**					
Actively seek to discover each student's spiritual condition and attitudes?					
Openly share your personal spiritual pilgrimage?					
Guide students to apply Bible truth in practical ways to life situations?					
Pray regularly for the needs of your students?					
Age Level **How often do you . . .**					
Consider the characteristics of the age group you teach when preparing your lessons?					
Plan ways to accommodate different skill levels of students in your group?					
Individual **How often do you . . .**					
Know the specific interests and needs that make each student unique in your group?					
Use varied teaching approaches to accommodate the different learning styles of students?					

ORGANIZING A TRAINING MEETING

A good training meeting requires the following:

★ advance scheduling, marked on the training calendar every teacher receives at the beginning of the year;

★ advance publicity (church bulletins, postcards, posters at church, etc.) stating the reason for getting together;

★ personal contacts by a leader to secure commitments to attend;

★ provision for child care that does not burden the teachers;

★ clearly defined starting and ending times on which people can depend;

★ excitement over those who attend, not complaints about those who are absent;

★ positive and enthusiastic leadership of activities and discussion focused on one or two topics that will help teachers improve their teaching;

★ prayer for each other and the children and families in their classes;

★ follow-up by leaders to inform staff members who were not present (consider a make-up meeting for people who have schedule conflicts).

During the meeting, you may want to provide some time for teachers who teach the same age level to meet together to choose responsibilities, plan materials, learn the suggested songs for upcoming lessons. Adapt this sample agenda as needed.

SAMPLE
MEETING AGENDA
(60-90 minutes)

5-10 minutes	Icebreaker activity
5 minutes	Welcome, prayer and announcements
20-30 minutes	Teacher training (watch video, discuss article, etc.)
15-20 minutes	Teachers' planning and sharing time
10-15 minutes	Devotional and prayer time
5-10 minutes	Refreshments

HELPFUL HANDBOOKS

Many churches develop a handbook for their children's ministry staff. These handbooks may be brief, providing only the most basic policies and procedures that must be understood by anyone working in the ministry.

More extensive handbooks may also provide information about teaching philosophy, age-level characteristics and teaching skills. The handbook is updated and distributed to each staff member at the beginning of the teaching term and also to new teachers as they join during the term. It is a simple way to be sure all staff have gotten the same information. Here is a sample of topics to be included:

★ Mission or vision statement, core values

★ A letter from the senior pastor conveying support of children's ministry and thanking volunteers for their service

★ Standards for teachers (screening policies, expectations)

★ Several key articles which present key elements of teaching that your volunteers need to know ("Bible Learning Activities: Hands-On Discovery Learning" on pp. 147-148, "Schedule: Goals and Methods That Work" on pp. 205-208, "Teacher's Role: What Do I Do?" on pp. 223-224)

★ Classroom procedures (class time schedule, attendance, greeting and dismissal procedures, name-tag procedures, field trip and party procedures, supply procedures, etc.)

★ Age-level policies (who belongs to which class, promotion times and policies)

★ Discipline procedures, safety and emergency procedures

★ Child-protection policies (diapering, bathroom assistance, child abuse and prevention, illness guidelines, teacher-to-child ratios)

★ Copies of needed forms (incident report, resource request, registration form, parental permission form, medical release form, etc.)

★ Copies of maps of the church campus, children's area, etc.

★ Current year's calendar, including scheduled training events, special events, etc.

★ Procedures for teachers (finding substitutes, budgets, supplies, space use, etc.)

While handbooks are valuable and can serve as a ready reference, don't assume that passing out a handbook (or even reading it aloud in a teachers' meeting) is a substitute for continuing training. It's only one part of a comprehensive training program.

HOW CAN YOU SHOW VOLUNTEERS THE VALUE OF WHAT THEY DO?

Although teaching children may be its own reward in many ways, volunteers in children's ministry can never receive too much encouragement and appreciation! You can demonstrate in meaningful ways that your church values highly the people who give their time and energy to teach and assist children. Here are some ideas:

★ Leave a small, inexpensive gift for each teacher (snack, cookies, unique supplies, etc.) occasionally during the teaching term with a note that tells a specific reason that you appreciate him or her.

★ Designate a Sunday at the beginning of each teaching term or program to dedicate or recognize those who will be teaching or helping in the coming days. Serve refreshments after the service for a "Meet the Teachers Reception" to honor these volunteers. List teachers' names in the bulletin or a newsletter.

★ Invite children and their parents to offer their thanks to a teacher through homemade cards or treats at holidays or a teacher's birthday.

★ Plan an annual event to honor teachers. Include the teachers and their spouses, family or other guests. These can be major events with decorations, special foods and entertainment or they can be low-key and informal. The goal is that the event be sufficiently well planned so that it communicates to the teachers that they are important enough for the children's ministry leaders to have gone to some trouble in their behalf.

★ Give thank-you gifts and cards at the end of the school year or at the end of a teacher's term of service. (A card or handwritten note may be more meaningful than giving every volunteer the same low-budget gift.

That sort of giving may seem to devalue a volunteer's individual contribution.)

★ Show appreciation with an attractive award certificate for each teacher. Include a gift certificate to a favorite restaurant or a Christian bookstore.

★ Have children create artwork or write notes of appreciation to be given to teachers.

A MONTH OF APPRECIATION!

Designate a month as "Teacher Appreciation Month" in your church. Some churches incorporate this into the month of October (Clergy Appreciation Day and Sunday School Teacher Appreciation Day both fall in October) or the month of February ("We Love Our Teachers" Month). Using an entire month gives you time to plan and the chance to expand on appreciation ideas that you might want to do more than just one time. Plan ways to honor teachers throughout the month.

★ A Sunday morning breakfast (sit-down or buffet, with or without a program; celebrate each department's teachers on a different Sunday to keep logistics from becoming too cumbersome)

★ A presentation honoring teachers, made up of photos and/or videos of teachers in action (show in a church service or at a teacher appreciation program)

★ Provide corsages and boutonnieres for teachers to wear so that everyone in the congregation can recognize them.

★ Each Monday morning, make it a habit to write one or two personal notes of appreciation. (Invite your team leaders or age-level coordinators to do the same!)

★ Challenge your church choir to write and sing a song to honor children's ministry volunteers!

★ Have a poetry contest: Poems must be written to honor either a specific volunteer or volunteers in general. Give a small prize and invite the winning author to read his or her poem at a church service or appreciation event.

★ Invite your creative teens to take their video gear around the church to get video greetings and messages of appreciation to be shown to teachers at a service or appreciation event.

RECOGNIZE VOLUNTEERS BIRTHDAYS!

Send each volunteer a birthday card signed by the Children's Ministry Director. Sound impossible? It can be done! (Most of the process could easily be done by a faithful volunteer.) First, be sure you have accurate birthday information for every volunteer. Purchase cards, address envelopes, place cards inside (don't seal them) and then note each person's birthday in the spot where the stamp will be placed. Then organize and file cards by date. Check the card file every Monday. When cards are pulled for the week, sign and add a personal note, seal, stamp and mail! It is a small but important way to affirm and show your appreciation of your volunteers.

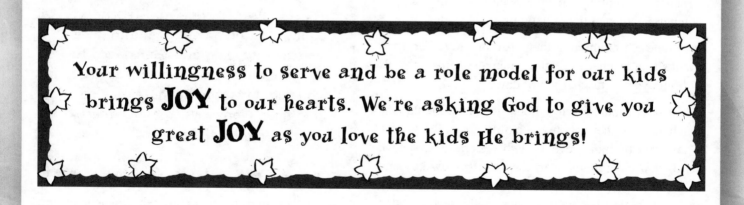

Your willingness to serve and be a role model for our kids brings **JOY** to our hearts. We're asking God to give you great **JOY** as you love the kids He brings!

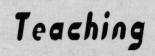

Teaching

HOW DO I DEAL WITH THESE PEOPLE?

What should I do when teachers don't get along?

Occasionally, you may find that for one reason or another, the teachers in a particular class do not develop a friendship and find it difficult to work together.

First, prayerfully try to determine if there is a particular factor that could be the root of the problem (teachers disagree on discipline methods, one teacher is always late, too many children for the number of teachers, etc.). Try to correct that problem.

Second, consider adding a teacher to the team. Sometimes a third party can help smooth out a troubled relationship.

Third, switch teaching assignments. One teacher may have a preference for another age level. Be sure to try steps 1 and 2 first, however.

How can I get my teachers to try something new?

It is a common pattern for most people to teach the way they have always taught. The best way to encourage a teacher to try a new activity, to practice a new skill or to modify a class schedule is threefold: First, in a teacher training meeting, give teachers time not only to learn about but also to practice and role-play a new skill or activity. Teachers are much more likely to try something they have already practiced and feel confident doing.

Second, provide teachers with an opportunity to observe the new activity, skill or schedule in action. You may find that the teachers in one class are more open to making a change than other teachers. Begin with that class and invite other teachers to observe. After the observation, answer questions and then invite each teacher to take a turn leading the activity or class. If possible, observe the teachers and affirm them for their positive actions, giving a few helpful hints if needed.

Third, begin something new at the start of a new school year or new teaching term. Whether it is a new check-in procedure, a new class schedule or a new curriculum, clearly communicate to all teachers (and parents if needed) what is being changed and what benefits will result.

What can I do with a person who volunteers but does not seem to be suited to children's ministry?

This is where the application process is vital. First, be sure the person has an application on file (every volunteer should have an application on file—even if the person has been working in children's ministry for years). Then personally interview the person. If you feel you need more background information, talk with the references listed on the application. If after your church's approved application process has been completed, you still feel that he or she would not be suitable, express your appreciation for his or her interest in children's ministry and offer an alternative job that enables the volunteer to serve in a more appropriate capacity (preparing lesson materials or bulletin boards, shopping for supplies, etc.). If you feel the person needs to develop teaching skills further before you assign a job, place the volunteer alongside an experienced teacher who is skilled at training and can help you observe the volunteer. If you have no appropriate jobs for the person, talk with other church leaders to identify another area of service and then lovingly direct the person to the leader.

How can I get my teachers to arrive on time?

First, make sure that all teachers are aware of what time they are expected to be in their classrooms. (Each job description should include a starting time!)

Second, during training, emphasize the benefits of teachers' being present and well prepared when children arrive: Children feel welcome and can immediately begin learning. Also emphasize the likely consequences when teachers are not present: Children and parents feel unsure about who is in charge and chaos often erupts!

Third, permanently assign one of your helpers or greeters to the door of that classroom. This will keep children safe until the teacher arrives.

Fourth, if the teacher's lateness is a perpetual problem, talk with that volunteer and invite him or her to take a different position, perhaps preparing materials or doing other support activities that have no time restriction. Be understanding of difficulties but firm about your commitment to both the safety and the learning of the children.

One underlying issue may be that some children (other teacher's children, etc.) arrive much earlier than other children. If so, set aside an area where they can be supervised while participating in several unstructured activities (watching a video, free play, coloring, etc.) so that all teachers have the time free to fully prepare for the teaching session.

What do I tell a parent who wants to teach his or her own child in Sunday School?

First, ask open-ended questions to find out the parent's reasons for wanting to teach the class. If the parent's concern is that the child will not be comfortable without him or her, invite the parent to observe quietly at intervals, without the child knowing, so the parent can see how well the child adjusts. If the parent simply wants to be acquainted with the children in the child's peer group, serving as an occasional substitute or a helper in the child's class may work out quite well. However, (especially with younger ages) a child often finds it difficult to understand the change in the parent's role as a teacher in the classroom. The child frequently behaves in an entirely different manner! Normal interaction with other children suffers.

Suggest other ways parents can assist in a child's class: preparing materials, providing snack, etc. It's also good to encourage parents to teach in a class of children similar in age to that of their own child. Parents benefit greatly by seeing typical behavior patterns and seeing how skilled teachers interact with children. Some parents find it helpful to teach the next older age as a way to prepare for their own child's growth. Suggest this as an option. Others feel more comfortable teaching the next youngest age, using experience gained from their child at that age.

How can I prepare for last-minute teacher substitutions?

When recruiting teachers, develop a list of people who are willing to be on call as last-minute substitutes. Often, people who teach children during the week but who don't wish to teach regularly on the weekend make excellent substitutes because of their knowledge of children and experience in guiding classroom activities. Administrative leaders can benefit by substituting periodically, too. Teaching or helping in a class from time to time is essential to stay in touch with practical needs.

Provide the substitute with a copy of the schedule and lesson for the class and a list of children's names. If name tags are not already available, make them for each child to wear. Also make sure that all supplies are readily available. If you are unable to provide the substitute with the appropriate lesson plan, be prepared in advance by having a generic lesson or two planned along with the necessary supplies. Store the lesson and supplies in a "substitute" box.

One of my teachers continually says her class is difficult or out of control. How can I determine specific ways to help her?

Ask the following questions to plan ways of improving the situation:

★ Is the number of teachers appropriate for the size of the class? Look at the chart of recommended teacher-to-child ratios on page 45. You may be able to handle a group of children with fewer teachers, but the results are that teachers often spend much of their time providing crowd control or dealing with discipline problems.

★ Are the teachers present consistently so that relationships are being built and consistent classroom procedures are being followed?

★ Is the class offering enough variety of learning activities and thus meeting the needs of active children? Observe (help in) the class several times in order to fully answer this question. When teachers have unrealistic expectations (for example, sitting still for extended periods), problems often result.

★ Are children being offered choices? Allowing children to make some of their own choices (which learning activity to participate in first, what materials to use, etc.) will help avoid discipline problems. Children's behavior is more positive when they are doing something they have chosen.

★ What is the pattern of problem behavior? Does it happen only at a certain time, such as when children first arrive or during the large-group Bible story time? If so, help a teacher see ways to change procedures during the difficult time. For example, make sure teachers are present and prepared when children first arrive so that children are immediately involved in an appropriate activity, or have teachers sit among children during large-group times, so they can redirect children's attention if needed.

★ Does a particular child need one-on-one supervision? For some children who consistently struggle with behavior, it may be helpful to ask an adult volunteer to participate in classroom activities alongside the child, building a friendship with the child and being available to redirect the child's behavior as needed.

★ Does the teacher need additional training? It may be helpful to ask the teacher to work alongside a more experienced teacher or to participate in one or more training meetings or conferences.

All of these questions are best answered through your own observation. Then you can address the areas of need with kindness, understanding and sensitivity. You can also invite the teacher to complete one of the personal evaluation forms on pages 66-68 to help him or her identify areas of teaching that need to be improved.

How do you get teachers to come to training sessions? When is the most effective time to schedule teacher training?

Talk with several leaders and teachers to determine the best incentives and the best times for teachers in your church to meet. Some possibilities:

★ Hold meetings on weeknights when the church calendar is relatively free of other meetings; providing dinner and child care will eliminate the two most likely excuses for not attending!

★ Have training sessions during a time when teachers are already planning to be present (Wednesday night for Sunday teachers, Sunday meeting for Wednesday teachers, etc.) Another idea: On one Sunday during regular class time, obtain substitutes, or during a special program for all ages, hold a training session.

★ Have a Saturday-morning brunch or a Sunday after-church luncheon and offer both food and child care!

★ Offer the same training session at two different times. Invite teachers to choose the time that is best for them.

Refer to pages 64-70 for more information on how to schedule and lead training meetings.

What should I say when a parent wants to know if an older sibling can stay and be a helper in a younger child's class?

If the younger child is new to your church, you may want to invite the older child to stay and assist in the class for a week or two. Make it clear that this solution is for a limited time. Explain to the parent, "It will be fun to get to know your daughter, but the activities in the class aren't designed for her. She will have a better time and learn more in a class for her own age. I'll be glad to introduce you to her teacher."

A good rule of thumb for teen helpers is for a separation of about 10 years of age to exist between preschoolers and helpers and at least 5 or 6 years of age with children and teen helpers. If helpers and children in a classroom are too close in age, the teachers often find that the helper's "help" is minimal. (It is recommended that helpers for toddlers be at least 12 years old and that helpers for infants be at least 16 years old.)

We do want to use teenagers as helpers for our staff. What guidelines should we follow?

Many churches plan effective ways of training and using youth in their children's ministries—always as helpers and never as teachers by themselves. Here are some guidelines for setting up an effective youth helper program:

First, determine with your church staff and youth leaders the minimum age and grade level for youth helpers. Consider these other possible requirements: parent's permission to participate, regular attendance at church youth classes and worship services, attendance at a specified number of training classes and a recommendation from a youth supervisor or leader in the church. Youth should also complete a volunteer application form (see pp. 59-60).

Second, plan one or more training classes for potential youth helpers that include their parents. Including parents in the classes is helpful, not only because it acquaints the parents with what their children are doing, but also because it encourages parents to follow up at home on the training.

At the training classes, provide job descriptions. Explain classroom procedures and safety guidelines. Role-play some common situations in which youth helpers serve. Emphasize that the job of a youth helper is an important task because of the way in which positive experiences influence children and because of the service youth helpers provide to the church family. Clearly state to helpers how important it is that they recognize they are there to help. Help them formulate questions they can ask a teacher to find out how best to help. Remind them that their purpose is to focus on children, not on other helpers. Set up a time for teachers to give feedback on additional training that is needed for youth helpers.

Third, limit the number of youth helpers who will be assisting with one group at a time. If there are too many youth helpers, the helpers may focus on each other rather than giving attention to the children.

When teachers are absent and forget to call, we can't get substitutes. What on earth can we do then?

Remember that the rule of thumb for classroom safety is at least two adults in each classroom. If you are unable to provide an emergency substitute, a parent may be asked to lead or help in the classroom, provided that there is another adult or teen helper. Consider asking administrators or other leaders to help out in a pinch. If there are not enough adults for a class or classes to remain open, place children in nearby classes with children of similar ages, provided the teachers of those classes have space, enough materials and have agreed to the change ahead of time. (Note: In an emergency, a class may need to be closed for the safety of the children. Make sure this procedure has been approved by your church leadership before it is necessary to close a class.)

If this situation becomes a recurring problem, begin immediately to prayerfully enlist new teachers who will take this vital ministry more seriously. If a haphazard approach to ministry is tolerated, people will assume that it is OK.

A Place for Kids

Facilities and Equipment

Welcome to the place where you can imagine the children's ministry environment of your dreams!

Here are complete physical descriptions of well-designed and well-equipped children's ministry rooms, as well as a basic materials list, how to set up a resource room, the benefits of developing a quality facility, and more.

WHAT MAKES EACH CHILD FEEL WELCOMED, LOVED AND VALUED?

We love to see children come to our classroom doors full of enthusiasm and ready for whatever is coming next! But some children reluctantly sidle up, act clingy or are clearly anxious. Although their negative reactions may be unrelated to their being at church, we're wise to be aware of the ways we can head off some of that negativity by making each child feel welcomed.

A WELCOMING PLACE

Take time to look thoughtfully at the areas of your church where children's ministries take place. Then consider the places in your town where children love to gather. What are those places? What features of those places send the message to kids, "This place is for you. It was created especially to make you want to come here!" (In addition, consider what features are designed to actually appeal to adults, so they want to bring their kids!) Based on features that have genuine child appeal, look at your children's ministry area again. Ask, "If we could make this place more kid friendly, how would it change? What features could it

incorporate? What might this physical space look like? Changes need not be cutesy or especially appealing to adults. The space may not need to be a particular color or have special lights or fog machines. But it is important that the features of the room tell a child, "This place is for you because we think you are important. We welcome you in to this place!" (For more information about facilities and equipment, see pp. 81-87.)

WELCOMING PEOPLE

The first moments of a child's experience at church will have great impact—for better or for worse. When a child comes to the door of a room whose interior looks like a famous pizza restaurant or an amusement park and he or she seems overwhelmed and hesitant, we may wonder, *What is wrong? Didn't we make it look welcoming?* But if a child is ignored at the doorway of an attractive room, this tells the child that no matter how much fun this place looks to be, he or she is not likely to be treated as an individual. "You can be part of this gang if you are bold enough to step inside!" is what the environment alone can tell a child. No matter how visually appealing and exciting a place may look, children are still human beings. They look for other human beings to whom they can relate, whether in a nursery or a preteen hangout room!

Ministry to children begins by welcoming them. Making children feel welcomed and comfortable is life-changing stuff! A friendly person at the door sees a child. He or she gets at the child's eye level, smiles, gives a pat or hug around the shoulder and talks to the child, repeating the child's name. This amazing person then explains the activities in which the child may engage. Something powerful happens—a child is included! Community is created, there and then!

Greeters should work in teams so that one may always be at the door while another guides a child to an appropriate area. Even in very small classes, greeters at the door free the teachers to interact with children already in the room. Instead of being constantly distracted, teachers and children can integrate new arrivals easily and effectively. And don't forget to give greeters the honor they deserve—they are tremendously important! (For a job description for greeters, see p. 52.)

WELCOMING PROGRAMS

The program is what happens to a child once he or she is inside the door. It may be large group or small group, entertaining or interactive, quiet or loud. But what makes a program say, "Welcome!" to a child? What program makes a child feel, "They value me here. They care about me. They think I can do things!"

Here are three questions to ask about a program (for more information on curriculum selection, see pp. 33-35):

1. Is the program age appropriate? For example: Second graders yawn and roll in their seats, counting ceiling tiles during a program that is absolutely riveting the attention of the fifth graders. Are the second graders feeling that the adults chose this program especially for them? Not at all! Rather, they are exhibiting normal signs of restlessness that result from a program that is not designed in an age-appropriate way. Read the recommended session schedule (see p. 207) for information on effective learning for children.

2. Is the program different from what kids do at school? When a program seems like school, children quickly revert to school behavior (that skill we all learn—feigning attention while ignoring the proceedings around us!). Most children believe that if they wait quietly and patiently and don't volunteer (what some schoolteachers call "being good"!), they can wait out this experience, too. So a program needs to catch children's interest, engage their minds and bodies to tell them, "This is not school!"

However, this does not mean that a program needs to scream, "FUN! FUN! FUN!" every minute. Children are already distracted and overentertained. We do them a disservice if we do not provide the meat of what matters forever and show them how to chew on it! Children need some quiet time and a safe place for age-appropriate, interactive discussion that helps them not only to learn Bible facts but also to understand how Bible truths work out in their own daily lives. Fun is not the only purpose of children's ministry—because God did not create us with a need for perpetual fun but with a need for relationship with Him! No amount of fun will satisfy that need. Fun is often the by-product of activities that engage and excite children about what matters! (Rather than asking if a program is fun, determine whether a program is lively, engaging, interesting and conducive to children's discovering truth for themselves. Refuse to be intimidated by those who whine, "This is boring!" Determine what their actual concerns are. Then address those concerns by involving those children in the learning process!)

3. Is the program going to make a difference in children's lives? First, understand the aims and goals of the program itself. List aims you believe should be achieved in your situation. Without knowing specific aims for ways a program may effect change, there will not be clarity about what result to expect! (For more information about goals and aims, see pp. 9-10.) Because this is spiritual ministry to children, don't settle for child care or entertainment. Talk with and listen to teachers to see if they feel the aims of the lesson are being met. (For more information on assessment tools, see pp. 16-25.)

No room will be perfect. No one program will fit all needs. Not every child will care if he or she is greeted at the door. But when we create a welcoming place, we remind ourselves that we need to honor the children whom we want to disciple into wholehearted followers of Jesus Christ. And as we honor them, we honor Him who said, "Let the little children come to me!" (Matthew 19:14).

Facilities

HOW DOES A PLACE HELP CHILDREN LEARN ABOUT GOD?

Teaching and learning can occur almost anywhere, but the surroundings can draw students toward learning or distract them from it. Furniture can make a room comfortable so that learning is the focus or uncomfortable so that attention is lost and restlessness results. Equipment can help or hinder communication; room arrangements can aid the building of relationships or can make them difficult. Walls can reinforce learning or create distraction, depending on their use.

BENEFITS FOR CHILDREN

We're wise to remember that God created children with certain physical and learning characteristics that we need to carefully consider when we plan the physical spaces in which they are taught. While our facilities never will be perfect (nor do they need to be), it is important to evaluate them regularly and improve them in light of what we learn.

Children work, play and learn with their bodies as well as their minds and hearts. The younger the child, the greater the need for physical space. Children need rooms that are equipped for action. Open space, properly sized equipment and safe and interesting materials make children feel that the rooms at church belong to them and are good places to be. When a physical space is welcoming to children, teachers find children are more receptive, so it is easier to effectively teach the Bible and communicate God's love!

In addition, classrooms that are inviting in appearance make it easier to recruit teachers and helpers. Adults are as affected by the visual aspect of a room as children are. Teachers need space that is clean, organized, welcoming and spacious. When teachers are frustrated by poor maintenance, disorganized supplies or crowded conditions, they are not likely to return.

SUFFICIENT SPACE

For younger classes, determine how many children a room can adequately handle. First, measure the length and width of your room. Multiply these two measurements and then divide the answer by 30 feet (9 m) to determine the number of children who should be present in the room at one time. Once each year (usually several months before children are promoted into new classes), reevaluate room designations by considering the number of children and their ages. Assign classes according to the chart on this page.

Keep in mind that younger children are likely to be stressed by large groups, even with an adequate amount of space and an adequate number of teachers. If your rooms are so large that there are more than 20 children in a room, use sturdy dividers or other furniture to create smaller areas within the room for small groups of children to meet.

Just because children have moved into elementary school, do not automatically assume that they will be able to sit still for extended periods of time! Although they may be able to sit for longer periods, children still need to move frequently. They still learn best by using their entire bodies. Space needs to be adequate so that they can participate in activities that stimulate their senses, engage their minds and involve their bodies. That requires space!

THE RIGHT LOCATION

The ideal location for early childhood classrooms is at ground level, with quick and easy access to a safe (fenced) outside area, to parking and to restrooms.

R= Recommended   A = Actual (what you now have)

	Column 1 Maximum Attendance per Department		Column 2 Optimum Room Dimensions and Approximate Square Footage		Column 3 Floor Space per Person		Column 4 Student Ratio for Small Group Class	
	R	A	R	A*	R	A+	R	A
EARLY CHILDHOOD **Ages 0 to 1**	12-15		24'x36'=900 sq.ft.		30-35 sq.ft.		1:3 or 4	
Ages 2 to 3	16-20		24'x36'=900 sq.ft.		30-35 sq.ft.		1:5	
Ages 4 to 5	20-24		24'x36'=900 sq.ft.		30-35 sq.ft.		1:6	
CHILDREN **Grades 1 to 5/6**	24-30		24'x36'=900 sq.ft.		25-30 sq.ft.		1:6 to 8	

Notes

*To figure room square footage, multiply the length of the room by the width.

+To figure floor space per person, divide room square footage (see column 2) by department attendance (see column 1).

(Consider reserving the portion of your parking lot nearest the early childhood rooms specifically for parents with young children.) Classrooms for children in elementary school should be easily accessible to parents who will be checking them in and out. Having a safe outdoor area available to these classrooms makes it easy for classes to move outdoors for some activities, especially if indoor classroom size is limited.

Make sure classrooms are clearly marked and that ushers, greeters and the welcome/information-center staff know the locations for each age level. Large churches often provide a labeled map to direct parents to the appropriate rooms for their children's classes. A small church may provide information on a white board placed on an easel near an entrance or at a central gathering area.

Furnishing for Learning

Floor Covering. Select a durable floor covering that is easy to clean. Vinyl flooring or linoleum in a subdued pattern is usable for many activities. Washable carpeting provides a quiet, relaxed atmosphere and helps to control sound. Many churches combine vinyl flooring and carpet in a room so that messy activities can be done over vinyl flooring with a carpeted area available for being seated on the floor. Carpet squares or a sturdy area rug on which children may sit is needed if there is no carpeting at all. (Note: Keep cleaning materials for all surfaces easily accessible to adults but safely stored away from children.)

Ceiling, Walls and Windows. Acoustical ceilings deaden sounds. Walls also should be insulated to block sound and be furnished with some sound-absorbing materials. Use wall paint that can be easily washed (usually semigloss). Windows should be made of clear shatterproof glass. Securely fasten window screens. Window coverings are needed only to reduce glare or to insulate against heat or cold.

Lighting and Color. Lighting should be even and without glare in all parts of the room. Soft pastel colors help to create a warm, cheery atmosphere. To brighten rooms that are dark on gloomy days, use a soft yellow or pink wall color. To reduce glare in a sunny room, select pale blue or green colors. Bright colors can be added as highlights but should not overpower the room environment. (See pp. 88-89 for further guidelines on wall treatments.)

Toilet Facilities. Toilet facilities that immediately adjoin each room are desirable for children aged two to five, with a child-level sink and drinking fountain in each. Elementary classes should have easy access to nearby restrooms that are designated for their exclusive use.

Electrical Outlets. Electrical outlets should meet local codes, be equipped with safety plugs and be out of children's reach. Outlets on each wall eliminate the hazards of extension cords.

Room Temperature. Children need a comfortable room temperature. Radiators or floor heaters should be covered to avoid accidental burns and adequate ventilation is also needed. A room filled with active children can get stuffy very easily, making children restless and uncomfortable.

Use the form on page 84 to evaluate each of your classrooms.

ROOM EVALUATION FORM

Class Name

Date _____

Evaluated by _____

Room

Put an X in each box where improvement is needed

The Classroom					
Adequate space?					
Quick, easy movement from large to small groups?					
Adequate lighting from windows, fixtures?					
Proper ventilation?					
Controlled temperature?					
Floor and ceiling absorb sound?					
Bulletin boards/wall displays at students eye level ?					
Bulletin boards current and uncluttered?					
Provision for darkening room for videos?					
Electrical outlets accessible/adequate?					
Room attractively decorated?					
Walls clean, cheerful in color?					
Walls need repair/painting?					
Toilet, sink facilities easily accessible?					
Handicap access to room?					
Any doors that could be taken off small rooms to facilitate movement?					
Any walls that could be removed to give more flexibility?					
Adequate storage facilities?					
Floor coverings adequate, clean?					
Classroom Equipment					
Furniture/equipment easily moved to provide flexibility?					
Classroom materials available, so students have easy access?					
Tables, chairs the right size?					
Any excess furniture that could be removed to provide more space?					
Any additional furniture/equipment needed?					
Any furniture/equipment needing repair/painting?					

EQUIPMENT AND FURNITURE

Consider these lists of equipment and furniture as ideals for which to strive—it can be overwhelming to think about providing all this equipment at once! Develop priorities by which the most necessary items are purchased first. After you've obtained the basics, continue to evaluate the priorities of your classrooms, upgrading or adding equipment as your church budget allows.

When selecting equipment, it is wiser to buy a few well-made items than many less expensive (and less durable) ones. Equipment of superior quality is well worth the investment in terms of years of hard wear. Regularly examine equipment and furniture for hazards such as cracks, splinters or missing parts.

RECOMMENDED SIZES FOR TABLES/CHAIRS

Age Group	Chair: Height from floor+	Tables: 10 inches (25 cm) higher than chairs	Tabletops: Durable and washable
Ages 2 to 5	10-14 inches (25-35 cm)*	20-24 inches (50-60 cm)	Approx. 30x48 inches (75x120 cm)
Grades 1 to 6	12-16 inches (30-40 cm)	22-26 inches (55-65 cm)	30x48 inches (75x120 cm) to 36x60 inches (90x150 cm)

Notes:
+Stackable chairs that do not collapse are preferable to folding chairs.
*In Early Childhood rooms, no adult-sized chairs are necessary, as teachers should sit at child's eye level.

Entrance Furniture. Coat racks near each classroom's entrance are necessary pieces of equipment. Coat hooks and a shelf can be mounted on the wall either in the room or in the hall outside your classroom door. A sign-in table or counter is helpful near the entrance. (See pp. 109-110 for more information on check-in procedures.)

Tables and Chairs. All children learn best when they are comfortable. Tables and chairs in the correct sizes are essential. Select chairs that are sturdy and not easily tipped over but are light enough for children to move. Tabletops should be durable and washable. Avoid tables that seat more than six to eight. Rather, select tables that allow the teacher to be within arm's reach of all children.

Round tables have the advantage of having no corners, but rectangular tables are less expensive and are more efficiently used for art activities.

Storage Space. Ample storage space for each class is necessary. For teacher's materials, if possible, mount cabinets about 50 inches (127 cm) from the floor. Installation at this height frees the floor space below the cabinets to make more room for children's learning activities.

If storage space in the classroom is limited, keep only basic supplies (glue, scissors, markers, crayons, etc.) in the classroom. Keep additional supplies (construction paper, cardboard tubes, beanbags, etc.) in a central supply room (or resource room) from which teachers obtain needed supplies on a weekly basis. Many large churches find that it is more cost effective to maintain such a central storage area. (See pp. 92-93 for more information about resource rooms.)

Make sure that each classroom has a designated area (cubby, table, clear floor space, etc.) for children to place take-home materials (activity pages, art projects, take-home papers, etc.) during the session. Some churches provide a labeled paper bag for each child to use for carrying materials home. Labels include the child's name and the lesson's Bible verse. Children may decorate the labels when they first arrive in the classroom.

ENOUGH SUPPLIES

Active children need to participate in a variety of Bible learning activities, and they need the proper equipment to do it. Use the following list as a guide for learning activity materials that should be on hand in every room:

Basic Materials

★ Appropriate scissors for children in that room (include scissors for left-handed children)

★ Beanbags, soft balls in various sizes

★ Bible-times clothing box (fabric strips or old ties for headbands and belts, fabric sections with neck holes for tunics)

★ Butcher paper and poster board

★ Children's music CDs and player

★ Collage materials (yarn, ribbon, cotton balls, chenille wire, etc.)

★ Construction paper in a variety of colors

★ Discarded magazines and catalogs

★ Glue (bottles and sticks)

★ Markers (washable ink), crayons and chalk

★ Newspaper or plastic tablecloth (to protect surfaces during projects)

★ No-rinse hand disinfectant, premoistened towelettes or paper towels

★ Paint smocks (or old shirts)

★ Plastic or paper dinnerware (plates, bowls, cups, napkins, utensils, etc.)

★ Play dough

★ Stapler and staples

★ Tape (masking or painter's tape, transparent tape)

★ Yarn

WELL-ARRANGED AREAS

Having enough space and the appropriate furniture and supplies is only part of providing good facilities. How the furniture is arranged in the room has a significant impact on a teacher's ability to involve children in class activities. In general, children need to be able to move from tables to another open area of the room and back to tables during a session. (If adequate space is not available indoors for active games, designate a safe outdoor area for games.)

More time can be spent in learning when movement between activities can be done quickly and easily. Tables should be easily movable to create a variety of room arrangements. Facilities that are arranged in a manner conducive to a variety of groupings and arrangements also allow for variations in attendance.

A room does not need to be completely or perfectly furnished for effective learning. Staffing a room with several loving, concerned teachers and a few quality pieces of basic equipment for firsthand learning experiences makes the room ready for action!

THE FACTORS FOR SAFETY

In determining room layout, keep in mind these safety guidelines:

★ Arrange furniture so that there are no hard-to-see blind spots. This makes supervision much simpler.

★ Bolt shelves and cabinets to the walls.

★ Attach safety hinges to doors, so they open and close slowly, preventing caught fingers or toes.

★ Evaluate the ways in which children will move from one area of the room to another to make sure movement is not impeded.

★ Do not block any entrance, exit or adjacent hallways with unused furniture. Every exit should be clearly marked. Contact your local fire department or state-licensing agency to help you determine proper placement of fire extinguishers, fire alarms, emergency exits and other safety considerations. (For example, all doors, even when locked, should be operable from the inside.) Post fire and other emergency (tornado, storm, earthquake, etc.) plans in every classroom, preferably by an exit door.

★ When children are present in the room, do not stack chairs on tables.

★ Check with your local fire department before hanging items from the ceiling. Moving ceiling tiles is sometimes a violation of fire safety codes.

Adapt the room arrangement on page 87 to your facilities. Avoid creating rooms that are too small to be used as your children's ministry needs change over the years.

Since welcoming and checking in children are important safety aspects of children's ministry, plan furniture and facilities to make check-in and check-out procedures flow smoothly. (For more about these procedures, see pp. 109-110).

ROOM DIAGRAM
Elementary—Grades One to Five/Six

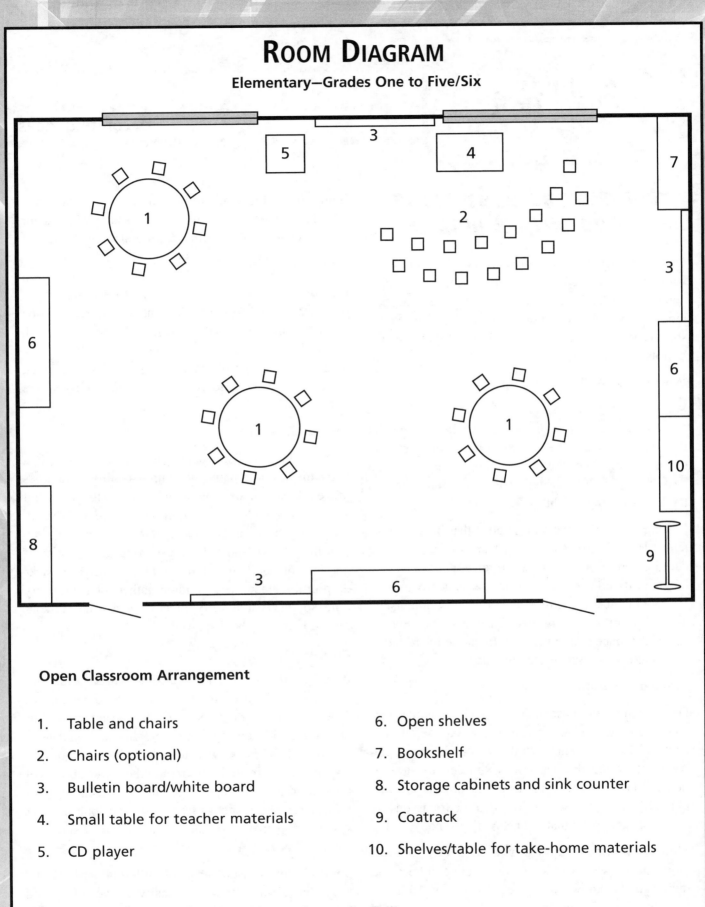

Open Classroom Arrangement

1. Table and chairs

2. Chairs (optional)

3. Bulletin board/white board

4. Small table for teacher materials

5. CD player

6. Open shelves

7. Bookshelf

8. Storage cabinets and sink counter

9. Coatrack

10. Shelves/table for take-home materials

Note: Rectangular rooms provide maximum flexibility.

WHAT'S THE BEST THING TO DO WITH A WALL?

Unless you teach out of doors, every classroom has a wall or walls. Whether those walls reinforce learning depends on what is presented on them. Color, line, pattern and texture draw children's attention. They can lift spirits and pique curiosity. Here are tips for making the best use of any wall!

Worthwhile Walls

Walls that are the most useful contain a balanced amount of display. Like a piece of art, the elements on the wall should lead the eye, while reinforcing (instead of distracting from) the proceedings in the room. The best displays will be visually interesting and related to the lessons being taught.

Posting an item on the wall implies that it has importance. However, if items are put up because they are cute instead of because they are related to the lessons taught or if items remain on walls permanently or even for months at a time, their importance is diminished and their purpose is forgotten. Change items frequently (at least once a month), so children are interested to see what is new in their classrooms.

Limited Decoration

Decoration is not a case of "if less is good, more is better." View the walls as a canvas for expressing both content of and responses to the lessons being taught. Avoid cluttering the walls with unnecessary decorations. When too many pictures and objects are displayed on the walls, children cannot focus on the lesson-related items that are being displayed.

Murals are often suggested as a good way to cover large, empty wall spaces, and they help children (and their parents) know that the church is a welcoming, friendly place. However, even Bible-story-related murals that are well-planned and attractively painted limit the flexibility of a room. Add a mural to only one wall in a classroom so that ample space remains for lesson-related items. Permanent murals limit the use of a room by other age levels or by other programs such as Vacation Bible School. Also, because one of the best uses of a wall is to present new and fresh visual elements, a mural, no matter how attractive, tends to be overlooked after initial interest has waned. Instead, invite children to create lesson-related murals on large lengths of butcher paper. Easily posted at eye level, these murals are quickly replaced, improving visual interest.

Bulletin Boards

Hanging large bulletin boards in each classroom is a good display alternative if church facility guidelines prevent taping or stapling things to the walls, if no wall space is available or if classroom spaces are shared. Place bulletin boards at the eye level of the children (not the adults) who will be gathering in the room. If possible, one bulletin board should be placed as a backdrop in the area where children gather for Bible story time so that Bible story pictures and other lesson-related items can be displayed.

Ideas to Try

If no bulletin board space is available in a room, consider dedicating a rolling bulletin board to each class. Teachers may display lesson-related posters and children's artwork during class sessions and update it throughout the year. Or extend level-loop indoor/outdoor carpeting from the floor onto the lower portion of the wall to provide an area suitable for attaching items using T-pins or the hooks from hook-and-loop fastener systems (Velcro). (For more information about wall color, see p. 83.)

Some churches install strips of bulletin board material so that display items can easily be tacked up and then removed. Other churches use various types of trim materials (rickrack, colored tape, bulletin board borders, etc.) to define a focal area in which teachers can display posters, Bible story figures or Bible verses.

Consider using simple visual treatments to define space and to create a focus that draws attention to the Bible story. To add a colorful backdrop for a Bible story area, drape a length of lightweight fabric across a wall area or a corner (secure with pins, tacks or staples). Create a three-dimensional paper tree trunk from brown paper grocery bags twisted together and stapled to a wall. Add green paper leaves above the trunk or invite children to add blossoms or leaves.

IS SHARING SPACE SOMETHING WE CAN DO WELL?

Rarely does any group have the luxury of being the only group to use a room. In many churches, most rooms are used frequently throughout the week. By following certain guidelines, you can help your staff share the rooms.

Guideline 1: As often as possible, assign rooms for use by groups of the same or similar age. Establish a plan for scheduling use of the classrooms. Changes in schedule should be approved and communicated to all teachers involved.

Guideline 2: At least once a year, schedule a meeting with the teachers or leaders of all groups that use a room. Allow time for each person to describe what his or her group does in the room and the reasons why certain facility issues are important. When people meet together and talk about the goals of their programs, they become more accommodating to each other's needs. Help the people who share a room come to an agreement on what furniture, equipment and supplies will be shared and what will have restricted use. Establish guidelines for the use of shared resources. Discuss how each group is to leave the room for use by the other. Clearly communicate the guidelines to all staff who use the room. If the staff teach or lead the same age level, offer training to the teachers and leaders at the same time. (If you are unable to schedule a time when users of shared facilities can meet together, the leaders of each program should meet and develop a plan for sharing, and then communicate that plan to all who share the space. Many churches find it helpful to create a master plan for room setup in order to cut down custodial work.)

Guideline 3: Provide adequate storage space for each group's supplies. If this cannot be done in (or very near) the room, provide portable storage containers (available at office-supply stores) for transporting needed items from a storage area. (See pp. 92-93 for more information on storage.)

Guideline 4: Provide appropriate display space for each group. It's important for each class or group to have something displayed that reflects its interests. Assign specific display space in a room to each group that regularly uses the room. Portable bulletin boards can be rolled or carried into a room as needed. Hinge bulletin boards so that they can easily be turned from one side to the next. Mount displays on butcher paper that can be attached to classroom walls for display and then rolled up for storage. If possible, request that any displays be limited to seasonal art that is appropriate for all groups using the room.

Guideline 5: Plan for adequate custodial help to handle movement of furniture and equipment to prepare a room for use by different groups. Each group should provide the custodian with a clear diagram of how the room should be set up. If paid custodial help is not able to handle room setup on a regular basis, enlist volunteers to do the job so that teachers are not burdened with the task. You may also wish to post the room diagrams on classroom walls so that other groups who use the classrooms know how the room is to be arranged after their use.

Guideline 6: Develop creative solutions for seemingly unsolvable problems. For example, move a portable divider in front of stacks of unsightly desks or adult chairs or drape them with colorful fabric. One or two adult chairs can be used as a supply shelf for the materials needed by a class of young children.

Guideline 7: If classrooms are used by a school, it is helpful to develop written guidelines for issues such as rent, storage, repair, maintenance, standards for use of rooms, etc. When staff changes occur at the church or at the school, review and update the guidelines. It is often helpful if one or more members of the church serve on the school board and if school parents and church members cooperate in facility cleanup projects.

If a teacher brings to your attention that items are not being put away properly in other programs, quickly meet with teachers of that program to go over the agreed-upon guidelines. Quick action will avoid allowing these lapses to become a bone of contention that hinders both programs from being effective. Often a simple reminder resolves the problem (at least for a while), but be open to changing the guidelines if they are proving unworkable. Periodically remind teachers in all programs that sharing facilities requires that some concessions must be made on all sides.

Supplies

WHAT'S THE BEST WAY TO KEEP IMPORTANT SUPPLIES AVAILABLE?

A resource, or supply, room stocked with supplies, audiovisual equipment and curriculum resources should be readily accessible to all classroom areas. Most teachers are unlikely to walk very far to pick up items before class, so a large facility may need more than one such room. (Some churches provide coffee and snacks for their teachers in their resource rooms as a way to build friendships and interaction among teachers.) A well-maintained resource room frees up classroom space and makes the jobs of teachers and helpers easier.

If your church does not currently have a resource, or supply, room, begin with a large cabinet in a central location. Label shelves in alphabetical order. Place items in clearly labeled transparent plastic boxes or other containers. (Consider gluing a sample of what's inside the box to the outside of the box if possible.) Using the list on pages 95-96, prioritize the needs of your church and begin with those items. Don't be afraid to ask church members to donate recyclable items such as egg cartons, cardboard tubes, etc. Place an item in the church bulletin or ask an adult class to adopt the resource cabinet as its service project.

There is another side to donations, however. When asking for donated items, it is important to be very specific in describing the materials needed (for example, donated fabric should be washed, books should be in good condition, etc.). Many times churches become the recipients of donated castoffs that are not appropriate for group usage or that don't enhance the goals of your program. Thank the donor, saying "We'll check to see if this fits our needs. We will pass it on to other children if it is not something the children in our program are able to use." Give unneeded donations to an organization that repairs toys for reuse by charitable groups. If any donated item is unsafe for use by children, it is best to discard the item (with no guilt!).

Maintain an up-to-date alphabetical list of the items (and their locations) that are stored in the room and post it near the door. Storing items in labeled clear plastic boxes makes it easy to see what is in a box and when there is a need to purchase additional items. Containers such as ice-cream buckets can be kept in the resource room for teachers to use in collecting items and returning unused items. An individual who is unable to teach in the children's ministry but enjoys shopping or recycling may enjoy being the resource room coordinator!

Look through the next quarter's curriculum for items teachers might need in the coming weeks. Inform teachers regularly about new additions to the resource room. If there are certain kinds of activities you wish to encourage teachers to do, be sure that the resource room is well stocked with the needed supplies. Periodically ask several of your regular teachers to suggest frequently used items that could be added to your resource room. Adapt the list on pages 95-96, giving a copy to each teacher and displaying it prominently in the resource room.

Set up a system for filing and storing visual resource materials (flannel figures, posters, videos, DVDs, etc.) as well. (If your church uses recyclable curriculum, do the same with the curriculum pieces that are currently not being used.) Post a clear description of the storage method and use large, resealable plastic bags to store a many items as possible so that they are easy to see without opening the package. Arrange resources by age level, in alphabetical order.

Depending on your church's procedures, you may allow teachers to purchase classroom supplies on their own and then turn in receipts for reimbursement. (Simply set a maximum dollar amount of supplies that can be purchased without prior approval.) You may also choose to use supply request forms which teachers must turn into you at least a week before the supply is needed (see sample supply request form on p. 94).

It's also good policy several times a year to ask teachers to clean out their classrooms and return to the resource room those leftover items that are still usable. Do this before making up a list for the next shopping trip or bulletin request for donations.

Requests for repair of classroom equipment and materials can be handled easily by having a form like the one on page 94 available in every classroom for teachers to fill out and leave on the table for the janitor or other designated repair person to pick up and complete each week.

Supply Request

Date

Name and Phone Number

Class

What do you need?

How many do you need?

When do you need it?

Comments

Repair Request

Date

Name and Phone Number

Class

What needs repair?

Level of urgency
(before midweek,
before next weekend,
when convenient)

CHILDREN'S MINISTRIES SUPPLY LIST

- ❏ Aluminum foil
- ❏ Art foam (also called fun foam)
- ❏ Baby-food jars
- ❏ Baggies in various sizes
- ❏ Balloons
- ❏ Balls (foam, playground, tennis)
- ❏ Beads
- ❏ Beanbags
- ❏ Beans
- ❏ Bed sheets (for covering floors)
- ❏ Burlap
- ❏ Burlap sacks
- ❏ Butcher paper rolls (brown, white, various sizes)
- ❏ Buttons
- ❏ Cardboard sheets
- ❏ Cardboard tubes (toilet paper, paper towel)
- ❏ Carpet squares
- ❏ Catalogs (discarded)
- ❏ CD/DVD/cassette player
- ❏ Chalk (white, colored, sidewalk)
- ❏ Chenille wire in assorted colors and lengths
- ❏ Chimes (tone, handheld)
- ❏ Clothespins
- ❏ Coffee cans (various sizes) with sharp edges removed
- ❏ Coffee filters (basket-style, white)
- ❏ Confetti (in a variety of shapes)
- ❏ Construction paper (in various sizes and colors)

- ❏ Cotton balls (white, colored)
- ❏ Cotton swabs
- ❏ Craft sticks (several sizes)
- ❏ Crayons
- ❏ Crepe-paper streamers
- ❏ Extension cords
- ❏ Fabric scraps
- ❏ Farm animals (small, plastic)
- ❏ Felt
- ❏ Film canisters
- ❏ Flowers (plastic, silk)
- ❏ Foil pie tins
- ❏ Food coloring
- ❏ Glitter
- ❏ Glitter glue
- ❏ Glue (large refill, small bottles, sticks)
- ❏ Hole punches (handheld)
- ❏ Index cards (large and small, white and colored, lined and unlined)
- ❏ Jingle bells (several sizes)
- ❏ Latex examination gloves
- ❏ Leaves (fall, artificial)
- ❏ Magazines (discarded)
- ❏ Magnetic strips
- ❏ Magnifying glasses
- ❏ Markers (washable, in a variety of colors; also permanent markers and dry-erase markers for dry-erase boards)

- ☐ Masking tape (wide, narrow)
- ☐ Measuring sticks
- ☐ Muffin cups
- ☐ Muffin tins
- ☐ Nature items (rocks, feathers, shells, pinecones, pebbles)
- ☐ Newspapers
- ☐ Oatmeal containers
- ☐ Offering containers
- ☐ Packing peanuts (cornstarch-based, Styrofoam, in a variety of colors and shapes)
- ☐ Paint (watercolors, liquid tempera)
- ☐ Paint smocks (or old shirts)
- ☐ Paintbrushes
- ☐ Painter's tape (several colors)
- ☐ Paper bags (grocery, lunch-sized)
- ☐ Paper clips
- ☐ Paper fasteners
- ☐ Paper plates (large, small)
- ☐ Pasta (dried, variety of shapes)
- ☐ Pencils
- ☐ Picture file (Bible stories, animals, nature, food, people)
- ☐ Play dough and tools and cookie cutters
- ☐ Pom-poms
- ☐ Poster board
- ☐ Puppets
- ☐ Raffia
- ☐ Rhythm instruments
- ☐ Ribbon (curling)
- ☐ Rope
- ☐ Rubber bands
- ☐ Rulers
- ☐ Safety pins (large, small)
- ☐ Salt
- ☐ Sandpaper (variety of grits)
- ☐ Scarves
- ☐ Scissors (adult-sized, child-sized, left-handed)
- ☐ Scratch paper
- ☐ Seeds (a variety)
- ☐ Shells
- ☐ Stamps and stamp pads
- ☐ Staplers and staples
- ☐ Starch
- ☐ Stickers (stars, happy faces, hearts, etc.)
- ☐ Strawberry baskets
- ☐ Straws
- ☐ String
- ☐ Tablecloths (plastic)
- ☐ Thumbtacks
- ☐ Tissue paper
- ☐ Tongue depressors
- ☐ Toothpicks
- ☐ Transparent tape
- ☐ Trim
- ☐ Twine
- ☐ Utensils (plastic knives, spoons, forks)
- ☐ Wallpaper samples
- ☐ Waxed paper
- ☐ Wiggle eyes
- ☐ Yarn

WHAT'S THE BENEFIT OF OUTDOOR PLAY AND ACTIVITIES?

An outdoor play area for children is a great resource for meeting children's need to move (and to make noise!). While a child's time at church will include much more than outdoor play, there is great benefit when children are able to connect their enjoyment in play with the people and places where they learn about God. As children enjoy supervised outdoor playtime, they build friendships with each other. Teachers can informally build with children relationships that communicate God's love.

Outdoor play space for elementary ages may serve a variety of purposes: free play, organized games, outdoor classes and social time. It is not generally used as frequently as are early childhood play areas. A large, level grassy area, far away from traffic hazards, serves nicely (since playground balls often end up in the street). Stagger outdoor play schedules so that the area is not overcrowded. Depending on your situation, your church may or may not wish to add any equipment to the area.

Consider the following guidelines for play areas:

Guideline 1: Fence it. Completely fence any play area to be used by younger children with fencing that meets safety standards (heads or hands cannot be caught in fence, fence is tall enough to discourage climbers, etc.).

Guideline 2: Vary surfaces. Provide both soft surfaces (grass, sand) and a hard surface for a variety of play experiences. Smooth cement is preferred over rough concrete or asphalt. Avoid slippery surfaces such as gravel. Remove tripping hazards. Separating a sand area from a cement area with at least a strip of grass or ground cover will minimize sand drifting onto the cement causing the cement to become slippery.

Guideline 3: Locate sand far from classrooms. If planning a sand play area, locate it in an area farthest from classroom entrances so less sand will be brought indoors on children's feet and clothing. Cover sand areas with heavy-duty plastic netting when not in use to keep animals out of the sand.

Guideline 4: Plan for shade. Be sure there is an awning, overhang, leafy tree, etc. for at least a portion of the outdoor area. Make sure trees and plants are not poisonous. (Note: When children are outdoors, watch for signs of overheating and have drinking water available on hot days.)

Guideline 5: Buy the right equipment. If you choose to add play equipment to the area, purchase good quality, age-appropriate equipment. Display a sign telling the ages for which each play area is designed. Equipment should offer as much variety as possible.

Guideline 6: Make safety first. While church volunteers might build playground structures, strict safety standards must be adhered to for the safety of the children and to protect your church from liability in case of injuries. Be sure there are no protruding bolts or hooks around which children's clothing may become entangled and no sharp points or edges that may injure children. Never allow children who are too old or too young to play on playground equipment.

Pay special attention to the surface beneath playground equipment. For safety, sand areas need a minimum depth of 12 inches (30.5 cm) of loose fill. If properly installed, rubber tiles, hardwood fiber/mulch and safety-tested rubber mats are also options for playground surfaces. Safety surfaces should extend 6 feet (1.8 m) in all directions from playground equipment. Spaces that could trap children (between climbing rungs, etc.) must measure less than $3^1/_2$ inches (9 cm) or more than 9 inches (23 cm). Guardrails and protective barriers should be a least 29 inches (73.5 cm) high. Make sure that all playground equipment is regularly inspected and maintained by adults who are knowledgeable in playground safety, and consult an expert for help in designing at least a part of the playground so that it is suitable for children with disabilities.

When returning from outside play, provide a way (sink or hand wipes) for children to wash or clean their hands.

Guideline 7: Develop large muscle skills. Outdoor toys such as balls in varying sizes, jump ropes, hula hoops, etc., encourage children to develop large-muscle skills. Plan a way to store these items so that they remain in good condition.

Guideline 8: Supervise carefully. During all outdoor play times, adults should be alert to look for potential hazards, guide children in safe use of equipment and be available in case of injury. Expect teachers to be involved with children as they play rather than using the time for adult conversation. As with indoor activities, two adults should be present at all times.

(Note: Free information regarding recommendations for outdoor play areas are provided by both state and federal agencies and are available on the Internet. If your church has a weekday school or day-care facility, consult with your state's licensing agency for safety standards and the need for inspection by playground specialists.)

OTHER OUTDOOR OPTIONS

Since most events in the Bible took place outdoors, it stands to reason that there is great value (with any age group) in occasionally moving outside the walls of the building for learning activities, outdoor play or organized games. Consider these ideas for outdoor use:

Change the setting to increase interest. Every group needs variety to avoid falling into a rut. Simply moving out of doors can increase childrens' enjoyment and interest in the same activities they would have done inside.

Add a biblical flavor. Since so much of the Bible happened outside, taking a class outdoors for some stories can help students feel more a part of the action.

Pray and meditate, alone or together. Give children time to walk or sit outdoors for group or personal prayer to the God who made the world they see.

Serve a snack. Even crackers and water taste better eaten out on the lawn or under a tree!

Make friends and hang out. Time before and after a session can be as important for learning as the class session itself. In the same way, conversation-friendly places outdoors can be just as important as the insides of classrooms. Besides the parking lot, teachers and children benefit by an outdoor place where they can talk about questions that came up during class or where they can simply get to know each other better. Lawns, benches, patios, shade trees and even fire pit areas can become pivotal places where we learn, talk, listen and build each other up in Christ!

A Safe and Healthy Place

Policies and Procedures

Here is an overview of important information about the factors of health and safety in dealing with children.

Use this information to set up policies and procedures to make your children's ministry a safe and healthy place.

Includes suggestions and tips for cleanliness, safety and health guidelines, check-in forms and ways to respond to illnesses and emergencies that will help you and parents make this environment one where children can come freely and parents can leave them confidently.

WHAT POLICIES WILL HELP US KEEP THE CHILDREN SAFE AND HEALTHY?

Cleanliness is more than half the battle.

Keeping things clean is always an issue of concern in any program involving children. You may want to provide charts (see samples on p. 103) on which to record cleaning assignments. (If you share facilities with a school, preschool or day-care program, coordinate cleaning with the leaders of those programs.)

★ Plan which tasks will be done by teachers and which will be done by the custodian.

★ Vacuum carpets or mop the floors after each day's use, cleaning up any spills immediately.

★ Store all cleaning supplies out of reach of children, preferably in cabinets or closets that have either locks or safety latches. Make sure teachers are informed as to the location of the supplies and cleaning equipment that they are likely to need. (Teachers are not likely to clean up well if supplies and equipment are not conveniently available.)

★ Schedule long-term cleaning tasks such as washing windows, curtains, blinds, shelves and chairs. Shampoo carpets once or twice a year.

One often-overlooked detail in keeping rooms clean is dealing with the leftover items that seem to accumulate. Sunday School papers, jackets, Bibles, hair clips, small toys, used coffee or punch cups, cookies, etc., often appear in rooms. Each teacher can be asked to dispose of such items in the trash or in a Lost and Found Box, or whoever is responsible for locking up classrooms can collect such items at the end of the session.

Hand washing is vital.

Frequent hand washing does much to prevent the spread of germs. Encourage staff to wash their hands

before beginning their teaching assignment, before handling food, after going to the bathroom, after any contact with body fluids and after cleaning equipment or supplies.

Wash hands with running water and antibacterial soap, rubbing front and back of hands together for 15 to 30 seconds. Dry hands with disposable towels. Use a disposable towel to turn off the faucet so that hands are not contaminated again. Display hand washing instructions (see p. 104) near each sink.

Ask your teachers to plan time for children to wash hands before eating. If your classrooms do not have nearby sink facilities, provide a commercial no-rinse hand disinfectant solution, premoistened wipes or paper towels for teachers and children to use.

Hand Washing Is the Best Prevention

Wash and wipe your hands together, live in health forever!

Take time to wash:
- ✔ when you first arrive
- ✔ before handling food
- ✔ after using the restroom
- ✔ after any contact with body fluids
- ✔ after cleaning up

Everything you ever wanted to know about washing hands:
- ✔ wash with running water and antibacterial soap
- ✔ wash front and back of hands
- ✔ wash for 15-30 seconds
- ✔ turn off faucet with disposable towel
- ✔ dry hands with disposable towel

Daily Room Care

Today's Date _____

❏ Wash Tables

❏ Wash and Disinfect Equipment
as Needed

❏ Disinfect Furniture, Tables,
Door Knobs and Light Switches

❏ Vacuum Rug and Mop Floor

❏ Spot Clean Spills

Long-Term Room Care

Room _____

MONTHLY _____

Date _____

❏ Wash Windows

❏ Wash Rugs

❏ Wipe Off and Disinfect Furniture

SIX MONTHS _____

Date _____

❏ Wash Window Treatments

❏ Shampoo Carpet

YEARLY _____

Date _____

❏ Wash/Paint Walls

Hand Washing Is the Best Prevention

Wash and wipe your hands together, live in health forever!

Take time to wash:

- ✔ when you first arrive
- ✔ before handling food
- ✔ after using the restroom
- ✔ after any contact with body fluids
- ✔ after cleaning up

Everything you ever wanted to know about washing hands:

- ✔ wash with running water and antibacterial soap
- ✔ wash front and back of hands
- ✔ wash for 15-30 seconds
- ✔ turn off faucet with disposable towel
- ✔ dry hands with disposable towel

Write guidelines for infectious diseases.

The health and safety guidelines developed by your church should include guidelines for responding to children who have hepatitis (HBV) or AIDS or who may be HIV positive. Write procedures for handling these diseases in conjunction with churchwide guidelines. Include facts about the disease, information about the infection-control procedures followed in your church (e.g., cleaning procedures, etc.) and confidentiality policies. Because laws about the treatment of people with infectious diseases are subject to change, it is best to consult a state health agency and a competent local attorney for further information about state and federal laws at the time you are developing your church's health policies.

The best way to prevent the spread of blood-transmitted infections is to utilize universal precautions. "Universal precautions" refer to the manner in which body fluids are handled, and it means that the blood of everyone is considered potentially infectious. Train all children's ministries staff members in the use of universal precautions. Latex examination gloves should be readily available for staff to wear in helping children who are sick or injured and when contact with blood, open sores, cuts or the inside of a person's mouth is anticipated. Staff members with open sores on their hands should also wear gloves. Open sores elsewhere on the body should be covered with an adequate-sized bandage. Store gloves in all children's classrooms, in the kitchen and on the playground. Clean blood spills with bleach.

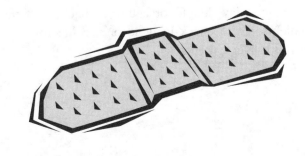

Accidents will happen!

Your staff members need to be familiar with efficient procedures for handling accidents, even though they may never need to put the procedures into practice. Often, a quick hug and sympathetic ear are enough to calm a child's outward distress. However, teachers need to be watchful no matter how slight an injury appears. Here are observation questions to post for consideration:

★ Is the child unresponsive?

★ Is the child having difficulty breathing?

★ Is the child's cry unusual?

★ Is the child's pulse weak or rapid?

★ Is the child vomiting?

★ Is the child's skin broken?

If any of these questions are answered in the affirmative, call for medical help and/or provide treatment immediately and call the parents.

Each classroom should have an up-to-date first-aid manual (available from your local American Red Cross) that is clearly in view and a first-aid kit stored out of children's reach. Once a month check the kit contents and replace items as needed.

Staff should also have quick access to a telephone if emergency medical services are required. Post emergency phone numbers (9-1-1 or local hospital, law enforcement and fire departments and poison control centers) near each telephone, along with directions to your facility and to the building and/or room.

Consider these additional tips for handling accidents:

★ During each session, designate a person in the building or on the premises who is trained in CPR for children. (Provide CPR and first-aid classes for staff on a regular basis.)

★ Never hesitate to offer first aid to an injured child, but wear disposable gloves while cleaning up blood or other bodily fluids. Have latex examination gloves available at all times (see information about universal precautions on p. 105).

Any time a child sustains an injury, verbal and written reports need to be completed. (See forms on p. 107.) Parents and a designated person on the church staff should be informed of the injury, the circumstances in which it occurred and how the injury was treated. (Follow any guidelines that have already been established by your church.) Follow up the injury with a phone call to the parents the day after the injury took place to determine if further injuries have developed and to express your care and concern for the child involved.

If a staff person, whether paid or volunteer, is injured while serving in ministry, follow the insurance and liability procedures your church has already established for employees and volunteer workers.

Expect emergencies.

All churches should have planned procedures in case of fire and/or emergency evacuation. Depending on your church's location, you may also need to provide information for emergencies such as earthquakes, tornadoes and floods. Ask your local American Red Cross to provide you with the appropriate posters and/or handouts to display or have on hand. Summarize pertinent emergency information at teacher training meetings or in a teacher handbook.

★ Plan who will alert teachers to evacuate their classrooms.

★ Plan and post two emergency exits from each classroom and have fire extinguishers on hand. (Ask your local fire department to help you determine the safest routes and where fire extinguishers should be mounted.) Designate a meeting place for all children and staff.

★ Keep emergency supplies (snacks, disposable gloves, first-aid kit, flashlight, portable radio, water, etc.) elsewhere on the church premises, in a place quickly accessible to teachers in case of evacuation.

★ Always have at least one working flashlight available in each classroom, in case of a power outage or if an evacuation takes place at night.

★ Make a plan for how teachers will communicate with each other and with parents in case of emergencies (phones, cell phones or walkie-talkies). Be sure teachers have your cell-phone number stored in their own cell phones!

Be alert to allergies.

More and more often, children seem to have mild to severe allergies to common substances (milk, wheat, eggs, dust, peanuts, tree nuts, insect stings, animal dander, etc.). Symptoms of an allergic reaction may include itchy skin, rashes (hives), runny nose, itchy and swollen eyes, swelling around the mouth and in the throat, wheezing or difficulty breathing, vomiting, diarrhea, nausea and abdominal pain. These symptoms usually develop fairly quickly after a child touches or ingests a substance to which he or she is allergic.

Symptoms may be mild or very severe, depending on how much of the substance the child was exposed to and how allergic the child is to that substance. A severe reaction can include anaphylaxis (difficulty breathing, swelling in the mouth and throat, decreased blood pressure, shock and even death).

Whenever children will be using a substance (such as wheat-based play dough) or eating a snack, post the ingredients at the check-in table or use the form on page 108 to alert parents.

PARENT NOTIFICATION

I Was Hurt Today (But I'm OK Now!)

Where I Was: _____

_____

What Happened: _____

_____

_____

_____.

_____ **helped me by**

_____.

CHURCH OFFICE NOTIFICATION INJURY REPORT

Name, Age and Gender of Child Who Was Injured

_____

Address/City/Zip _____

Name of Parent _____ **Phone Number** _____

Date and Time of Accident _____

Describe in detail how the child was injured, including location, names and actions of all children and adults involved.

_____

_____

Describe the child's injuries and what action was taken to treat the injuries.

_____

How and when was the parent notified?

_____

Please list names and phone numbers of witnesses to the accident.

1. _____

2. _____

3. _____

Additional Comments _____

Your Name, Address and Phone Number _____

_____

Parent

ALERT!

Today we will be using/eating

in class. Please let us know if your child has a sensitivity or medical concern related to this substance.

THANK YOU!

Parent

ALERT!

Today we will be using/eating

in class. Please let us know if your child has a sensitivity or medical concern related to this substance.

THANK YOU!

WHAT'S THE VALUE OF ACCOUNTING FOR OUR KIDS?

Regardless of the size of your church, it's vital to evaluate the number of children in your programs and make decisions that affect their safety. (In an increasingly litigious society, volunteer teachers and helpers need consideration for their safety as much as the children do!) It's important to establish procedures that are clearly stated and faithfully followed so that each child and volunteer is protected.

Leaders need to decide if parents will be asked to check in their children at a counter or reception area, or if they may bring their children directly to individual classrooms. The physical size of your church campus, the number of people attending your church and the number of children in your program will help determine how extensive the check-in procedures should be. (It is recommended that children up through grades 3 or 4 be required to be checked in and out by a parent or other designated person.)

Registration Cards or Forms: At the beginning of the school year or whenever a new child joins your program, the child's parents should complete a registration card or form. Use names and addresses for maintaining home contacts (mailing birthday cards to children, sending invitations to special events, absentee follow-up, etc.).

A church may choose to ask a parent to complete a more extensive registration form. This often includes the name and phone number of the family doctor, name of a person who will care for child if parent cannot be reached, food allergies or other medical condition information, medical insurance information and a liability release statement to be signed by the parent. If your church takes photos or video footage of children's programs, you may also wish to include a photography or video release in the registration form. (It is often not legal to photograph children who are wards of the state; this may also be a concern for children who are party to a parent's legal actions such as court orders.) When creating a more extensive registration form, it is wise to consult a book about church-liability issues and/or contact a lawyer who is familiar with the laws in your state for help in designing a legally appropriate form.

Adapt the sample registration and medical release forms on pages 110-111 for your own church. (Note: Some churches provide registration cards with space for all children in the family to be listed so that parents do not have to fill out multiple cards. Cards are then photocopied and distributed to each child's class. This also tells teachers which children are siblings.)

SUNDAY SCHOOL REGISTRATION

Child's Name _____ Today's Date _____

Age _____ Gender _____ Birth Date _____

Address _____

City/State/Zip _____ Phone Number _____

Food Allergies (if any)

Special Needs (if any)

Parent/Guardian Name (include address and phone number if different from above)

Parent Name (include address and phone number if different from above)

Siblings' Names and Ages

Parent Participation: I would be willing to help with

_____ Snacks   _____ Games   _____ Art   _____ Music   _____ Drama

_____ Other _____

MEDICAL AND LIABILITY RELEASE FORM

PARENT PERMISSION/RELEASE FORM

(Church Name)

(Address)

(Phone Number)

Child's Name _____

Birth Date _____ Grade _____

Address _____

City _____ Zip _____

Phone Number _____

Date(s) of Activity _____

Authorization of Consent for Treatment of Minor

I, the undersigned parent or guardian of _____,
a minor, do hereby authorize any duly authorized employee, volunteer or other representative of the (church name), as agent(s) for the undersigned, to consent to any x-ray examination, anesthetic, medical or surgical diagnosis or treatment, and hospital care which is deemed advisable by, and is to be rendered under the general or specific supervision of, any licensed physician and surgeon, whether such diagnosis or treatment is rendered at the office of said physician and surgeon or at a clinic, hospital or other medical facility.

It is understood that this authorization is given in advance of any specific diagnosis, treatment or hospital care being required, but is given to provide authority and power on the part of our aforesaid agent(s) to give specific consent to any and all such diagnosis treatment or hospital care which the aforementioned physician in the exercise of his or her best judgment may deem advisable.

This authorization shall remain effective from _____ to _____.

Signature _____

Check-In Forms: A typical check-in form asks for the child's name and age, parents' names and where they can be located. Parents sign the form when leaving and picking up their children. Encourage everyone, even your most regular attendees, to completely fill out these forms. Make the forms easier for parents to complete by reducing the amount of time it takes to fill in the desired information. For example, provide forms with children's names and ages already preprinted. Visitors add their names at the bottom of the list. You may also preprint the variety of locations where parents might be, asking parents to simply check off the appropriate locations.

Whenever a class is eating a snack or using a substance that might be of concern for children with allergies, diabetes, etc., post a note at the check-in area telling parents what is being offered. (See sample form on p. 108.)

Name Tags: Depending on the size of your church, you may choose to provide each child and teacher with a name tag. Have blank tags available for visitors. (Add the date of the visit on the back of the tag to help keep track of when the visitor becomes a regular attendee!) Even if name tags are not regularly used in a classroom, they can be helpful when a substitute is present.

Child and Parent Identification: Many churches have developed a system for child identification that ensures children's safety and their release only to approved adults. Teachers are then protected from parent complaints and from legal action in instances of custody disputes.

Consider these ideas for child identification systems, choosing one that best fits your church. You can make your own tags or coupons (see samples on p. 114) or purchase commercially made child-parent identification systems. Contact your local Christian bookstore for possible sources.

• Coupon with Date and Child's Name—Coupon is given to parent when the child is checked in. Only the person with the coupon is allowed to pick up the child at the end of the session.

• Number ID—Card or paper with date and number assigned to the child. A tag with the corresponding number may also be attached to the child's name tag.

• Pagers—Numbered vibrating pagers are given to parents when their child is checked in. The child is dismissed to the parent when the pager is returned.

• Wallet-Sized, Permanent Identification Cards—These cards, with parents' and children's names and personal family identification number, can be given to parents. A child is only released to an adult who shows the identification card.

• Photo ID—Take a photo of each child with his or her parent or others who may pick up the child. Mount photos on a bulletin board near the entrance to each room. Children are released only to those shown in the photo. Have an instant camera available to photograph visitors. This is especially effective in nursery and early childhood programs.

• Parent Designation—Provide a section on the check-in form in which the parent writes the name of the person who will be picking up the child. Person picking up the child would be requested to show identification if not known to the child's teacher.

• Computer Check In and Check Out—Terminals are available at the welcome area or other entrance points. Parents or other designated individuals sign children in and print out a receipt that identifies them at check out.

Whatever system you choose, stress the importance of faithfully following the guidelines. Better to have a parent a little put out with having to provide identification than *not* having a child because he or she is missing! If a parent is impatient or reluctant to follow the procedures, explain, "I know it takes a few minutes extra to sign in (Nathan), but thank you for taking this time to help us make sure that all our children are kept safe."

Check-In   Date _____

Child's Name	Grade of Child	Parent's Name	Write Your Location in Church Buildings				Sign-In Time	Sign-Out Time
			Sat. P.M.	Sunday 8:00	Sunday 9:15	Sunday 11:00		

Identification Tags

Community Church
Children's Ministries

Name _____

Number _____

Date _____

To protect your child, please return this coupon
to the teacher when picking him or her up.

First Church

Child Security Tag

Date _____

This tag must be returned in order for
your child to be released from the classroom.

We appreciate your cooperation!

Your child's number is _____.

HOW CAN WE BEST MAKE OUR CHURCH A SAFE PLACE FOR CHILDREN TO GROW SPIRITUALLY?

Emotional and spiritual safety is important. Meeting a standard for children's physical safety is not only a good thing, but it is also required by law! Safety in the emotional and spiritual realm is equally important. But it may be overlooked or minimized, even at church. However, it should be a priority, for it is an integral part of helping kids know Christ and grow in Christ!

Emotional and spiritual safety sends a message. Every child who participates in our children's ministries deserves and needs to know that he or she is valued, loved and protected. Everything we say or do as leaders and teachers should communicate that message. Our goal is not only that children gain "book knowledge" (know the Ten Commandments or the books of the Bible, etc.) but also that their lives be transformed through knowing God's Word, understanding what it says and then learning how to apply it daily. Because we have the world's highest goal, we must be sure that children receive the world's highest message by our behavior—a biblical message of love and care.

Emotional and spiritual safety creates an environment for growth. Children's lives can be hurried, complicated and confusing. They may come to our programs carrying far larger burdens than we imagine! The church should be a place where it is emotionally safe for children to talk about what is going on in their lives and where it is spiritually safe for them to ask hard questions and be heard, acknowledged and

answered. When we are committed to children's emotional and spiritual safety, we nurture their growth into wholehearted followers of Christ.

Core beliefs are the basis for providing safety. When adults hold the following core beliefs, they are ready to foster emotional and spiritual safety for children:

Servanthood. Believing that we are all here to love and help each other.

Value. Believing that each child is valuable as a person, both to God and to us. Children will know they matter to God only when they see they matter to us.

Faith. Believing that every child can have a bright future in God's family. Children need for us to see their spiritual potential.

Trustworthiness. Believing that a child's trust is a delicate gift that must be treated with care.

Honor. Believing that when we honor a child, we honor Jesus.

Some actions that foster emotional and spiritual safety:

★ Placing oneself at a child's eye level.

★ Listening with interest to what a child has to say.

★ Giving frequent and genuine smiles and safe touches.

★ Using a child's name lovingly and often.

★ Telling a child the truth and making truth understandable to him or her.

★ Being honest when you don't know an answer by saying you don't know.

★ Finding an answer and reporting it to the child.

★ Giving a child a choice in activities.

★ Phrasing directions positively so that a child knows what he or she can do.

★ Helping a child take responsibility to change problem behavior.

★ Helping the child find ways to change negative behavior rather than making negative comments about the child's character.

★ Making sure no child ever feels he or she is a burden or a problem.

★ Making sure no child receives a negative label but does receive words of love and blessing.

These actions flow from the beliefs above. Beyond being professional, Christian teachers are called to live in ways that genuinely display Christlike character.

Teachers must be trained. Because we already have been trained in certain ways to talk to children, relate to children and discipline children (often without knowing we were absorbing that training), we must teach and learn emotionally and spiritually safe ways to talk with, relate to and to discipline children. Teachers need a chance to think back and recognize the ways of dealing with children that were modeled for them (often in their own childhoods) that were or were not helpful. (For more on teacher training, see pp. 64-70.) As leaders, provide teachers the opportunity to talk openly about ways to improve their communication with children. Brainstorm examples of positive, helpful things to say, not just cautions about negative, hurtful comments.

Safety

WHAT ARE THE BEST WAYS TO KEEP CHILDREN SAFE? ARE WE PREPARED TO DEAL WITH CHILD ABUSE OR ABUSE ALLEGATIONS?

We're not eager to think we'd ever need to put into action those policies and guidelines we develop to prevent or report child abuse. However, the adage "better safe than sorry" was never more applicable than in this case. For every child—from a baby in the nursery to a teen at a youth event—our churches need to be absolutely safe and trustworthy. Follow the strategies below to help ensure the safety and trustworthiness that should mark our children's ministries.

1. Develop a Child-Safety Policy.

Developing a policy for preventing and reporting child abuse and endangerment is a necessary step toward keeping the children of your church safe. It is truly worthwhile to develop a written safety policy. A safety policy should include

★ guidelines for teacher selection (including application forms, personal interviews, follow-up of references, fingerprinting and criminal-history checks);

★ policies to be followed in the classroom and on any church-sponsored outing (number of adults required, name tags, check-in and check-out procedures, restroom guidelines, etc);

★ reporting obligations on the part of a teacher if child abuse is observed or suspected;

★ step-by-step plans for responding to an allegation of child abuse or to a volunteer who repeatedly fails to follow child-safety policies.

A simple equation to motivate you: Lack of Policy + Intent = Potential Abuse.

2. Agree to Support a Child-Safety Policy.

Submit the child-safety policy to church leaders for approval. It is vital to have both agreement and awareness of the policy. For this reason, all staff members should read the safety policy and sign a form verifying their compliance with the policy each year. It is best to introduce the child-safety policy by explaining its purpose: to make your church the safest place it can be for the children in your community and to protect teachers should unfounded allegations of abuse or child endangerment be made. Use the sample safety policy and introductory letter on pages 119-121 as guides in developing your own procedures.

It is also recommended that an attorney evaluate your policy to be sure it conforms to your state's laws regarding the reporting of child abuse. Depending on the kinds of ministries your church provides, you may also need to check with your state's social services department to determine which (if any) licensing laws apply to church programs (day care, preschool, summer sessions, after-school care, etc.).

It might be wise to also invite a security professional who attends your church to read the policy and also to observe a typical session for the purpose of recommending security improvements that could be made (especially if your group of children is large).

Don't be shy about letting people know that only certified individuals may interact with the children in your ministry. When such policies are in place, parents feel assured that your children's ministry is free from child abusers.

3. Implement the Child-Safety Policy.

For everyone to see: Post a child-safety policy checklist in every room where it is easily seen. This checklist serves to remind teachers and helpers of policies as well as telling parents what standards are in place. Include information about the number of adults required, positive discipline techniques, bathroom or toileting policies, child-abuse definitions, etc.

With new volunteers: In the delight of finding another willing volunteer, don't forget to clearly explain the church's policies for volunteer staff. Each volunteer must first have an application on file, have a background check and have regularly attended the church for a minimum of six months to a year (or whatever your church's policy specifies). If a new volunteer has not yet met the attendance time requirement, be ready to suggest another way that person might help in the children's program (decorate bulletin boards, help with mailings, etc.).

When you see a breach of the child-safety policy, take time to privately talk to the volunteer about the situation. Don't assume the worst: The volunteer could have simply forgotten or misinterpreted policy information. Response to this question then prepares you to address the problem. Review the policy with the teacher or helper. Review steps outlined in the policy that will be taken if a teacher or helper repeatedly deviates from the policy.

Child-Safety Policy

We desire to protect and support those who work with our youth and children. These policies to prevent child abuse, neglect or any unfounded allegations against workers or teachers address three major areas:

1. Worker selection
2. Worker practices
3. Reporting obligation

Selecting Children's Workers

• All paid employees, full or part-time, including clergy, and all volunteer workers should complete a Volunteer Application Form.

• A personal interview will be included as part of the selection process.

• Where circumstances merit, personal references listed in the application will be checked to further determine the suitability and character of the applicant. The reference check shall be documented.

• All workers with children should normally be members of First Church or have been attending First Church for a minimum of six months.

Safety Policies for Children's Ministries

• Volunteers and other workers are encouraged to be in public areas where both the children and teacher are visible to other people.

• All drivers transporting children on out-of-town activities shall be a minimum age of 25 and maximum age of 65 and shall complete and have approved a Driver Form.

• The desirable minimum age for all drivers for in-town activities is 25. No one under age 18 will be permitted to drive for any church-sponsored activity.

• Children's workers should not provide transportation to and from church on a regular basis.

• For overnight outings and camps, whenever both genders are present as participants, both genders need to be present in leadership.

• For outdoor activities, participants are to be in groups of at least three.

• Counseling is to be by a leader of the same gender and is to be done in public areas where both the child and leader are visible to other people.

• Each group of children should have at least two workers who are not related to each other, at least one being an adult, present at all times.

• For children, infant through kindergarten age, the desirable ratio is one worker for every five children. For grades one through five, the desirable ratio is one worker for each six to eight children.

• Window blinds and doors are to be kept open (or doors should have windows). A supervisor or designated adult representative will circulate where children's activities are occurring.

• When taking children to the restroom, workers should supervise children of the same gender. The worker should stay out of the restroom at the open door until the child is finished in the stall. Workers enter to assist only when necessary.

• In the nursery, diapers are to be changed only in designated areas and in the presence of other caregivers.

Reporting Obligation and Procedure

1. All workers are to be familiar with the definitions of child abuse (see below).

2. If a worker suspects that a child has been abused, the following steps are to be followed:
   • Report the suspected abuse to your supervisor.
   • Do not interview the child regarding the suspected abuse. The interview process will be handled by trained personnel.
   • Do not discuss the suspected abuse. It is important that all information about the suspected child abuse (victim and abuser) be kept confidential.

3. Workers reporting suspected child abuse will be asked to complete the Suspected Child Abuse Report (available from your state's Department of Social Services). Confidentiality will be maintained where possible. This report must be completed within 24 hours.

4. Once a suspected child abuse case has been reported by a worker to a supervisor, it will be reported to the designated reporting agency.

Definitions of Child Abuse

Defined by the National Committee for Prevention of Child Abuse

Physical Abuse

Nonaccidental injury, which may include beatings, violent shaking, human bites, strangulation, suffocation, poisoning or burns. The results may be bruises and welts, broken bones, scars, permanent disfigurement, long-lasting psychological damage, serious internal injuries, brain damage or death.

Neglect

The failure to provide a child with basic needs, including food, clothing, education, shelter and medical care; also abandonment and inadequate supervision.

Sexual Abuse

The sexual exploitation of a child by an older person, as in rape, incest, fondling of the genitals, exhibitionism or pornography. It may be done for the sexual gratification of the older person, out of a need for power or for economic reasons.

Safety Policy Introductory Letter

IMPORTANT: *This is a sample form, not intended to be reproduced. Adapt to your specific needs.*

(Date)

(Church Name)

(Address)

(Phone Number)

Dear _____ ,
(name)

Here at First Church we believe that having a well-thought-out Child-Safety Policy is part of the wisdom to which Christ calls us. We are aware that even with such a policy in place, we remain dependent on Christ and His ultimate protection. However, this policy will give us confidence that our children and youth will have a safe environment in which to learn and grow in their Christian faith.

We are asking that everyone in the children's ministries complete the required forms and attend a training session about the Child-Safety Policy. The next training session is scheduled on (date). We thank you for your help and cooperation in advance.

Our efforts in this area are a bit like a CPR class. You never expect to have a problem, yet you take all the precautions you possibly can. You train in order to know how to respond if there is a situation calling for action, believing and praying that it will not be needed.

Thank you for caring about children and youth and helping them grow in the nurture and admonition of the Lord.

Sincerely,

_____

(name)

_____

Pastor

HOW CAN WE BE SAFER, HEALTHIER AND HAPPIER?

What should we do if a child gets sick during class?

Sometimes a child develops symptoms of illness during a class session. The child may be in pain, appear lethargic, have a flushed face or sudden rash, cough frequently and sound congested, or exhibit discharge from the nose or eyes. If any of these symptoms appear, contact the parent immediately. Request that the child be taken home for his or her own comfort and health. Until a parent arrives to pick up the child, keep the child isolated in an area of the classroom or in the children's ministries coordinator/director's office if needed.

How can we be prepared for bathroom accidents?

It is not uncommon for younger children to occasionally forget to go to the bathroom in time. Treat bathroom accidents in a manner-of-fact way. "Cody, I see we forgot to take you to the bathroom on time. Let me help you clean up." Have spare sets of clean clothing (including extra underwear) in several sizes on hand in the resource room for children. Thoroughly clean and disinfect the area where the accident happened. Consider putting together for each classroom an accident kit that contains cleaning materials and appropriately sized, gender-neutral clothing.

A parent called recently to tell us her daughter had come down with chicken pox in the afternoon after attending Sunday School in the morning. What do I need to do?

Occasionally, a child may develop symptoms of a disease later in the day after participating in a class or activity at church. In these cases, it's helpful to send or post a notice to alert parents to the possibility that their children had been exposed to the disease. Include possible symptoms and the time period in which children may show symptoms of the disease (see sample below).

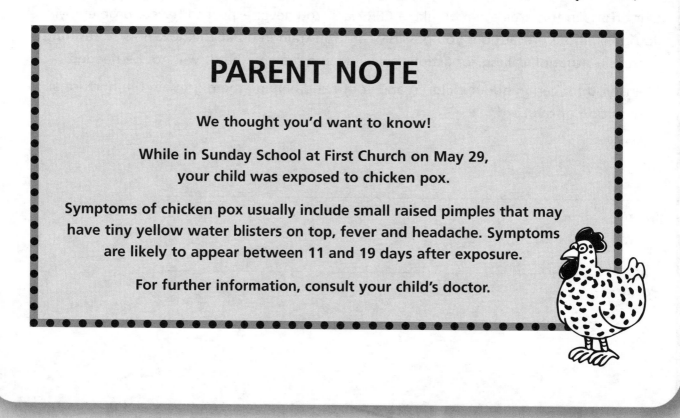

PARENT NOTE

We thought you'd want to know!

While in Sunday School at First Church on May 29, your child was exposed to chicken pox.

Symptoms of chicken pox usually include small raised pimples that may have tiny yellow water blisters on top, fever and headache. Symptoms are likely to appear between 11 and 19 days after exposure.

For further information, consult your child's doctor.

A Home That Enriches

Parents and Families

Welcome to ways to reach out, teach, mentor and encourage families to become the best they can be in Jesus Christ!

This section gives guidelines for communicating with parents, keeping records and getting useful information that will help you support families in a variety of ways to draw them into their most important role: nurturing their children toward Christ.

HOW CAN WE HELP THE WHOLE FAMILY GROW TOGETHER IN JESUS?

Once a teacher has prepared lessons, played games, told stories, taught Bible verses, shared snacks and sung songs every week, it may feel like quite a stretch to try to connect with each child's family as well! But learning about the family of each child doesn't really add more work. Rather, it helps give understanding of the home "roots" from which each child has grown. This enriches teaching and improves a teacher's ability to minister to that child and his or her family. Teachers and families are blessed in the process!

Make it clear that your church values family outreach and support as an important task. Consider recruiting a Family Outreach Coordinator (see p. 54 for a job description). The coordinator serves as the point person to both organize and administer a variety of programs and outreaches for families within and outside the church.

Use these three built-in ways your church can reach out to support the families each child represents:

1. Teacher Touches. Help teachers know the families of their students by providing teachers with up-to-date rosters. List each child's name, address, phone number, birthday, family or parent e-mail address and both first and last names of parents and siblings. Compile rosters from registration forms (see sample on p. 110) or family information sheets (see sample on pp. 127-128). Update the information throughout the year.

At each classroom door, display a roster of names (including pictures, if possible) to make it easy for parents and children to find classrooms and feel welcomed.

If teachers' rosters also list the names of children from church families that are not actively involved, teachers can then periodically contact these children and families to personally invite them to attend a class or special program. Suggest that teachers use lists to make contacts informally (in the church parking lot, at an adult event, in the grocery store, at the mall, at the park, etc.).

Communicating by card or phone call with each child during the week could be overwhelming! But an attainable goal to encourage your teachers to strive for is to communicate with at least one child and his or her family each week. Make the goal seem possible by giving each teacher a contact kit: a class roster, enough note cards to send one to each child, a pen, decorative stickers, postage stamps, etc. Seal all items in a resealable bag. Label with the teacher's name.

To help parents get to know a child's teacher, give parents copies of the Teacher Get-Acquainted Form (see p. 126) at the beginning of the term. Parents may use this as a guide for getting to know their child's teacher(s) and get the information they need most.

Teacher Get-Acquainted Form

Teacher's Name _____

Teacher's Address _____

Teacher's Birthday _____

Teacher's Phone Number _____

Teacher's E-Mail Address _____

What is the best way to find out what Bible verses and Bible stories are being taught?

_____

_____

What is the best way to contact you?

_____

What is the best time of day to call you with questions or concerns?

_____

What are ways I could help in class? Outside of the class time?

_____

What have you noticed about my child?

_____

How may I pray for you in your ministry?

_____

Comments my child has made about the class:

_____

_____

Family Information Sheet

Names of Children	Birth Dates	Grades in School
1.		
2.		
3.		
4.		

(Use the back of this form if you need more space.)

Name of Parent/Guardian

1.

Attend this church? (y/n)

Address

City

Zip Code

Telephone

Home

Work

Cellular

E-Mail

Name of Parent

2.

Attend this church? (y/n)

Address

City

Zip Code

Telephone

Home

Work

Cellular

E-Mail

Mail any information from the church to:

Activities your family might enjoy (check all boxes that apply):

- ☐ Beach/Swimming
- ☐ Camping
- ☐ Group Bike Riding
- ☐ Hiking/Walking
- ☐ Holiday Celebration
- ☐ Kite Flying
- ☐ Museum Excursion
- ☐ Park Day/Play Date

- ☐ Pet Show
- ☐ Picnic
- ☐ Service Project
- ☐ Single Parent Group
- ☐ Sports Day
- ☐ Tea Party
- ☐ Zoo Trip

Add your own ideas below:

2. Visitor Thanks. Pay special attention to the ways in which visitors are contacted in the week or two after their first visit. In addition to mailing personalized "thanks for visiting" cards or letters, consider giving each visiting child a small bag containing several inexpensive gift items (stickers, crayons, etc.) as well as printed information about your church.

Give visiting families a Welcome Pack when they visit. Include information about church programs, stickers or inexpensive books, registration cards, letter from a parent describing the benefits of participating in church programs, refrigerator magnet with church information, etc.

3. Parent Perks. Plan a series of parent events that include parent-education classes to provide parents with strategies and guidelines related to common parenting issues. Invite a speaker (a knowledgeable person in your church or community) to address an issue of interest to parents—discipline, family activities to do at home, holiday celebration ideas, safety in the home, etc. Include a time for parents to talk together and trade ideas and thoughts about the challenges of child rearing. Offering six to eight sessions over a period of several months will encourage participation by parents whose time is limited.

One to three times a year, plan a "Family Growth" meeting that focuses on ways to teach children spiritual truths to help the family grow in Christ. Present information found in relevant articles (see pp. 185-186, 189-190, 197-198) as the basis for this meeting. Allow time for

FAMILY-FRIENDLY OUTREACH EVENTS

New families may feel that everyone else at church seems to know each other. This can cause them to feel like outsiders. To help new families get acquainted and feel that they are part of the group, design several outreach events yearly! Here are a few ideas to inspire you:

- Social times and simple parties coinciding with fun activities

- Game night (when families bring table games to play together)

- Kite day (bring and fly kites together at a nearby park)

- Music and potluck evening (bring food, instruments and music to share)

- Pet show (showing real or stuffed animals)

- Cookie share (every family brings a batch of their favorite cookies or children bake cookies together with adults).

- Indoor picnic (every family brings a lunch and a blanket to share)

- Movie night (bring a favorite flavor of popcorn to share, stop the movie for a popcorn-related game)

These simple ideas can be made as elaborate as your imagination allows! Keep in mind the goal of developing the event in ways that will make new families and children feel welcomed and included.

brainstorming as well as questions, so parents can both learn new information and share their best ideas on the topic.

Send out copies of articles of special interest to parents from reproducible parenting resources.

Plan ways the church can support a family when a new baby is born or when a child or parent is ill (meals, transportation, child care, etc.).

Develop an Intergenerational Prayer Partners Group: Link older members of the church family with parents of growing children. Encourage growth of these relationships by providing complete contact information, birthdays, ages and interests of children, etc. (See the Family Information Sheet sample on pp. 126-127.) Prayer partners can share requests and encouragement by phone, e-mail or personal meetings.

Establish a library area near children's classrooms. Stock it with books about child rearing, activities to enjoy with children, age-level characteristics, etc. Encourage parents to sign out these books, returning them in a week or two. Invite parents whose children have grown older to donate books or other resources they found helpful as parents of young children.

Connect grandparents to young families by forming a Grandparents' Club. Invite senior adults who do not have grandchildren or whose grandchildren do not live nearby to join in informal meetings with young families—particularly those whose parents are no longer living or who do not live nearby.

Once a month, offer babysitting free to parents of young children during the dinner hour. Parents can eat at home or at a restaurant, enjoying a special time of "adults only" conversation. Include these guidelines: (a) parents reserve space a week ahead of time; (b) when checking in their children, parents leave a phone number where they can be reached and sign a permission slip.

Families

HOW DO WE MAKE SURE EVERYONE KNOWS?

Unless there is an intentional effort to communicate with families, it's likely that a number of your families will go for years without understanding basic policies others take for granted! You can't guarantee people will read or remember the information given out, but you can make it available. Here are some proven ways to accomplish good communication with families:

Family Welcome Center. The easiest way to ensure that you regularly interact with parents is to establish a consistent location where parents may sign in their children, receive information about their children's classes, register for various children's events, get name tags, etc. Consider the traffic pattern both before and after your church's services. Set up a table or counter at a convenient location that is visible but out of the traffic flow. (Large churches may need several such locations.) Post a large, clear sign where new parents can see it above the crowd and get to the table easily.

Post a list of all classes, the locations where they meet and the names and phone numbers of the teachers. Keep available a good supply of current brochures describing your children's ministry. There also needs to be a person at the location who is knowledgeable about the programs and can answer parents' questions accurately.

Recruit another person to act as a greeter for 10 to 15 minutes before and after the start of a session who is then free to attend an adult class or worship service. This tandem effort will ensure a smooth and welcoming start for new families.

Classroom Signs. Outside every class, mount a sign with the name(s) of the teacher(s). Also mount (outside or inside the class) a poster with candid snapshots of teachers in action with students. Add labels with the names of the people pictured and update the photos periodically. Particularly in a large church in which parents may be unfamiliar with their child's teacher, these signs and photos will help to create a sense of connection. Such signs also help teachers feel a sense of responsibility and ownership!

Handbook or Brochure. Another key method to communicate with parents is to develop a handbook or brochure that describes the programs and procedures of your children's ministry. Update the handbook at least once a year or more often, if your programs change significantly throughout the year.

Give the handbook to all parents when they register their children in your program or whenever a family visits your church. Make sure that each teacher also has a copy. Provide copies in the church entryway and make sure that ushers know the location of the books, so they can give them to interested visitors. The handbook should include information on the following topics:

★ The goals and purpose of your ministry

★ Well-child guidelines for children coming to church

★ Greeting and dismissal policies, check-in and check-out procedures

★ Your church's plan for child and parent identification

★ How you would like parents to provide information about the child (name of child and parents, phone numbers, allergies, etc.)

★ Programs available for all ages of children, time schedules (include both starting and ending times), room locations for different ages, campus map

★ A summary of a typical session plan and descriptions of other programs for families and parents

Parent Newsletters. At several significant times throughout the year, it is helpful to send newsletters to parents. (Some churches develop monthly letters.)

These newsletters help parents understand how they and their children can best benefit from the programs available.

The most effective times to send newsletters are at the beginning of the school year, at the start of holiday seasons and at the beginning of summer vacation. Holiday times are natural opportunities to contact parents. Parents are often looking for ways to help their children experience the spiritual significance of such holidays as Christmas and Easter. Some parents just need to be reminded that your children's ministry provides one of the best ways to help a child discover and enjoy the rich meaning of the holiday. Always include information and an invitation to a specific program in your ministry, including the time, place and age groups involved.

Class Activities. You may attach by the entrance of each classroom a small white board on which the teacher writes a few comments about activities in which children participated.

Parent Observations or Open House. Periodically invite parents to schedule a Sunday when they will observe a full or partial class session with their child's teacher. Participating in activities with their child will give parents firsthand knowledge of what happens in a program and may increase interest in helping in children's ministry! A small church may schedule all parents to visit on the same day, but a large church will want to stagger parent visits.

If a number of families are new to your church, offer a facility tour for children and their families. Distribute copies of your handbook. Answer questions about the policies and programs of your children's ministry. Provide a brief time with refreshments for teachers and parents to talk together. You may wish to invite a parent whose child has been participating in Sunday School (or another program) to attend the open house or tour to tell how their family has benefited from the church's children's ministry.

Families

HOW CAN WE BECOME AWARE OF AND HELPFUL TO CHILDREN AND FAMILIES AT RISK?

"At risk" is a term that originated with the medical field to indicate the state of a body that had been assessed and found to be likely to contract a particular disease. More recently, both the concept and the term have been used by social services and educational agencies to categorize children who are likely to have difficulty in school, likely to be victims of certain abuses and injustices or likely to be in need of intervention (foster care).

Our purpose is never to label children. But because we are committed to Jesus' mandate to help them and their families in His name, we need to understand how the category of "at risk" is defined and how these children may be viewed so that we can understand the criteria by which school and social agencies may evaluate them and plan the best ways we can help them.

The United States Census Bureau defines "children at risk" as persons younger than 18 who are characterized by:

having one or more disabilities

having been retained in at least one grade

speaking English less than "very well"

living with only one parent (or with neither parent)

living in a family who has immigrated in past 5 years

living at an annual family income below $10,000 (or established poverty level)

living in a home where neither parent/guardian is employed[1]

State educational agencies look to any or all of these factors to define risk: illness; disability; premature birth or birth trauma; slow growth; frequent illness; developmental delays; parents who punish rather than teach; parents who have substance abuse or illness issues; parents who ignore, give little affection or overindulge a child.

These very different criteria are included to show that we're probably all at risk by someone's standards! But the Census Bureau report cautions that evaluating either risk or well-being is quite subjective: What may be seen as danger by one may be seen as opportunity by another! The Census Bureau points out that no one can ever say for certain that any factor or set of factors necessarily constitutes a true risk to an individual's well-being or future. To this we add that God says that with Him, all things are possible (see Matthew 19:26)! These factors are simply one way to help us evaluate and give meaning to what we might be seeing.

When a child or a family in your ministry exhibits traits from the aforementioned lists, here are steps to take to provide the best help possible:

1. Be prepared. Keep up-to-date information on file about care programs available through your own church, other local churches, aid agencies and county or state relief agencies. Learn what steps need to be taken to get the kinds of help offered. Knowing what processes these agencies require makes you better able to help. (If your church has a significant number of families or children in need of these kinds of services, recruit a volunteer "children's care pastor" to keep current information on local helping agencies, be familiar with their policies and processes and to help families with paperwork, transportation, etc.).

2. Get to know the family. The intention of a home visit is not to nose around or report parents to the authorities but rather to show genuine compassion. Families in crisis usually have multiple needs.

Observe and respectfully ask questions. Where can your ministry and your church best serve their needs? Do they need housing? Food? Clothing? Transportation? Child care? Parenting classes? Your church may not be able to meet all the needs, but if you are prepared, you may well be able to open the door of access to agencies that can help.

3. Treat the child and the family with all the respect Jesus Himself would get from you. (This will require that we drop all issues of social inequality at the foot of the Cross. Many families in crisis have been embittered by the rejection of churches whose Christlike words did not match their actions.)

4. Keep good records. First, because these children and families are so often overlooked or pushed away, keeping complete records is a way to remind ourselves of their importance. Second, there may be so many transitions that it's difficult to keep track of what happens to them without written notes. Third, because these families are often evaluated by state agencies, good records may help to show a level of involvement at church that would be an otherwise unseen part of a family's stability. (As one seasoned director advises, no matter what else you purge, keeping records for as long as the children are in your program is good policy.)

5. Pray regularly for the needs of these children and families. God commands us to defend the poor and the victims of injustice or abuse (see Isaiah 58:6-11). These children desperately need caring adults to pray for them, to see and talk about God's good plans for them and to live before them in a trustworthy, Christlike way.

6. If a child has difficulty socializing or getting along with others, recruit a teacher assistant whose job it is to accompany the child during the program. This person need not do anything but be the child's friend and model appropriate behavior.

7. Because these children are often having difficulty with schoolwork, consider providing a tutor from your congregation. You might even consider setting up an after-school tutoring program or a mentoring program. Recent studies show that when an adult intervenes in the life of an at-risk child for at least 9-12 hours per week, a solid impact is made in the child's life!

Note

1. Robert Kominski, Amie Jamieson, and Gladys Martinez: *At-Risk Conditions of U.S. School-Age Children: Working Paper Series No. 52* (Washington, D.C.: United States Census Bureau, Population Division, Education and Social Stratification Branch, 2001), n.p.

Families

HOW CAN WE BEST MEET THE NEEDS OF THE FAMILIES WE SERVE?

Some parents regularly check their children into our children's program and then leave the church campus. What are effective ways to get them to stay?

When a parent leaves a child at church and goes off to eat breakfast or read the Sunday paper, the action tells everyone that while church is fine for kids, it has little value to the parent (except as a free babysitting service). The parent misses out on spiritual life, relationships and important information. The child is not encouraged to understand the lifelong value of being part of the church.

But as we address several solutions, we need to first know that every time a child comes to church, for whatever reason, by whatever means, we have a great opportunity to build God's love into that young life forever. We're wise to gladly make the most of it, even if a parent never shows the slightest interest!

Second, a parent might not be a believer and/or may not feel comfortable attending adult classes or worship services. Plan and publicize classes designed specifically for these parents (parenting skills, family life, Bible study for nonbelievers, etc.). This creates value for them and gives them a place to build relationships with others having similar interests.

Consider inviting parents to a group or activity you think would be interesting to them. Then call the parent twice: first, to invite the parent and second, to confirm a time and place you will meet the parent. Meet the parent at church at the agreed-upon time and place. If possible, attend the service with the parent. Or introduce him or her to others who will invite the parent to sit with them for several weeks. (Sitting with a visitor is a small act but is immensely valuable in making that person feel comfortable and welcomed. Consider recruiting a group of regular members to this ministry!)

Consider that for some parents, having an hour or two to spend with each other while children are in a class is seen as more valuable than any program the church is offering.

This circumstance is especially true if both parents work full-time outside the home. If this situation describes many of the parents in your church, realize that your church will need to develop alternative ways of ministering to these parents (family events, short-term groups, once-a-month activities, etc.) that help parents build their own relationship as well as their participation in the church family.

Third, involve the parents. Even if parents are nonbelievers, ask their help with their children's group! If their children are enrolled, they are likely willing to bring snacks and craft materials or send out absentee postcards. This not only makes the parents into contributors but also gives teachers and helpers a chance to build relationships with them!

Fourth, provide transportation for children when parents may be unable to do so. Arrange for carpools with church families or arrange for the church van to pick up children and bring them to church. This shows the parents you value their child and models for them the importance you place on being at church!

A growing number of our children live under shared custody arrangements. Some attend only every other Sunday. Some attend only once a month. How can we best support these children and their families?

The situation of every child whose parents are divorced is different. Some may initially feel grief or guilt when their parents separate. Other children may not even remember when their parents divorced and are comfortable with two homes, two churches and two routines. For some children, one or both parents may be living in a second marriage or with an uncommitted mate. None of these factors is in the control of children. Your goal as a teacher is to welcome each child into your class, loving and accepting the child regardless of his or her home situation or attendance pattern.

If a parent is an every-other-weekend parent, encourage him or her to continue to bring the child to church as often as possible. Avoid implying that the child is in any way missing out on the opportunity to grow as a member of God's family. Keep good records of both parents' contact information and the schedule the child is likely to keep. This prepares you to faithfully mail Sunday School or other materials to that child when he or she is not in class. Along with a short note from you, this mailing takes only a little time and money, but it provides continuity, keeps the child thinking about spiritual matters and shows that you think about the child, whether he or she is present or absent. If you have a number of children who are regularly away from church due to every weekend visitation, consider scheduling weekday events or after-school programs to provide them with Christian education.

In addition to providing practical assistance for their parents, if needed, consider offering divorce-recovery or grief-support classes for children coping with a difficult family situation. Make it a point to recruit helpers from among the parents of these children, so they not only learn how to help and support their own children but also hear information that will benefit them!

The parents of two children in our children's ministry seem to regularly complain about the care their children receive. What is the best way to respond to these parents?

When talking to a parent who has a complaint, listen closely to what the parent is saying. Ask open-ended questions that help the parent describe the situation and his or her feelings. This will ensure you have all the needed information to respond to the complaint. If a problem has occurred due to an oversight or mistake, apologize and thank the parent for bringing the matter to your attention.

If the complaint is related to an ongoing situation, invite the parent to suggest specific actions that he or she believes would remedy the existing problem. Let the parent know you will do your best to resolve the situation. Follow up the complaint by letting the parent know what changes have been made, if possible.

If the complaint is not really valid, thank the parent for voicing concern, but point out why the class or program operates as it does.

What can we do to make parents feel that they are part of the team?

First, be sure that parents understand what programs are available and the reasons behind them. Help them understand the schedule and operation of the classes in which their children are enrolled (check-in, snacks, etc.). Because we live in such a consumer-centered culture, some parents may not even realize that classes are taught by volunteers instead of paid professionals! Help parents understand that this volunteer team effort is the result of people who love God and children enough to sacrifice time and effort to teach them. Invite parents to observe a class or to help during a session. Generally, parents who observe or help with a class quickly understand the challenges and benefits of your programs!

Some churches make their children's classes a cooperative venture: They make it clear to parents from the outset that if children are enrolled in classes, each parent is expected to contribute time to helping in class. Parents who understand this are usually willing to help in an assigned way at an assigned time. (Having a system in place and a sign-up sheet at the check-in table will go far in simplifying the process. Don't expect a parent to contact you!) Parents who help are also exposed to Bible truth (sometimes for the first time) and to good teachers who model positive ways to interact with children. This will help them as parents and may lead them to take the next step to train as teachers themselves.

Occasionally, a parent will want to have both of his or her children in the same class, usually because one child becomes upset at being separated from the other. Should we let the children attend the same class?

This situation is most likely to occur when a new family begins attending your church. It is best to address the situation at the beginning. "We're glad to have Mariah and Michael attend the same class for one or two weeks while they get used to our church. But after several weeks, Mariah will probably be bored in Michael's class. Then it will be time to move her into her own class, so she can enjoy the activities of children who are the same age as she is. By that time, Michael should be comfortable in his class, too." Encourage the children to attend the class appropriate for the youngest child. The older child can participate and the younger child will become comfortable quickly in an age-appropriate class environment.

Teacher Training Articles
Sharpening Our Skills

This section contains concise, informative articles that deal with issues faced by teachers and others who work with children, whether veterans or new volunteers.

These articles may be used in two ways: preventive work in training staff before a problem occurs and as prescriptive correction to problem situations that may be encountered.

Distribute these articles in any way you choose or use selected articles that target an area you want to address as the basis for teacher training sessions. Either way, this resource provides instant and specific information for better training!

Children love to make things with their hands! As infants, they mold their baby food into lumps and then progress to sand castles, mud pies and twig figures. Creative art activities engage many of a child's senses, but the goal of art activities is not simply to make pretty objects to take home and show to parents. The end result of an art-based Bible learning activity is to provide a stimulating, multisensory way for children to learn and apply Bible truths to their lives.

PROCESS VERSUS PRODUCT

Art activities may sometimes have a "product" orientation: to create an attractive object for display by following directions accurately to reproduce a standard item.

But in the classroom, focus on a "process" in which the doing of the art is more significant than the end result.

The advantage to focusing on "process" is that in creating individual pieces of art, children are not judged by their artistic abilities. A child may be hesitant to participate in an art experience if he or she feels that his or her ability is lacking. No child should be judged by the ability to accurately draw objects or by who is the neatest in using scissors. All artwork has value!

At times, it is useful to create craft items, but the primary goal of art activities should be to allow self-expression. Simply putting together an object only demonstrates that the child can follow directions. Giving children the freedom to create their own art

BIBLE LEARNING ACTIVITY OR CRAFT?

Bible Learning Activity

• Children explore, create and discover with the provided materials.

• Teacher talks informally with children, asking questions and guiding the conversation toward the Bible learning aims; children talk with each other as well as with the teacher.

• Focus is on the process (including the use of materials), group interaction and the connection to the Bible truth.

• Children choose from two or more activities and choose how they want to complete the activity.

• Small groups work with one activity at a time and move freely from one activity to the other.

Craft

• Children follow predetermined pattern.

• Teacher gives instructions with little opportunity for children to talk.

• Focus is on the product.

• Only one project is offered and children are expected to produce a similar result.

• Children all work on the same project at the same time.

encourages self-expression, thinking skills, creativity and greater satisfaction in the final product. As children work, the observant teacher can gain insights into the child's interests and understanding. Also, as children are allowed to express their own thoughts and feelings, they come to feel accepted and valued.

There are two reasons for using art activities in teaching:

1. Allows children to be active, rather than passive, participants in learning;

2. Puts abstract concepts in concrete terms that children can comprehend.

TIPS FOR LEADING ART ACTIVITIES

Make the art relevant to the Bible lesson. There is a temptation to use art activities only as time fillers. It's easy to hand out pages from a Bible coloring book when the lesson runs short. However, even a simple creative art activity that invites a child to express his or her understanding of a Bible story or verse will expand the impact of a lesson on a child's life. Take advantage of the tested and proven ideas presented in your curriculum rather than spending precious time developing your own creative ideas each week. If, however, you need additional art ideas, consider these:

★ Illustrate scenes of a Bible story to make a book.

★ Cooperate with other students on a mural depicting Bible story scenes or contemporary situations in which children are obeying Bible truths.

★ Use paint or decorative markers and scissors to make praise banners, identifying reasons to thank and praise God.

★ Decorate the cover of a prayer journal to be used in class or at home.

★ Create puppets to use in acting out ways to demonstrate love for God and others.

As a child works on an art activity, ask questions to help the child apply the Bible truth: "What happened just before the scene you are making? Which person in this scene do you think is a good example to follow? Why? What could you do this week that would show kindness like the good Samaritan did? What are you doing in this picture that is the same as what Ruth did in our story? How would it help the person in your picture if (she) remembered our Bible verse today?"

Be prepared. Experiment with the materials and the activity before class to be certain that the activity can be finished in the time allowed and that it is not too difficult. Note tips for success that can be shared with the children. If needed, briefly show a sample of your finished creation when introducing the activity, but then put away the sample to allow children to create in their own way.

Reduce cleanup. Avoid messy cleanup by providing glue and glitter that come in easy-to-control squeeze pens or tubes. Use erasable colored pencils instead of permanent markers. Cover tables with newspapers or plastic tablecloths. Keep plenty of wastebaskets, paper towels and cleaning rags on hand. Have children wear paint smocks or large washable shirts over their clothes. Give children plenty of time to assist with cleanup. Cooperating together on cleaning up the art materials can be a teaching time for children. Establish a consistent place in your classroom where art projects are placed to dry. As much as possible, avoid art projects that need more than 5 to 10 minutes to dry so that students don't carry wet objects home. (It's best not to make art projects that need to be left at church to dry, because some children may not be back the following week for pickup.)

Praise the art and the effort. Consider children's art to be their gift to God. Even the simplest attempt is worthy of acceptance. Praise children for their effort, use of color, creativity or the joy they show while making the art. Children appreciate that their effort is honored.

Modern life makes many demands on families. A two-day weekend may not provide enough time to shop, visit friends and relatives, do homework, take family trips, participate in sporting events, celebrate family events, finish household tasks and relax. When Sunday morning rolls around, parents may feel too tired or too busy for church. Because most children are brought by their parents, it's important to recruit parents as your allies in helping their children establish good attendance habits.

ENLISTING PARENTAL SUPPORT

Educate parents. As you have opportunity through phone calls, personal conversation, class open house, newsletters and e-mail, help parents understand the importance of bringing their children to church regularly. A child who attends regularly is likely to continue church participation as an adult—not only because

the habit is established, but also because the child has built solid friendships through regular attendance.

Classmates at church may be from different schools or areas of town and may only see each other once a week. A student who attends infrequently does not have the opportunity to cultivate these significant relationships. As a result, the child may feel lonely or isolated at church and so becomes less interested in attending. Even if a child complains about activities or teachers at church, he or she often will remain eager to come to church to see his or her friends. Especially as children move into their teen years, it may be difficult to begin new friendships at church, so it is important for friendships to be established at an early age.

Communicate with parents. Maintain regular contact with parents as best you can. Look for opportunities at church events to introduce yourself and talk to parents. Ask parents for e-mail addresses so that you can keep them informed of lesson plans, Bible memory verses, needed supplies and special events. Always communicate

with parents in a positive manner. Be ready to share an activity the child particularly enjoyed. Parents will be interested in their child's class at church when they know what's going on. If a child is new to your class, be sure to find out if the child has food allergies, medications or special needs.

Host an open house. A good way to acquaint parents with your class is to invite parents to meet you and observe in the classroom. Provide refreshments and let parents participate in the lesson activities. If your classroom isn't big enough for all parents to attend at once, invite a different group of parents each week for several weeks in a row.

DEALING WITH SUNDAY MORNING CONFLICTS

Some of the children in your class (and their parents) may face the difficult choice of choosing between church and sports activities on Sunday morning. What used to be exclusively church time can now be crowded with children's sports functions. There are no easy solutions to this situation. Children may feel resentful toward church if they must give up all sports activities to attend Sunday services.

In addition to helping parents understand the impact of regular attendance at church, here are some tips for what to do if a parent tells you that the child will be missing your class for a sports activity.

★ If you have multiple services, suggest that families attend each week, even if they must attend a different service time.

★ Encourage the parent to involve the child in a church activity that meets at another time (weekday, Saturday evening, etc.).

★ Invite the child to attend class dressed in his or her sports clothes, so the child can come directly before or after the sports activity.

★ Make plans to send lesson materials to the child each week (take-home papers and/or student worksheets provided by the curriculum, etc.). Encourage the parent to read and talk about the materials with the child.

★ Look for ways to continue your relationship with the child: Send an e-mail each week, schedule a class event (picnic at the park, pizza party, etc.) at a nonconflicting time. Send birthday or we-missed-you cards from yourself (or schedule a time during class for students to make these cards).

Attention Deficit

Although ADD and/or ADHD affect only 2 to 5 percent of school children, this small percentage translates into over 2 million children in the United States alone. You may have a child in your class who has been diagnosed with ADD/ADHD. If you are not a professionally trained educator, however, you may know little about these disorders. With patience and good teaching skills, most ADD/ADHD children can be taught successfully in your class. Place a priority on developing a good relationship and ongoing communication with the parents of children with ADD/ADHD. These parents may need the support of the church in many ways (child care, access to trained counselors, prayer, etc.).

WHAT IS ADD/ADHD?

Attention deficient disorder (ADD) and hyperactive disorder (HD) are two types of attention deficient disorders. Often the terms are used interchangeably. Children who have both types of disorders are ADHD. Research has shown that ADD and ADHD are biologically based and not a result of poor parenting or not learning to obey. These children will not grow out of these disorders. Over half of the children with ADD/ADHD will continue to exhibit symptoms as they mature.

Children with ADD/ADHD may have difficulty focusing on and completing tasks. They may be easily distracted and may not listen when a teacher talks to them. They can be forgetful, inattentive to detail or careless with objects. These children find it difficult to follow instructions or organize tasks. They act impulsively and sometimes recklessly.

Sometimes called hyperactive, children with ADD/ADHD can seem like fast-running motors that never shut down. They might squirm, fidget in their chairs or find it difficult to sit for a long time. They sometimes prefer to run around the room. They talk nonstop, blurt out statements and interrupt when others speak. They find it hard to take turns or wait in line. ADHD children might find it difficult to work quietly. If ADD/ADHD is left untreated, the child may be unsuccessful in school, at work and in getting along with others.

More boys than girls are diagnosed with ADD/ADHD because the symptoms are less visible in girls. Because girls with ADD/ADHD may not be treated as often, they may drift through school with mediocre grades and few friends and not live up to their potential.

Only a trained professional counselor or physician is qualified to diagnose a child with ADD/ADHD. Neither a teacher nor a pastor can assume that a rowdy child has or does not have these disorders merely by watching his or her behavior. If a child exhibits the symptoms of ADD/ADHD to the extent that your class activities are regularly disrupted, your supervisor may wish to talk gently with the parents to ask for their advice on how to better meet the needs of the child. No child should be labeled with this disorder without a qualified diagnosis.

HOW CAN I TEACH THE ADD/ADHD CHILD?

Medication. Many, but not all, ADD/ADHD children take prescription medicine as part of their treatment. Such medicine, however, only relieves the symptoms and does not actually cure the disease. This medicine is not a tranquilizer that makes the child compliant, or a magic cure-all. Teachers and pastors are not qualified to prescribe or handle these drugs. If medication is required, the parent or a qualified medical professional should administer the dosage to the child.

A child may show some side effects, such as loss of appetite, sleep problems, moodiness or fatigue, when ending the medication or changing the dosage. Because some parents do not medicate their children when their children are not in school, you may see these side effects during class.

Student attention. Part of a child's treatment is training the child how to concentrate and pay attention. In addition to the tips included in this article, consult the parents, a health specialist, educator or reference books for additional information on teaching the ADD/ADHD child.

You may wish to also enlist the help of another adult who is willing to be trained in helping the ADD/ADHD child. During class, the adult mentor stays near the child and is ready to offer one-on-one direction as needed. In some cases, it may prove helpful to have the adult provide patient and loving one-on-one guidance rather than pressing to have the child try to fit into what the other children are doing.

While the following teaching tips are useful when teaching all ages, these tips are particularly important if you are teaching children with ADD/ADHD.

★ Provide colorful posters, markers and chalk as well as a variety of visual aids.

★ Use sound and music to signal to the child when it's time to listen.

★ Speak clearly and look for visual cues that the child is listening.

★ Use words the child will understand. Be specific.

★ Draw a square around information on a chalkboard, poster or white board to show the student where to look. Use a flashlight to draw a child's eyes.

★ Use a variety of storytelling techniques including props, first-person stories, skits. Avoid having any presentation extend too long. Be brief and change to a new activity at the first sign of restlessness.

★ Try to eliminate or soften outside sounds that could distract a student: a loud air conditioner, street noise, hallway traffic, music or talking in a nearby room.

★ Keep room decorations attractive but simple. Take away all unnecessary materials and furniture that could distract the child. Erase the chalkboard or white board after the information has been presented.

★ Cover all but a few lines of a book page as the child reads it so that the child is better able to concentrate on a few lines at a time.

★ Avoid lag time. Have materials and multimedia prepared for quick use. If the rest of the class is doing an activity that requires a significant amount of time, have alternate activities on hand for the ADD/ADHD child to do when his or her attention wanders.

★ Let the child sit close to you and away from doors and windows. Make eye contact when speaking. Surround the ADD/ADHD child with well-behaved children.

★ Maintain a regular class routine. ADD/ADHD children do not cope well with change. Give choices within appropriate boundaries.

★ Before a child begins a task, be sure the child clearly understands the directions. Don't embarrass the child but do have the child repeat back or write down the instructions for clarity. Encourage the child to ask for assistance if he or she gets stuck. Keep projects simple, with a minimal number of directions. Give simple instructions, one at a time, and repeat instructions if necessary. Show patience and understanding when a child is unable to remain focused on a task.

★ Give age-appropriate rewards for completing tasks within a reasonable time limit. ADD/ADHD children may work slowly and may grow frustrated if they cannot keep up with the pace of other children's work. Be available to give assistance and encouragement if the child gets stuck.

Being diagnosed with ADD/ADHD is not an excuse for the child to misbehave. Establish class rules ahead of time and talk about the consequences of not following the rules ("If you want to play this bowling game, you need to wait in line for your turn"). Redirect children's behavior in a fair, kind and calm manner. Avoid confrontation, ridicule and criticism. Do not announce to the entire class when the child needs to take medication or that the child has ADD/ADHD.

Most of all, give plenty of positive reinforcement and affirmation when the child does well. Show love and affection with more than words. Children will pick up your caring feelings by seeing your facial expression and actions.

Bible Games

Incorporate a variety of games into your lesson plans to help motivate children's enthusiasm. Avoid the temptation, however, to use games just to fill time or to work off childhood energy. Instead, choose games that help you reinforce the lesson. Children may not be aware of the direct learning value of a game, but they will learn as they participate enthusiastically just because they enjoy the game.

Bible games are best played to develop cooperation within teams, not competition between individuals. With teams, as each person shares his or her talents, students learn to cooperate and build up the community of Christ. The emphasis is on the group's goal, not individual accomplishment. Students are given the opportunity of learning to be fair, to be honest and to take turns. Providing both active and quiet Bible games ensures that children of varying learning styles will be able to participate in games that appeal to them.

ACTIVE GAMES

Active games require an open space free of obstacles so that children can move and run. These games help provide a change of pace when students have been sitting for a while, or during special events such as Vacation Bible School, retreats or camps. Active games can be played outdoors on a level grassy playground area or indoors in a church gym or fellowship hall. Some active games can be played in classrooms if space is cleared by moving tables and chairs to the side of the room.

Think of these games as "play with a purpose." The object of these games is not to build muscle or stamina but to encourage teamwork and reinforce biblical truths. Popular active games are finding hidden objects, relays and tossing games.

QUIET GAMES

Quiet games can be done with students sitting at a table or on the floor. These games often require the use of a worksheet or activity page and are often more knowledge oriented than active games. Quiet games may include mazes, codes, ordering words of a Bible verse and jigsaw and crossword puzzles. They can be played individually or in teams, with each student answering a question or getting help from teammates.

TIPS ON EFFECTIVE GAME LEADERSHIP

★ Alternate active and quiet games to keep student interest high. Children who are not skilled in active games may feel more comfortable participating in quiet games.

★ Avoid using strenuous active games when children are dressed in clothing that parents do not want to have soiled. If needed, provide smocks or large shirts for children to wear if children will get wet or dirty during the game.

★ Always think of safety first. Make sure there are no sharp edges or points on game items. Never let students run with scissors, sticks, spoons or hard objects. Only use soft foam balls indoors and never allow balls to be thrown at someone's face. (Keep adhesive bandages on hand for an accidental cut or scrape.)

★ Practice the game before class to be sure that it will work and it is not beyond the students' skill level. Make sure the jigsaw pieces fit, the clues are accurate, and the maze can be solved.

★ Keep the game simple. Especially with younger children, the concept of working as a team to accomplish a task may be difficult. Games such as relays or games based on familiar children's games are easy for teachers to explain and for children to understand. Most of the game time should be spent playing the game, not explaining complicated rules. Demonstrate exactly what the children are to do. Give students a practice round or a warm-up try so that they don't feel anxious or frustrated in playing the game.

★ Alternate the ways teams are selected so that children have opportunities to interact with a variety of classmates. Avoid letting children select their own teammates so that no one will feel left out. Teams can be formed by children wearing the same color of clothes, children with birthdays in the same month, children who have the same type of pet, the same number of letters in their name, initials of their first name, hair color or drawing names from a hat.

★ Make games as noncompetitive as possible. If prizes are given, be sure each child receives a token for participating. No one should feel left out or as if he or she lost out. Consider using terminology such as "first winners" and "second winners" to help all children feel valued and still encourage healthy competition.

Bible Learning Activities

Children learn best by what they do, not what they hear or see. Thus, choose activities that reinforce the focus of a lesson. How does a teacher select the best activities for the class? How does the teacher lead students to gain the maximum amount of learning from these activities?

SELECTING LEARNING ACTIVITIES

Suitability. As you look at activity ideas in your curriculum, ask yourself, *Is the activity appropriate for the age, number of children, interest and skill level of my class?* While young children may enjoy using puppets, they may not be able to actually make puppets. Older children may feel that some activities are too childish. Because of their learning styles, the students may enjoy doing certain activities more than others. Inner-city churches may have different challenges than suburban or rural congregations. An effective curriculum will provide you with varied activities from which to choose so that you can customize your lesson to the needs and abilities of your class.

Don't let having a small classroom or limited budget prevent learning from taking place. Rather than focusing on limitations, think of ways to creatively use the available resources. Instead of buying expensive maps of Israel, ask a church member who has visited there to share slides and photos of the trip. If there is no money for art supplies, ask church members to donate paper and markers. If a classroom is too small for games, make arrangements for the students to use the fellowship hall or an outdoor patio.

Teachability. Does the activity support the objectives of the lesson? Or is the activity only a fun time filler? While children love to have fun, and your classroom should provide times of fun, it is also necessary to provide a good balance of activities that help students discover how to apply the Bible concept to their daily lives. Does the activity clearly present the teaching objectives? If the activity is too complicated, if it hides or distorts the teaching objective, find another activity that requires less explanation. Look for activities designed to help students learn to use the Bible and Bible reference tools.

Life-related. Your lesson may have one Bible truth for the students to grasp, yet student learning should connect that truth to everyday life. For example, the lesson may focus on obeying God by being honest, but an effective game activity will help each student to name situations and ways in which to show honesty.

LEADING LEARNING ACTIVITIES

Tell the purpose. Tell students *why* they're doing an activity. They may see the activity as a fun thing to do, but use your conversation to point students toward a higher purpose: "We're going to make a scene of the Israelites escaping from Egypt to help us remember we can trust God to take care of us."

Give clear directions. Children grow frustrated if they don't understand what to do. Explain clearly what is expected and how students can accomplish their tasks. Write directions on a chalkboard or large sheet of paper for reference. Have supplies nearby and organized.

Let children work at their own pace. Once the project is explained and students begin working, avoid micromanaging. Avoid the temptation to "do it for them" and let children proceed at their own pace. Let students make choices and mistakes. Allow students the freedom to ask for help instead of anticipating their needs. Have additional activities on hand or books to read for students who finish quickly instead of making the slower students rush.

Use guided conversation. Use comments and questions during the learning activity to help students connect the activity to the lesson's Bible truth. "I see you've drawn a picture of a way to show patience at home. What is a way to be patient at school?" or "Thanks, Nathan, for helping clean up the spilled glitter! That's what the Bible tells us to do."

Summarize what was learned. Near the end of the session, ask students to summarize what they learned about today's Bible truth. "What was one important thing learned by the boy who shared his lunch?" If students cannot answer the question, then more learning is needed. Ask additional questions, or tell an example from your life to extend students' interest and learning.

Share learning with others. Information is best used when it's passed on to others. Teaching is the best way to learn. Encourage students to share what they learned in class with their parents and friends. Let students lead an activity for a class of younger children. Students can share their learning by giving short talks to the congregation during worship or a church event. Children who are shy about public speaking can write statements for other students to read. Artwork can be displayed during an open house.

Bible Study

Passing on the living Word of God to the next generation is the most important and daunting task a teacher can do. Most new teachers approach teaching the Bible with trepidation. "I don't know much about the Bible!" "I haven't been trained in teaching methods or in theology!" "I haven't done this before!" "I'm not good enough!" "What if I say something wrong?"

Some of God's greatest heroes didn't feel up to the task, either. When Moses heard God's call, he complained that he had no credentials, he didn't know enough, he worried about failure, he didn't speak well, and finally in desperation, he begged God to send someone else! Does this sound similar to modern-day excuses?

Such fears can be relieved through Bible study and spiritual growth. God does not give you tasks without His promise of help. Daily personal devotional time will strengthen you for your work.

PERSONAL BIBLE STUDY

Study the lesson. This may sound obvious, but study the lesson's Bible story. While you may not present all that you learn to the class, studying the passage will equip you to teach, answer questions and apply the lesson to your own life. Begin your study early in the week so that you have time to reflect on what the lesson passage is saying to you.

Some teaching curricula have devotionals and study aids in the teacher's manual. Take advantage of these gifts and use them in your personal study time. The Bible is not so mysterious that only the super saints can understand it. God wants His Word to be known! Come to Bible study with assurance that God will open His Word and make it clear.

Establish a regular time and place. Try to establish a regular time and place for study. If one tries to fit in study "when there's free time," there usually isn't any.

You may need to wake up a few minutes earlier, stay up a little later at night or refrain from taking on one more activity. Even when people feel they can not fit lengthy uninterrupted study time into their schedules, it is important to make this time a priority. A short time every day might be great for some teachers!

In a busy family, a person may be hard pressed to find quiet time. Use your children's nap time or school time as study time. The working person may squeeze in study during a lunch hour or study in a quiet office before or after other employees arrive or leave. Some people may be able to concentrate on the train or bus going to work!

Clear the air. Some people like to begin study time with confession. Remember that through Jesus' sacrifice all sin is forgiven and all things are made new. Say a brief prayer of confession and then move forward with confidence and grace.

What's the point? Begin by reading through the lesson passage several times for meaning. If an overly familiar story seems dry, read a different translation.

Determine the main concept of this passage. First, what did God tell the people of that era? Second, what is God saying to me today? When reading about Jesus telling a rich man to sell all that he owned and give it to the poor, God may be telling you to be more generous with your time or possessions.

Meditate. Spend some quiet moments reflecting on the main point. Perhaps reread a verse that was especially meaningful. Think of ways to apply the main point to situations in your daily life. After reading, write your thoughts in a journal or practice being quiet so that you can hear God. You may find it helpful to keep a prayer journal or underline a special verse.

After considering the message of the passage for your own life, look at the lesson aims to see the suggested focus for using the lesson with children. Begin to pray that God will help you guide your learners toward that goal. Most of all, remember Jesus' promise that the Holy Spirit will guide you into all truth. Invite God to lead and teach you.

Get the background. The Bible was written in another time, place and society with many customs different from today's customs. The various books were written for specific purposes and persons. The Bible makes more sense when one knows how and why each book was compiled. Find information on the Internet, or invest in a good Bible dictionary, commentary, maps and reference books. Read what scholars say about the passage. Look up Bible characters, place names, and unusual words or customs. It is usually not necessary or even useful to share all that background with children. Simply look for insights that help you better understand the passage.

OTHER GROWTH OPPORTUNITIES

Adult study groups. Take advantage of adult Bible studies provided outside of the Sunday morning educa-tional hour. Some adult studies meet in homes on week-nights for casual discussions; others are formal lessons taught by a lay leader or the pastor. Many churches offer short-term courses. If there are no classes available, contact the pastor or education direction for assistance in participating in or starting an adult Bible study.

Corporate prayer. Take advantage of prayer groups, prayer chains and special worship services of prayer and praise. Use the time to pray for the students, other teachers, the unchurched in your community and for yourself.

Retreats or seminars. An all-day Saturday seminar or weekend retreat is a great pick-me-up for the burned-out teacher. Take time away from the demands of work, family and church to relax and be refreshed at a retreat center or campground. Ask your pastor to recommend opportunities for Bible study conferences or retreats.

Bilingual Teaching

America is a land of immigrants. In recent years, even rural communities have welcomed newcomers from different nations. Some of these immigrants who come to church may speak only their native languages, or a limited amount of English. The language barrier can present a challenge for the English-speaking classroom. Through patience and effort, English-speaking teachers can make the new students feel welcomed as they adapt to their new home.

"Bilingual" refers to a person who is fluent in two languages. In American churches, this may be English and Spanish, English and Korean, English and Tagalog—the possibilities are endless! It can also refer to classroom or church service where two languages are used.

"ESL" stands for English as a second language. In addition to their native tongue, these people learn English. Children of immigrant parents often master English rather quickly; however, in the meantime these children struggle to understand a strange language.

Also a person may be able to speak a second language but not read it. An ESL child may be able to follow simple verbal directions in English but not read from an English Bible. A child often understands spoken English better than he or she can speak or read it. If you have several ESL children in one class, you may find their understanding of English is at different levels. If so, give verbal information to the child with the best English skills, so he or she can help the others understand.

Get help. Try to find at least one bilingual teacher, assistant or translator for your class if you have ESL children. The role of this person is to assist ESL children with directions and activities rather than translating the entire lesson word for word. Being bilingual does not mean a person is skilled at rapid, accurate translation.

Use visual aids. Although visual aids are useful for any classroom, they take on special importance with ESL children. Every child can understand pictures and photos. The visual aids give children a focal point during discussion and storytelling. Be sure that the visual aids contain mostly pictures and few words. Pantomimes and puppets are also good ways to present a story to ESL children.

Provide written materials. ESL children will be happy to read along with the rest of the class, or you may provide classroom materials in the child's native language. Some bilingual church members may be able to translate student pages, if necessary. (Note: The American Bible Society offers Bibles in many languages.)

If a translator is available, you may wish to provide a list each week with the Bible verse, key lesson points and directions for activities in the child's native language. This list can be on a poster, written on a chalkboard or presented as a handout. When writing a second language, pay attention to special characters and accent marks which could change the meaning of a word.

Learn the language. Take the time to learn a few phrases, greetings and directions in the second language so that you can communicate with ESL children. Over time, add to your vocabulary as you talk with children and their parents. If you fail to learn correct pronunciations, don't panic. ESL children will find it humorous!

Involve the students. ESL children can easily complete art projects, play games and sing songs. As you give instructions, demonstrate your actions. Find out what customs the ESL children have for Christmas and Easter and incorporate these into the class.

As ESL students become more proficient in speaking English, encourage them to become involved in class discussions. Don't push children past their comfort zone or beyond their speaking abilities, yet provide a safe place where they can practice their new language.

ESL children may make mistakes as they learn English, but avoid the temptation to correct their speech. Repeat or rephrase what they said correctly and thank the child for participating. Your friendly smile can communicate your care for the child just as much as your words.

Begin a second class in a second language. If the church has several ESL students who speak the same language, one option is to start a second class conducted in the native tongue. The advantage is that the class can flow smoothly without having to stop for translation, which frees up for time for learning.

A child's time at church is limited to a few hours a week at best. In order to make effective use of these hours, develop classroom habits to gain attention, so children follow instructions quickly. Children will respond to specific attention-getting techniques when they are an established part of class routine.

COMMUNICATING WITH CHILDREN

Catch their eye, and then use your voice. A child responds best when directions are given specifically to him or her, not shouted across the room to everyone. Be sure the child is listening before speaking. Go to the child and bend down to his or her level. Say the child's name to emphasize that you want to speak with him or her.

Keep it short and simple. Give a clear, brief direction of what you want the child to do. Long, detailed or vague instructions will confuse a child. Instead of ordering, "We must get our coats off the table, so we can use the crayons," simply say, "John, please hang up your jacket."

Keep it positive. State requests in a positive, rather than negative, manner. Instead of saying, "Don't leave the paint bottles open and let the paint dry," say, "Jill, please put the lid back on the paint jar."

Speak naturally. Adults have a tendency to talk down to children, use a high-pitched voice or overemphasize words. Use a natural, calm tone of voice. Never yell or speak harshly. Speak softly and cheerfully. Smile while speaking!

ATTENTION-GETTING TECHNIQUES

One good way to keep attention is to follow a routine in your class—particularly for younger children who respond well to familiar patterns and predictability. If the same schedule is followed in each lesson, children will know what to expect and be ready to calm down and be active when needed.

There are two types of attention-getting signals. The first is to indicate the next activity. When children see or hear the signal, they know it is time for storytelling or games or art projects, and they can get ready for that activity. By using the same signal each time for a specific activity, children know what to expect.

★ Play or sing a theme song for the activity. The children sing along as they gather.

★ Start a countdown "10 . . . 9 . . . 8 . . . ." with all children seated before "1."

★ Ring a bell, shake a tambourine, beat a drum, ring a tone chime, or shake a maraca.

★ Clap hands in a different pattern for each activity. Students repeat the pattern as they sit.

The second type of signal is to quiet children when they are talking too much or not paying attention. Children are more likely to respond to fun techniques than to shouting. Make a game out of quieting down. Teach one of these techniques at the beginning of class and soon children will respond. Thank the children who respond first. When the signal becomes ineffective after repetition, try a new technique.

★ Flick lights on and off two or three times.

★ Use a silent hand signal, such as holding up (two) fingers and stop talking. Students sit down and hold up (two) fingers until everyone is seated.

★ Hold up an object, such as a small toy, that is designated as the "attention grabber." Or put on a funny looking "quiet hat," scarf, gloves or sunglasses. When students see the object, they know it is time to be still.

★ Thank the children who are quiet first, and then give positive reinforcement to disruptive students when they settle down. Children often disrupt just to get attention and will be calmer when you give attention to their good behavior.

★ If helpers are needed for a project, select the children who are most attentive and quiet. Most children like to be selected to help and this will encourage them to be attentive. However, if the same children are selected each time, use another means to pick helpers.

★ Use Simon Says instructions, such as "Simon says, 'Get a marker!'" or "Simon says, 'Stand up and find a partner!'"

★ If there are other adult teachers or assistants in the room, take turns giving directions. Sometimes children stop listening when they hear the same voice all the time.

★ Try not to schedule a very quiet activity, such as prayer, after a rowdy game or busy activity. Give children a chance to "cool down."

★ Be prepared with an interesting lesson. Children give their attention when they are mentally engaged and enjoying the activities.

★ If the classroom noise level increases, start whispering and lean in toward children. They will be likely to respond in kind.

Characteristics

It's true that every child is different. However, there are certain characteristics that are the same about most children in a given age group. Let this guide serve not to pigeonhole the children you teach but to help you think of the best ways to relate to them based on their common interests and abilities.

WHAT TO EXPECT FROM CHILDREN IN GRADES 1 AND 2

Physical

These children are growing rapidly. Younger first graders may be physically more like preschoolers, while the ones moving toward third grade have hit a new level of physical maturity that shouts, "I'm not a little kid anymore!" Although these children may be expected to sit in school at this age, they still need frequent opportunities for movement during every class session. Small-muscle coordination is still developing and improving. Girls are ahead of boys at this stage of development.

Teaching Tips: Use activities that involve simple folding, cutting and writing skills. Always offer drawing in place of writing for those who struggle with writing. Give them frequent opportunities to change position and to move around the room or outdoors. Vary the kinds of activities to help keep attention high and discipline problems to a minimum.

Emotional

Children are experiencing new and frequently intense feelings as they grow more independent. Sometimes the child finds it hard to control his or her behavior. There is still a deep need for approval from adults and a growing need for approval by peers.

Teaching Tips: Seek opportunities to help each child in your class KNOW and FEEL you love him or her. Show genuine interest in each child and his or her activities and accomplishments. Learn children's names and use them frequently in positive ways. Smile frequently.

Social

Children this age are greatly concerned with pleasing their teachers. Each child is struggling to become socially acceptable to the peer group as well. The Golden Rule is still a difficult concept at this age. Being first and winning are very important; taking turns is hard! This skill improves by the end of the second grade. A child's social process moves gradually from *I* to *you* to *we*.

Teaching Tips: Provide opportunities for children to practice taking turns. Help each child accept the opinions and wishes of others and consider the welfare of the group as well as his or her own. Call attention to times when the group cooperates successfully and thank children for ways you see them sharing, taking turns, etc.

Cognitive

There is an intense eagerness to learn! Children of this age ask many questions. They like to repeat stories and activities. Their concept of time is limited. Thinking is here and now rather than past or future. Listening and speaking skills are developing rapidly; girls are ahead of boys. A child tends to think everyone shares his or her view. Children see parts rather than how the parts make up the whole. They think very literally.

Teaching Tips: Consider the skill and ability levels of the children in planning activities. For example, some can handle reading and writing activities while others may do better with music or art. Use pictures to help them understand Bible times and people. Avoid symbolic language, which often confuses them. Use a variety of activities to keep brains alert and functioning at optimal levels.

Spiritual

Children can sense the greatness, wonder and love of God when given visual and specific examples. The nonphysical nature of God is baffling, but God's presence in every area of life is generally accepted when parents and teachers communicate this in both their attitudes and their actions. Children can think of Jesus as a friend but need specific examples of how Jesus expresses His love and care. This understanding leads many children to belief and acceptance of Jesus as personal Savior. Children can comprehend talking to God anywhere, anytime in their own words and need regular opportunities to pray. They can also comprehend that the Old Testament tells what happened before Jesus was born and the New Testament tells of His birth, work on Earth, return to heaven and what happened in God's family on Earth.

Teaching Tips: The gospel becomes real to children as they feel genuine love from adults. Teachers who demonstrate their faith in a consistent, loving way are models through which children can understand the loving nature of God.

WHAT TO EXPECT FROM CHILDREN IN GRADES 3 AND 4

Physical

Children at this level have increasingly good large- and small-muscle coordination. The girls are still ahead of the boys. Children can work diligently for longer periods but can become impatient with delays or their own imperfect abilities.

Teaching Tips: Give clear, specific instructions. Allow children as much independence as possible in preparing materials. Assign children the responsibility for cleanup.

Emotional

This is the age of teasing, nicknames, criticism and increased use of verbal skills to vent anger. At eight years of age children have developed a sense of fair play and a value system of right and wrong. At nine years children are searching for identity beyond membership in the family unit.

Teaching Tips: Here is a marvelous opportunity for the teacher to present a Christian model at the time children are eagerly searching for models! Provide experiences that encourage children's creativity. Let all children know by your words and by your actions that "love is spoken here" and that you will not let others hurt them nor let them hurt others. Make your class a safe place where children feel accepted, where they are comfortable asking hard questions and where they may express their true feelings without fear of teasing.

Social

Children's desire for status within the peer group becomes more intense. This often leads to acting silly or showing off to gain attention. Most children remain shy with strangers and exhibit strong preferences for being with a few close friends. Many children still lack the essential social skills needed to make and retain friendships.

Teaching Tips: This age is a good time to use activities in which pairs or small groups of children can work

together. Create natural opportunities for each child to get to know others and to take on greater responsibility.

Cognitive

Children are beginning to realize there may be valid opinions besides their own. They are becoming able to evaluate alternatives, and they are less likely than before to fasten onto one viewpoint as the only one possible. Children are also beginning to think in terms of "the whole." Children think more conceptually and have a high level of creativity. However, by this stage, many children have become self-conscious about their creative efforts as their understanding has grown to exceed their abilities in some areas.

Teaching Tips: Encourage children to look up information and discover their own answers to problems. Provide art, music and drama activities to help children learn Bible information and concepts. Encourage children to use their Bibles by finding and reading por-

tions of Scripture. Bible learning games are good for this age and children are often eager to memorize Bible verses. Help children understand the meanings of the verses they memorize.

Spiritual

Children are open to sensing the need for God's continuous help and guidance. The child can recognize the need for a personal Savior. There may be a desire to become a member of God's family. Children who indicate an awareness of sin and concern about accepting Jesus as Savior need clear and careful guidance without pressure.

Teaching Tips: Give children opportunities to communicate with God through prayer. Help them understand the forgiving nature of God. Talk personally with a child whom you sense the Holy Spirit is leading to trust the Lord Jesus. Ask simple questions to determine the child's level of understanding.

WHAT TO EXPECT FROM CHILDREN IN GRADES 5 AND 6

Physical

Children have mastered most basic physical skills. They are active and curious and seek a variety of new experiences. Rapid growth can cause some 11-year-olds to tire easily.

Teaching Tips: 10-year-old boys will still participate in activities with girls, but by 11 years of age they tend to work and play better with their own sex. In your class provide some time for children to be grouped by gender, and some time when genders are mixed. This is a good age for exploration and research activities. Use active, creative ways to memorize Bible verses.

Emotional

Children are usually cooperative, easygoing, content, friendly and agreeable. Most adults enjoy working with this age group. Even though both girls and boys begin to think about their future as adults, their interests tend to differ significantly. Be aware of behavioral changes that result from the 11-year-old's emotional growth. Children are experiencing unsteady emotions and often shift from one mood to another.

Teaching Tips: Changes of feelings require patient understanding from adults. Give many opportunities to make choices with only a few necessary limits. Take time to listen as children share their experiences and problems with you. If your class includes sixth graders who are attending middle school, realize that these children are greatly influenced by their peers. They may show signs of low self-acceptance and need your care and support more than ever.

Social

Friendships and activities with their peers flourish. Children draw together and away from adults in the desire for independence. The child wants to be a part of a same-sex group and usually does not want to stand alone in competition.

Teaching Tips: Children no longer think aloud. Keeping communication open is of prime importance! Listen, ask open-ended questions, and avoid making judgmental comments to help them feel that it is safe to share freely.

Cognitive

Children of this age are verbal! Making ethical decisions becomes a challenging task. They are able to express ideas and feelings in a creative way. By 11 years of age many children have begun to reason abstractly. They begin to think of themselves as adults and yet at the same time are questioning adult concepts. Hero worship is strong.

Teaching Tips: Include many opportunities for talking, questioning and discussing in a safe, accepting environment. These are good years for poetry, songs, drama, stories, drawing and painting. Give guidance in a way that does not damage children's efforts to become thinking, self-directed people. Be aware of children with difficulty in reading. Plan other ways for them to gain information and be sensitive if asking children to read aloud.

Spiritual

Children can have deep feelings of love for God, can share the good news of Jesus with a friend and are capable of involvement in evangelism and service projects. The child may seek guidance from God to make everyday and long-range decisions.

Teaching Tips: Provide opportunities for children to make choices and decisions based on Bible concepts. Plan prayer, Bible reading and worship experiences. Involve children in work and service projects.

Children's Needs

Children don't arrive at the classroom with a blank slate. They have physical, emotional and social needs that can interfere with learning. They bring "baggage" of what has happened to them outside of class that can distract them from learning. Think about ways you can begin to recognize and deal with such needs so that the child's mind is free to learn.

THE CHILD'S NEEDS

Spiritual needs. Every child needs a relationship with Christ and to know that his or her sins are forgiven. Sometimes this important goal is lost when you struggle to provide for all of the student's other needs. At times you may need to step back and evaluate the ways in which this spiritual goal is being reached. Look for opportunities to share with children appropriate examples of how being a Christian has helped you. Invite children to tell what they know about becoming members of God's family. Listen to their responses to observe when a child indicates readiness to become a member of God's family. Pray for each child and ask God to give you wisdom in discerning his or her spiritual needs.

Physical needs. A child may have a difficult time focusing on learning if he or she is hungry or uncomfortable. Make sure that the classroom temperature is not too hot or cold, the air is not stuffy or smelly, the outside noises are not too distracting and the chairs are not too hard or wobbly. Clean up and brighten the room to make a pleasant learning environment. If children arrive without breakfast, provide granola bars, fruit, bagels or juice. A church located in a low-income neighborhood may want to sponsor a free meal program or a food pantry. The church may also need to provide clothing for children without warm coats or shoes.

Safety needs. Children need to feel secure and safe from harm. Establish an atmosphere of trust and love so that children feel comfortable in class. Follow your church's written procedures to protect children when they are picked up after class, being aware of restraining orders and not releasing children to noncustodial parents. Make sure there is an area in your classroom where children's belongings can be left without being stolen or destroyed. Let children know that you will not allow bullying in your classroom.

Social needs. Children want to be with those who love, affirm and accept them. They want friends and need to feel part of the group. They don't want to be ridiculed, criticized or ignored. Be sure that all children are included in class activities. Provide team-building and

trust-building exercises. Let children pray and sing together to form community. Demonstrate acceptance of a child who may appear to be different in some way. Your caring actions will teach more about God's love than your words.

Children want to feel important and respected. They want their contributions to class (singing, reading, art, discussion) to be valued and welcomed. They like their artwork displayed, their photos on the bulletin board and their names listed in the church newsletter. They like to hear the teacher say, "You did a good job!" A child who does not feel valued will be more likely to withdraw from the class and unwilling to participate.

SPECIAL CONCERNS

Sometimes children will tell you about a special concern or worry; most often, however, they will not. Without prying, make an effort to learn about students' everyday lives and be sensitive to children's emotions. Some children clearly express their feelings; others are quiet and moody. Some children with ongoing emotional needs or who are experiencing difficult times in their lives may need you to be nearby for support.

Family problems. Children are affected by the problems faced by their family members: an older sibling facing trouble with the law, parents getting a divorce, parent dealing with unemployment or financial difficulties. Even a normally happy event, such as moving to a new house, going to a new school, the birth of a new sibling or the remarriage of a parent can cause stress and anxiety. You can provide support, comfort and love. In extreme situations, you may need to intervene. (Note: If you see signs of possible physical abuse in a child, notify your supervisor and follow your church's established procedures.)

School situations. A student may have difficulty at school with low grades, a dislike for the schoolteacher, no friends, encounters with a bully, etc. Parents may demand that their child achieve high grades. Children may be overburdened and tired from too many after-school activities. Children want to feel popular among their classmates. There may be peer pressure to start dating or to have a "boyfriend/girlfriend" even among elementary-aged children. Students may feel pressure to buy expensive clothes or toys. Some children may even be approached by street gangs recruiting for new members. All of these concerns can prevent a child from concentrating in the classroom.

Emotional needs. A child may be dealing with an illness or disability that prevents him or her from functioning at peak efficiency. A child may have ADD/ADHD, depression, a mental illness or a learning disability. A child may be shy and find it difficult to socialize with other people. Some may have deeply rooted feelings of inadequacy or rejection. Some students come to class with "chips on their shoulders" and uncontrolled rage.

Intellectual needs. There are children who truly want to learn as much as they can. They are fascinated by the Bible, eager to serve God and willing to work hard. However, they feel discouraged and hindered by the students who don't share their interest. The effective teacher may need to find additional learning experiences for such children to keep their interest high.

You can do much to help meet students' needs. However, realize that you cannot solve every problem, make every student's life perfect, force people to change or make every situation right. You can forgive yourself for your human limitations, do your best to minister to your students and turn all things over to God. When you show that you are secure in your faith in God, your students are encouraged to also be confident of God's care in their own situations.

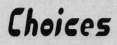

Choices

Adults often view themselves as the persons with the right knowledge and correct answers to give to uninformed children. As a teacher, you may think that it's easier and quicker to tell children what to do and how to think than to teach children how to make decisions for themselves.

There are many things that a child cannot control: who is in their family, where they live, what their parents' occupations are or which school they attend. Still, children do have a surprising number of choices that they make daily. The choices they make now will help them learn how to make significant decisions for the future. Look for ways to offer children practice in making appropriate choices.

WHY TEACH CHILDREN ABOUT DECISION MAKING?

To develop responsibility. Today, a child's biggest decision may be what kind of cereal to eat. As an adult, he or she must choose a career, a spouse, where to live, how to vote, and how to serve God and humanity. Making small choices now will give a child knowledge and experience which builds into greater ability to make important decisions later in life.

To develop confidence. A child who is not allowed to make little choices now will not feel that he or she can make good decisions later on in life. A child who is told constantly what to do can be easily swayed by other people. Children may later be resentful or angry about the choices made for them. A child without experience or confidence in decision making may make bad choices based on rebellion, emotion or lack of information.

To teach independence. A child will not be under the guidance of his or her parents forever. At some point the child must set his or her own course, start a new family and possibly move far away. Making good choices now will help a child move into mature independence.

To facilitate good behavior. Discipline problems can be averted when children choose what they want to do from among options you provide. Letting children make small choices in class will give them ownership of their learning and maintain their interest.

To make godly choices. A teacher can lead a child to God but the child must make the decision of discipleship for him- or herself. You cannot force a child to live the Christian life. By making good choices now, a child will be more likely to choose a lifestyle pleasing to God when he or she is older.

HOW DO I TEACH ABOUT DECISION MAKING?

Plan age-appropriate choices. Let young children make small choices (write or draw their answers to questions, which section of a mural on which to draw, etc.) and increase responsibility as the children grow older. Don't burden children with decisions beyond their experience and knowledge.

Be supportive. If a child wants to color a picture with only black and brown markers, that's OK. Children may not make the best or most rational decision, but affirm them as long as their choice is not disruptive, is not harmful to themselves or others or is not morally wrong.

Role-play. Older children can act out scenarios where they pretend to be in difficult situations, such as when they see another student cheating on a test. Act out different endings to the situation and discuss the best choice.

Provide active learning. Obviously, children are too immature to completely govern their lives. However, in the classroom, children will be more interested when they have some control over their learning. Allow children the opportunity to make choices in class:

★ Choose between two activities prepared in the classroom.

★ Choose the colors and materials for art projects.

★ Select which Bible verse to memorize.

★ Decide which part to play in a Bible story script.

★ Decide on a team name for a game.

★ Select a service project for the class.

★ Design a banner or a logo for the class t-shirt.

With active learning, be sure that all the students have an opportunity to make decisions. Be careful that one or two strong-willed students don't intimidate the more quiet children.

Experience consequences. When students make a less-than-perfect choice and it causes no physical or emotional harm to them or their peers, let them experience the consequences. Adults who constantly protect a child or cover for a child's mistake will not let the child learn the actual results of behavior. If a child is constantly late to class, don't wait to start a fun activity. If two children constantly distract each other, then tell those children they will need to be separated for a while. When children see that their behavior has consequences, they learn to make better choices.

Distinguish between good and evil. Modern society expects each person to decide what is ethically and morally right for him- or herself. But to make good moral choices, children need to know what God expects! While God allows people to choose their actions, His established behavior standards never change. Teach children what God expects from His children.

Use biblical examples. The Bible shows the consequences of good and bad decisions. The Israelites chose to worship an idol and God punished them. Mary chose to give birth to Jesus and helped bring salvation to the world. Use Bible stories to show child what great things can happen when decisions are made that honor God.

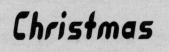

It's the most wonderful time of the year, but parties and visits to Santa can muffle the true meaning of Christmas for children. How can teachers at church reclaim this holy season for God's glory?

Remember that much of a child's response to Christmas is a reflection of what you model. Share your own feelings of joy, love and thankfulness for Jesus during this season. In class prayers, give thanks to God for Jesus. Avoid referring to Santa as a real person. It's OK to talk about Santa and Christmas gifts in the classroom, but keep the meaning of Christmas clear by frequently commenting, "Christmas is a special time of year because we remember how glad we are that Jesus was born. Jesus loves us all year long." Keep classroom activities low-key and avoid complicated art projects. Avoid the hurry and busyness of Christmas that often add to the stress in a child's life.

At the beginning of December, consider the schedule of lessons you plan to teach. Adjust your lesson plans as needed if many children in your class are likely to be absent during the holidays or if Christmas church events (children's choir rehearsal, etc.) will affect children's attendance.

CELEBRATION IDEAS

Each year, stores begin promoting the Christmas buying season earlier and earlier. In church, resist the temptation to rush into Christmas too soon. The church needs to set standards, not the commercial industry. Even if Santa has already arrived at the mall, wait to hang decorations in your classroom until the first Sunday of Advent.

Advent wreaths. In the rush toward Christmas, many Christians overlook Advent, the preceding four-week season of anticipation and preparation. Use this time to teach about Jesus' birth. Make or purchase a wreath for the class and teach the meaning of the lighting of the candles on the wreath. (Note: Information about Advent is available from your pastor, the Internet or devotional books.)

Nativity scene. Provide a nativity scene for your classroom or let students create their own scenes. Children can make their own class nativity scene by painting ready-made figures or by drawing a large butcher-paper scene. Depending on the age of your students, invite students to arrange nativity scene figures and use them in telling the story of Christmas.

Service projects. Involve children in service projects, so they turn their focus away from their personal wish lists. They can make holiday cards and cookies for homebound church members, buy toys for needy children, put together food baskets, serve at a church dinner or soup kitchen, sing carols at a senior center or host a party for younger children. If the children have a class gift exchange, set a one-dollar limit on purchases or give only handmade presents.

Creative storytelling. Since many of the children in your class may be familiar with the Christmas story, consider the following ideas to add interest:

★ Read the Christmas story from Luke 2:1-20, and then read one or more contemporary Christmas storybooks.

Ask children to evaluate the contemporary books by identifying which parts of the story match the biblical version.

★ Spread out a long length of butcher paper. Let children help you draw a road from Nazareth to Bethlehem, adding scenery, buildings, animals, etc. Move toy figures to indicate the actions of Mary, Joseph, the shepherds and the wise men.

★ Provide simple Bible-times costumes and props and let children act out the Christmas story. For another drama idea, provide paper bags and markers. Children make paper bag puppets to use in acting out the story.

Classroom Conversation

A child's education is not confined to hearing the Bible story or doing an activity—learning happens the moment the child steps into the church building. Before, during and after class, children are talking to their friends or teachers. These informal conversation times can be utilized to enforce the lesson concepts and to build a stronger bond between teacher and child. Don't dismiss these opportunities as "time fillers" or "shooting the breeze." Listen for cues and strive to guide conversation into a learning experience. Engaging a child in conversation makes class time an active, rather than a passive, learning experience.

CONVERSATION GUIDELINES

Encourage dialogue. Conversation is speaking **with** someone not talking **to** them. During informal conversation, allow the child to contribute and to talk about his or her interests. Adults may feel that children have little to offer in a conversation because of their limited life experiences and education. However, children can be surprisingly perceptive and entertaining. They relish conversation when adults treat them as persons worth listening to. Taking time for conversation says, "I love you" more clearly than words.

Listen up! The best conversationalist listens more than he or she speaks. When the other person is talking, most people tend to think ahead to reply and thus miss out on what the person is saying. When a child talks, concentrate on what he or say is saying. Let the child do most of the talking.

Listen to the child's attitude and how words are said. A child may say, "I'm fine" in a way that really means, "I'm sick" or "I'm upset." A teacher who hears anger, sadness or disappointment may want to investigate further and talk with the child about his or her problems.

Children have different priorities than adults do. They may consider their pets, their favorite superheroes,

their spelling tests or their games of soccer to be the most important things in their lives. Be interested in the child's world rather than judging it. Respond to the child's talk and ask questions. Children are always delighted when they know more than adults and they love to talk about their hobbies.

Watch for nonverbal clues. Some children simply don't speak a lot. They may be shy, may be frightened or may come from a family that encourages them to be quiet. They may communicate more with nods, shrugs or smiles. If a child doesn't speak much, continue to engage him or her in dialogue, even if the response is just a nod. When a child gets to know you better, he or she may begin to speak more.

TIPS FOR TALKING WITH CHILDREN

Be present. Stay with the children to be available for those unexpected moments. Avoid the temptation to

chat with the other teachers while the children are arriving or working on art projects. Sit at the child's level so you can always make eye contact when talking to him or her. Avoid interrupting or moving away when a child is speaking. Say the child's name when addressing him or her. Such actions tell children that you value their willingness to talk.

Be prepared. Know the lesson and the Bible well. A child may arrive to class with an unexpected question about something he or she heard, saw or read in the Bible. Allow a few moments to digress from the lesson long enough to deal with the child's question. The entire class may get interested in the answer and start the ball rolling for a new lesson idea!

Find out what's happening in the children's home lives. Then you can be ready to provide comfort for a child going through a difficult time. You may want to record in a computer file or on an index card brief notes about events or concerns in each child's life. Before class, use this record to remind you of what to talk about.

Relate Bible concepts to daily life. Affirm children when they do something well and show how they are living out God's commandments. "Thanks for taking turns with the CD player, Ashley. That's a good way to obey the Bible verse we talked about today." "Luis, I saw that you helped Nathan when the markers spilled. That's what the Bible talks about doing—helping others. Thank you." Look in your teacher's manual for conversation suggestions to help link activity to learning.

Ask open-ended questions. This not only starts a conversation but also helps the teacher to evaluate the student's learning and application. Look for ways to ask questions while children are engaged in an activity or talking about themselves. "What's it like going to a new school, Brittney?" or "Nico, how was the first day of school?"

Let children discover answers themselves. Instead of giving out all the answers, let children figure out the solutions. Rather than saying, "Here are ways we can show God's love to our families," say "What can you do to show God's love to your family?" Instead of saying, "Paul saw a bright light and heard God's voice on his trip to Damascus," ask "What does this verse say happened to Paul on his way to Damascus?" Rather than telling students that Jonah was sorry for his sins, ask them "How do you think Jonah felt when he was inside the big fish?" Then help children find and read the Bible references that hold the answers!

Creative Writing

In providing Bible learning activities that meet the varying needs and interests of children, one of the most useful and enjoyable activities is creative writing! If interesting activities are introduced with enthusiasm, even beginning writers will be motivated to join in. Every session doesn't have to produce a great art project or provide an active game—a pencil and paper can also be effective and fun teaching tools. For example, very often children will give more thought to writing answers than they will to giving quick oral responses.

Keep in mind that creative writing does not require a lot of training to use. Any child who can write can write creatively. Any adult who can write can guide students. Writing does not require a lot of materials, as do craft projects, or a large amount of space, as do some games. Writing can be an ongoing activity that can be stopped, stored on a shelf or in a drawer and restarted later. Writing activities can be completed as a group or by individuals. Writing helps the lesson move from head knowledge into heart knowledge as the child restates the Bible truth in a way that is personally meaningful.

In planning writing activities, two decisions need to be made:

1. Will others see the writing or is it only for the child's eyes? Some writing, such as personal feelings, is best kept private. Tell children in advance if this writing will be for sharing with the class or parents.

2. Will students write alone or with others? Some students may struggle with their writing skills and may be more comfortable working in a group. If children are not used to creative writing experiences or if their writing skills are just developing, they may feel more confident by participating in a group writing activity.

Give some simple but interesting suggestions to get young minds working. Begin telling a Bible story, then stop and let children write out an ending. Or give them a question to answer, such as How would you feel if Jesus washed your feet? or a sentence starter to complete, such as One way I can show I love God is by . . .

WAYS TO USE WRITING

★ Write a letter to a Bible story character (or write a letter from the character).

★ Write a letter or make a greeting card for a senior citizen, hospital patient, missionary family or absent classmate.

★ Write a Bible story as a newspaper article. "Flash! Big Flood Covers World!" "Soldiers Puzzled by Empty Grave!"

★ Write a cooperative free-style (nonrhyming) poem. Select a topic, such as "God's Power in Nature." Each student contributes one sentence. After class, arrange the sentences in order and write or type the poem. Reproduce the poem on colored paper and distribute copies to the class.

★ Write an "advice column." Give the students a question to answer, such as How can brothers and sisters in a family get along? or What should a kid do when his or her friend lies a lot?

★ Keep a prayer journal. In class, let students decorate construction-paper covers and attach blank sheets of paper. During the week, students write or illustrate prayer requests, Bible verses they have read, how they have helped others and their thoughts about God. Remind students that their journals are confidential!

★ Draw a Bible story as a comic page. This assignment is good for older students who love video games and graphic novels. Students who don't want to draw can write the captions and dialogue.

★ Use a computer. Many children are computer literate. If the church has a computer lab, let children type and print out their thoughts. They can e-mail messages to their home computers from church as reminders to pray or read the Bible during the week!

SPECIAL TIPS

Use colorful pens and paper. Children need not be restricted to regular lined white paper and blue or black pens. Use colored paper or parchment. Add stickers or let children decorate the margins of paper. Try recreating an illuminated manuscript similar to medieval times by letting students draw illustrations and fancy capital letters. Pens and markers come in many ink colors. Be sure each pen's tip is thin enough for easy writing. Older children may use pens with special calligraphy tips and ink cartridges. Avoid using tips that must be dipped in ink, as these tips could be messy.

Have a dictionary handy. While this is not a composition class, a child may want to use an unfamiliar word or just have difficulty with writing. A child may want to do better if the writing will be shown to parents. Help children find spelling and grammar helps as needed. Write Bible names and place names on a chalkboard or white board so that children can spell them.

Suggest alternatives to writing. Quite a few children may not feel comfortable doing a lot of writing. Children can speak their ideas into an audiocassette recorder so that their words can be transcribed after class. An ESL child can write in his or her native tongue and explain to the class the meaning in English. A child can dictate thoughts for the teacher to write down and then illustrate the words.

Death

Adults seldom talk to children about death until a loved one dies—a grandparent, aunt, uncle, a pet, a parent or even another child. A child with a terminal illness may be facing his or her own approaching death. This situation can be a sad, confusing and scary time for the child. An empathetic teacher can provide a safe environment in which a child may feel free to grieve and to ask difficult questions. (Note: If you become aware of a death in a child's family, make sure to alert the children's ministries coordinator/director for appropriate follow-up by the church.)

BIBLE STORIES ABOUT DEATH

The Bible gives many examples of how God's people deal with death in the family.

Genesis 23:1-2: Death of Sarah. "Abraham cried when his wife died. It's okay for us to feel sad when someone we love dies."

Genesis 49:29—50:14: Death of Jacob. "Joseph traveled a long way to bury his father. When someone in our family dies, he or she is usually buried in a grave. Visiting the grave is one way to remember the people we love. We can also go to the person's funeral and remember good things about the person, put flowers on the person's grave or even plant a tree or plant to remind us of the person."

Genesis 50:15-21: Joseph's brothers were afraid. "When Jacob died, Joseph's brothers were afraid that Joseph would hate them. When someone dies, we may wonder what will happen to us. But God is with us and continues to take care of us. We don't need to worry."

Luke 23:44-56: Death and burial of Jesus. "Jesus' friends were sad that Jesus died. They showed their love by burying Jesus and preparing spices for His body."

Luke 24:1-14: Resurrection of Jesus. "Jesus didn't stay dead. On the third day after Jesus had died, God raised Him from the grave. Jesus promised that when His followers die, they would live in heaven with Him and God our Father. Although we're sad when our friends die, we can be comforted because we know that people who are in God's family and who accept His love and forgiveness will be in heaven when they die."

John 11:28-38: Death of Lazarus. "Mary complained to Jesus when her brother Lazarus died. Sometimes we feel angry with God when someone dies. We might blame God for taking the person from us. God still loves us and knows we're just feeling sad. Jesus cried, too, when His friend Lazarus died."

ANSWERING QUESTIONS ABOUT DEATH

Children have many questions about the mystery of death. While adults may not know all the answers, they can provide a listening ear and caring heart to children in grief.

In discussing death, avoid euphemisms such as "the person is lost, sleeping, resting or on a journey." The child may interpret this literally and be afraid to fall asleep or go on a trip, or may try to find the "lost" person. Be honest in using words like "death" and "dying." Telling a child that God has "taken" or "called the person home" may cause a child to be angry with God for taking the person away.

Why do people die? "Our bodies wear out, like your toys wear out after you use them for a long time. After many years our bodies get tired and can't keep working. Sometimes people get sick and the disease hurts their body until it can't work anymore. But only our bodies die. The part of us that thinks and feels and loves keeps going. That's called our soul and it goes to live with God in heaven."

What is heaven like? "We don't know exactly what heaven looks like, but God promised it is a wonderful place with no tears or pain or sickness. God, Jesus, the angels and God's followers live there. Only God knows for sure who loves Him and who will be with Him in heaven. If we believe that Jesus is God's Son and ask God's forgiveness for our sin, we become members of God's family. God promises we will live with Him in heaven."

Why do little children die? "Because of sin, our world is not a perfect world. Anyone can get sick and die, although most of the time people do not die until they are old. Only heaven is perfect. There is no disease, sickness or death in heaven. But God is with us while we're on Earth and helps us when we are sick."

Does it hurt to die? "Sometimes people die quickly and sometimes it looks like falling asleep. No matter what happens to us, however, we know God is with us and loves us and takes care of us."

I thought mean things about someone. Is that why he died? "No, people don't die because of what others think or say. People die when their bodies get so sick or hurt that they don't work anymore."

Will my pet be in heaven? "The Bible doesn't say if our pets will be with us in heaven. However, the Bible does tell us that God loves animals. God cares for the animals, and He even knows when a little bird falls to the ground."

Sometimes a child needs closure for the death of a pet. The pet may have been euthanized and disposed of at a veterinary hospital without the child's being present. The class may say a prayer with the child: "Dear God, we thank You for (name of pet) and the joy it brought to (child). We remember the good times of playing with and caring for (pet). Be with (child) during this sad time and help us remember that You always care for us and the ones we love. Help us to always take care of Your creatures. Amen."

Discipline

The word "discipline" comes from the root "disciple" which means "student." Jesus' disciples were His students who learned from His words and actions. Maintaining discipline in the classroom should have the goal that each student is able to learn without distraction. Many behavior problems can be avoided with preventive methods that remove distractions. When problems do arise, behaviors can be viewed as learning opportunities in which the teacher can help a child understand how God's Word can make a difference in even difficult situations.

PREVENTIVE MEASURES

Love and pray for each child. Be a teacher who has a love for God and a love for children, remembering that when a child is the most difficult is the time the child most needs your understanding and love! Look for specific words and actions that will help each child feel loved and wanted. A child may come from a troubled family life or an overcrowded school. Church may be the one place he or she feels safe and appreciated! A child who feels accepted and cared for is likely to display positive behavior. When you pray for an individual child, it increases your love and commitment to them.

Plan a full lesson with choices of activities. Bored children are likely to be disruptive! Keep children interested from the first moment they walk through the door. Prepare a variety of things to do: music, stories, puppets, art activities, games, etc. A good curriculum will offer several choices of activities. As you get to know the interests and abilities of your class, choose the activities that will keep the children involved. Keep some basic game and art supplies on hand if the lesson runs short or if a planned activity doesn't work as well as you thought it would.

Keep the class moving. Children cannot sit still for long periods of time. They have short attention spans.

Video games and television have geared children to expect a constant flow of entertainment. Give students plenty of activities that let them move and play as well as quiet time. Avoid spending too much time on one activity; keep the energy level high by changing the pace and location of activities (sit on the floor to hear a story, complete an art activity seated at a table, etc.). If children display signs of disinterest (talking to each other, wandering away, etc.), be ready to move on to the next activity.

Prepare all needed materials. Children get restless if the teacher has to hunt for markers, find the missing CD or leave the room to make photocopies. Before class, make a list of all necessary lesson items, books, music, game materials, etc. Put all items in the room ahead of time so that they can be quickly retrieved. If the room is in use immediately before your class, place items in order of use in a container or on a movable cart that you can bring in to the classroom at the last minute. When using audiocassettes, CDs, videocassettes or DVDs, cue the material before class so that the music/program can be started immediately (and be sure you've practiced using the player). Make sure there are enough Bibles for children (if they don't bring their own) and some for visitors.

Use age-appropriate activities. The curriculum you use provides activities for the age level you teach. However, you may still need to modify activities to account for varying levels of skills. Offer drawing or writing as a way to respond to a question, or invite children to give oral responses. Especially in the first few weeks of your class, carefully observe students to evaluate their skills so that in the future you can plan activities better suited to their abilities.

Use sufficient staffing. Ideally, each class is led by two teachers with a ratio of one adult for every six to eight children. One teacher leads the activity while the other teacher(s) help guide behavior or assist students in completing activities. If your class is not sufficiently staffed, ask your supervisor for advice or invite parents to each take a turn helping in the class.

Set limits. Problem behavior occurs when children have unclear boundaries. Set several limits and follow them at each session: "When I flick the lights, I need for you to look at me." "We clean up after art projects." "We stay in the room during class time." Phrase your boundaries in positive terms, telling children what you want them to do rather than what you want them to stop doing.

Praise good behavior. Let children know that their helpful actions are appreciated. Children like to please you. Be sure that all children are affirmed.

Learn about the children. Some children have medical difficulties or special abilities that may cause unusual behavior or interfere with their learning. Talk to the parents and find out what can be done to enhance the child's learning experience.

DEALING WITH PROBLEM BEHAVIOR

Even with the best preparation, discipline problems will arise. Real-life, imperfect children will present teachers with a variety of problem behaviors. The goal at that moment is not just to end the disruption but also to help the child learn.

Avoid embarrassment. Whenever possible, talk to a child individually about a problem behavior. An embarrassed child may act up even more to "save face" in front of peers.

Avoid hostility. Teachers need to be levelheaded, mature adults who do not lose their temper. Shouting, berating, humiliating or grabbing a child are not forms of discipline but forms of abuse. When you find a child's behavior or attitude is causing you to get upset,

take a deep breath, whisper a prayer and seek to show love, not anger.

Be assertive. State what the child needs to do ("Keep your hands to yourself," "Listen when others speak") with firmness but not anger. If the child whines, argues or makes excuses, repeat the statement. Some children are skilled at manipulating adults with arguments or bargaining, so avoid debating with the child. When the child sees that the adult will not give in to his or her demands, the behavior is likely to cease.

Get the facts. Avoiding asking a child, "Why did you hit Tracy?" This question implies that if the child can come up with a good enough reason, the wrong behavior will be justified! The goal is not to get the child to explain or blame but to honestly confront what he or she did. So ask the child, "What did you do that was a problem?"

Facing the consequences. If a child continues to misbehave after you have tried to redirect the problem behavior, the child may need to forfeit a privilege related to the activity at hand. If the child misuses markers or game supplies, then he or she cannot participate in activities using those materials until more responsibility is demonstrated. Try saying, "I know you will have a good time playing this game, but until you can wait to take your turn with the beanbags, you'll need to stand here by me." Help children understand that the class will be more enjoyable for everyone when each child cooperates.

While it is preferable for discipline challenges to be handled in the classroom by the teacher, with the help of a supervisor if needed, there may be times when it is necessary to talk with parents about their child's behavior. Communicate positively with parents, asking them for advice on how to help their child participate more enjoyably and effectively.

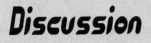
Discussion

Children like to speak their minds! The challenge is to keep the discussion focused on the lesson, to involve all children and to prevent distracting chatter. Children's learning will be much more effective when they are involved in the process of learning through discovery and discussion rather than through sitting and listening.

GOOD PREPARATION

Write good questions before class. Good discussions occur when the teacher knows what questions to ask. Study the class material thoroughly (even if it's a familiar Bible story) and think through the discussion questions provided in your curriculum. Think of additional questions to ask as well. Avoid questions with obvious one-word answers. Discussion grows out of questions that ask for opinions, ideas, reactions, etc., not just repeating factual answers. (This means you must begin preparation well before Sunday morning!)

Minimize distractions. Children are naturally curious and are interested in everything that goes on—whether it's the lesson activity at hand or not! Evaluate the distractions in your classroom by asking the following questions: Is there noise in the classroom from the choir warming up next door? Are people walking through the hallway? Are there toys or items scattered around the classroom that the children will want to play with? Are cell phones ringing? Do parents arrive long before the class ends and stand around outside the room?

Then consider these solutions: If outside noise is a problem, play a music CD or cassette as background to cover outside noise. Toy shelves can be turned to face the wall to help children avoid the temptation of playing with the toys. Arrange chairs so children are faced away from distractions. Remind teachers (and children!) before class begins to turn off cell phones. Keep in mind, however, that your reaction to distractions is the biggest factor. If you respond in a matter-of-fact manner, children will, also.

Limit the discussion. Children are not able to remain interested during long times of discussion. Children's physical requirements for movement need to be met. It's better to end the discussion time before children grow restless. Most discussions should be tied to some physical activity, either as an introduction to the activity, as a break during the activity or as a summary after the activity.

Involve everyone. Try to involve all children in a discussion. Start by asking several easy, low-threat questions that all children are capable of answering. Seek to involve the potentially disruptive child right at the start. Children are less likely to be disruptive when they're occupied. If a child looks restless, call him or her by name and ask a question. Also ask questions of children who have been quiet. Be sure not to ask a difficult question they may not know. One reason children may not participate is that they feel they don't know the answer and don't want to be embarrassed in front of their peers.

HANDLING INTERRUPTIONS

Get back on track. Despite the best plans, a discussion may veer off course. First, determine if the new topic is valid. Perhaps one child is overly focused on a small detail (such as how Joshua could make the sun stand still when in reality Earth moves) but the rest of the class is not interested. Acknowledge that the new topic is interesting and can be discussed at another time, and then return to the original topic. Restate the last question and if children do not respond, try another question.

If a child deliberately wants to get off the topic, use humor to return to the topic. If the children digress because they don't understand the topic or the question, use a simpler question or take time to explain the topic.

Discussion off the topic is not always cause for alarm. Sometimes a child needs to discuss a topic not on the agenda or finds an unexplored point in the topic. If the new topic will help children apply Bible truth to everyday life and will benefit the entire class, stay with it. If a child needs to discuss a special need, such as a death in the family, make time at the end of the activity for the class to offer support and prayer.

Go with the flow. Interruptions will happen. If the interruption is minor and the children are not unduly distracted, then ignore it and continue. Some interruptions require the teacher to stop and take care of matters: a child needs to leave early, an adult arrives to make an announcement or the air conditioner needs to be adjusted. Try to get the class back on track. If the class has grown too distracted, move on to another activity.

Be prepared for silence. Sometimes children will respond to a question with silence. This can be good if the children are pondering a deep question. It can be fatal if this is due to lack of understanding, embarrassment or boredom.

Give children a few seconds to think about the question. Ask for a visual signal (thumb up, fist on chin, etc.) when students think they may have at least part of the answer. Rephrase the question in case the first question was not understood. If children still are unable to answer, you might share the answer you would give and then move on to another question.

Some children may feel uncomfortable speaking in front of a large class. Divide the children into small groups of six or fewer in which to discuss the answers. Provide to each group large sheets of paper on which to write their answers. Then a volunteer from each group shares the replies with the whole class. Small groups are also good for discussing sensitive or personal topics, perhaps occasionally forming all-boy and all-girl small groups.

Sometimes children do not respond when the questions are too easy (Who are Jesus' parents?), too obvious (Does God want us to help our neighbors?), too personal (What sins have you committed this week?) or too difficult (According to legend, what are the names of the three wise men?). After class, revise the questions that failed to get a good response and use the improvements as a model for writing good questions for the next class.

Sometimes children will give the answer they think the teacher wants to hear. Write open-ended questions that are more challenging: How would you feel if you had been a shepherd who was off-duty the night the angels appeared? What do you think the blind man did after Jesus healed him? How can you defend your friend from a bully?

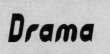

Drama activities provide children with stimulating ways to make Bible stories come alive and biblical concepts real. Children of all ages love to play act and pretend. Their natural creativity and lack of inhibitions make them natural actors.

Drama activities may sound complicated and hard to prepare, but with an emphasis on process instead of product, drama activities are easy to teach and do not require extensive rehearsal. The goal is for children to apply the concepts to their lives, not to give an award-winning performance. Thus, children of all acting abilities can participate. Here are a variety of methods to keep children acting!

TYPES OF DRAMA LEARNING ACTIVITIES

Act out the Bible story. After hearing or reading the Bible story, children act out the roles using their own words. (Younger children, or children unfamiliar with impromptu speaking, may simply pantomime the Bible story action as a narrator either tells the story or reads it from the Bible.) Costumes are not needed, although Bible-times costumes can be used if there are several on hand. Children may also enjoy resetting the story in modern times. Brainstorm possible situations and actions with children before inviting them to act out the contemporary version. Ask questions such as What kind of problems do kids your age have that are like the problem in the story? If Jesus walked into our (town) today, would anything happen that would be like our story?

Use puppets. Many children who would not feel comfortable acting out parts themselves feel confident when using puppets. Collect a variety of puppets to keep on hand in your classroom. Puppets can be inexpensive and simple, made from socks, small paper bags, gloves, stuffed animals, dolls or plastic foam "heads" decorated and put on long sticks. The "stage" can be as simple as a table turned on its side. For classes that plan to spend a lot of time with puppets, craft a more permanent stage by hanging cloth from a plastic (PVC) pipe frame. Puppets can be bought from educational or church supply stores, by mail order or over the Internet. Children enjoy using puppets to lip-sync along with prerecorded music.

Dress up in costumes. Keep a container on hand with old clothes and props. Many such items can be donated by church members or purchased inexpensively from thrift stores. Older children may want to make their own Bible-times costumes out of discarded fabric.

Role-play situations. In this type of drama activity, children act out a situation without a script. Children, grouped in pairs or trios, are either assigned or choose a topic, problem or question related to the Bible truth of the lesson. The children discuss possible situations together, plan a course of action and present the story to the audience with improvised dialogue. Role-play can be used to demonstrate examples of Christian living (confronting bullies, being caught in a lie, peer pressure, etc.) and helps children to see how biblical concepts can be lived out in everyday life.

Use "what if" questions. This method is similar to role-play except that each child pretends to be someone else—often a character in a Bible story. Drama activities like these help children develop understanding of a character's actions and explore other perspectives. Sample "what if" questions include What if you were David and God had asked you to fight Goliath? What if you were Moses and God had given you the Ten Commandments? What if you were a leper begging by the gate and you saw Jesus coming? "What if" questions can also be used to help children apply Bible truth to contemporary situations (What if you were a new immigrant to America and couldn't speak English?)

Pantomime stories. This is wordless storytelling, using pantomime movement and gestures. In pantomimes, encourage children to use exaggerated facial expressions and motions. As in the game of Charades, children enjoy pantomiming a story for others to guess.

Read skits. Older children enjoy reading and acting from scripts. Your curriculum may provide skit scripts or you can purchase books of plays. Costumes and sets can be as simple or elaborate as the children want to make them. Scripts are helpful for children who have difficulty thinking up their own stories and dialogue.

TIPS ON USING DRAMA ACTIVITIES

Although a stage is not necessary for classroom drama, open space is often needed so that children do not bump into furniture. If the classroom is too small to allow free movement, move the class outdoors or into a large unused room. Some churches have a stage in the fellowship hall that might be available during class time.

Some children feel uncomfortable speaking in front of others. Alleviate shyness by using puppets or pantomime. Another alternative is to let these children do the backstage jobs, such as gathering costumes and props or setting up the stage area.

Since the emphasis is on process and not product, it is not essential for children to give great acting performances or to repeat scripted lines perfectly. However, some children may want to clown around and act silly. Give the children a few minutes to play with the props and "get the sillies out." Then stop and talk about the story again to get the children in a focused frame of mind before they start again. Praise all of the children for their participation. Children with dramatic talent

may want to show off their skill. Let children use their gifts but also encourage other children to participate in starring roles as well.

If you are using scripts, provide highlighters for children to mark their parts. Explain any unfamiliar vocabulary ahead of time and help them practice pronouncing unusual words or names. If your group has more members than the script has parts, divide major roles between two or more "actors."

As with most learning activities, children benefit from repetition. Your children will be able to add expression and other dramatic effects each time they repeat a dramatic presentation. The more you use drama activities, the better your children will be able to act and the more fun (and learning!) all of you will have.

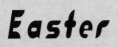
Easter is the most wonderful and important celebration in the Christian year. However, the increasing secularization of Easter threatens to make it little more than a time to gorge on candy and cuddle stuffed bunnies. As you interact with children during this time of year, use this great opportunity and privilege to present children with the true meaning of Easter.

Some of the aspects of Holy Week, especially the arrest, torture and death of Jesus, can be disturbing to children. Emphasize the positive aspects of the Last Supper and Easter: Jesus is alive today and loves every child. Students can be taught that Jesus laid down His life because of the sins of every person and as part of God's plan to demonstrate His love for us.

TEACHING THE EASTER MESSAGE

The trappings associated with Easter—baby animals, colored eggs, new clothes, spring flowers—can all be used to show and share joy because Jesus is living. Keep the focus of your conversation on the biblical truth that Jesus is alive and that Eastertime is when we celebrate His love for us.

If a child asks about or seems disturbed by Jesus' death on the cross, you can say, "When we see a picture of the cross or think about the sad day when Jesus died, it helps to remember that Jesus loved us so much that He was willing to let Himself be killed. The third day after Jesus died, God raised Jesus from the dead! It's good news for all people to know that Jesus is alive!"

EASTER CELEBRATIONS

Depending on the age level of the children you teach and the traditions followed in your church, consider incorporating some of these Easter celebrations into your class.

★ **Ministry baskets.** On Palm Sunday, children receive empty Easter baskets. During the week, children fill the baskets with small toiletry items or canned food. On Easter, the baskets are collected and distributed to families in need, a homeless shelter, food kitchen or residence home for youth. (Check with the organization first to get a list of desirable items.)

★ **Flowers on the cross.** Set up a wooden cross with two rows of nail heads protruding down the front. Children decorate the cross by putting fresh flowers between the nail heads. If a wooden cross cannot be used, then draw a cross outline on a large sheet of paper. Let the children color and glue paper cutout flowers on the cross.

★ **Easter egg hunt.** Use plastic eggs, but instead of filling them with candy, use strips of paper with Bible verses, pocket crosses or coupons for a larger prize, such as bookmarks, paperback books or music CDs. You may also fill eggs with items related to the Easter story (a small rock, a small piece of wood, a small artificial flower, etc.). Hide the eggs inside the church or on the church lawn. If the hunt is indoors, keep the hunt confined to one or two rooms. Separate children by age

so that the older children in their enthusiasm do not trample over younger children. Set a guideline for how many eggs each child is allowed to collect. Invite older children to prepare the egg hunt for younger children.

★ **Dramatics.** The events of Holy Week are full of visuals and spectacle. Provide palms and let children act out the story events of Palm Sunday. Bring in a basin of water to reenact Jesus washing the disciples' feet. Find a dark closet to represent the tomb, and have children take the roles of the women and the angel. Use costumes and props if possible. Taking part in the Resurrection story will make a dramatic impact on children.

★ **Flower celebration.** If the sanctuary is decorated with Easter lilies, after worship the older children and an adult supervisor can take the flowers to a hospital or nursing home. Or, several weeks before Easter, have children plant their own flower bulbs and care for the plants as they grow.

★ **Easter sharing.** Invite children to donate good-quality used clothing to a homeless shelter or relief organization. Encourage families in the church to buy clothes, socks or underwear for needy families instead of or in addition to buying new clothes for themselves.

★ **Worship participation.** Children learn an Easter song or skit that they present to the congregation during a worship service.

The physical appearance of your classroom will either contribute to or detract from the learning you want to take place. A well-furnished, clean room invites learning; a cluttered, drab space pushes children away. Many church programs meet in older buildings or overflow spaces that are not ideal; however, even these rooms can be furnished and upgraded for more effective class time.

No matter whether you are in a brand-new, up-to-date classroom or whether you have many improvements to make, remember that your friendly greeting is what will make your classroom a place that welcomes children.

EVALUATE YOUR ROOM

First Impression. Imagine that you are entering the room for the first time. What is your first impression on entering the room? Is the room attractive or uninviting? Is it gloomy or bright? If the room is dark, replace any burned-out lightbulbs and install more overhead lights or floor lamps. With permission and/or help from your supervisor, paint the walls a soft pastel, or hang attractive wallpaper. Clean the window blinds or put up colorful curtains. Clean the cobwebs from the corners, mop the floor and shampoo the rugs. Bad smells may be removed by a thorough cleaning with bleach. If unpleasant smells persist, use a room freshener or deodorizer.

Location. Periodically, take a close look at your classroom. Begin by considering the classroom location. Is the classroom easy to find? In some church buildings, rooms may be tucked under stairwells, hidden at the end of winding hallways or located a long distance from the main entrance. Visitors will be frustrated if they must search blindly for classes. If this is the case with your classroom, ask your supervisor if it is possible to move to a room that is closer to the front doors or easier to find. If it is not possible to move, post signs and arrows pointing the way to your room (and other classrooms as well). Display a detailed map by the facility entrance so that visitors can locate rooms. Position greeters in appropriate places to escort guests to the proper rooms.

Repairs. Take time to survey the room and list any repair needs. Are there cracks in the walls? Drips in the sink? Cracked windows? Broken furniture? Not only are such defects unattractive, but they can also be safety hazards. Alert your supervisor so that a custodian, parent or other volunteer can be requested to fix the problem(s). New furniture may be needed if the old furniture is beyond repair or unusable. If the budget will not support new furniture, seek out thrift stores or request contributions from members.

Learning Effectiveness. Regularly monitor the decorations and displays in your classroom. Is the bulletin board brightly decorated and attractive, displaying current items appropriate to your lessons? Are there colorful wall posters that appeal to the age of the children that you teach? Make sure to arrange for a place where children's art projects can be displayed, at least during each session.

Supplies. Consider how supplies and other learning materials are stored in your classroom. If space for storage is limited, make an effort to remove clutter frequently. Church classrooms tend to be used as catchall storage spaces! Take time away from class to inspect what's in the room. Are other ministries using the valuable closet space for their items? Meet with these ministries to see if other storage space can be found. Are there unusable items in the closets? Dispose of outdated curriculum, torn books, dried-up paints, broken items and unneeded furniture. Move old clothing and lost items to a lost and found box, or donate them to a thrift store. Set out the supplies needed for one lesson at a time. The rest of the supplies can be stored in a closet or a large container.

Storage Space. Some rooms simply need better organization. Put up a coat tree or coat pegs so that children can hang up coats rather than piling jackets on a chair. Bring in plastic bins to store books, papers and art supplies when not needed. Portable shelving is inexpensive and can be put in closets to increase storage space. Set up a bookcase to organize Bibles and storybooks.

Furniture. Use the furniture appropriate for the age group. For chairs, the floor to chair seat height should be 12-14 inches (30.5-35.5 cm) for first and second grades; 14-15 inches (35.5-38 cm) for third-fifth grades; and 16 inches (40.5 cm) for sixth graders. Tables are to be 10 inches (25.5 cm) above chair seat height. Make sure that there are enough chairs to include visitors and plenty of open space for activities. Enable children to be responsible for materials in the classroom by making sure there are shelves at the child's height. Are there furniture pieces that are not being used, or could they be replaced with closet shelving or storage containers?

USING TEMPORARY SPACE

The setup for some classrooms must be taken down and reset each week. This is often the case with a church that meets in a rented facility or a church that uses the classrooms for other functions during the week. Teachers in this situation may be limited by how much they can decorate and furnish the rooms. Here are some tips for coping:

★ Maintain a checklist of the basic supplies needed for each week. As the room is set up each week, mark the checklist to be certain that all items are at hand. With the checklist, make a diagram of the furniture arrangement so that the room can be reset the same way each time.

★ Think portable! Store items in wheeled bins or stackable containers that are easily moved. During the week, store bins at home or in a secured location, such as a locked closet. Instead of chalkboards, use fold-down easels with large writing pads. Use a small corkboard and easel instead of a bulletin board on the wall. Use folding chairs and tables, or if the space is too small for chairs and tables, bring in pillows or seat cushions on which children may sit. Keep your curriculum materials at home so that you only need to bring what is needed for each week's lesson.

★ If you share your room with other programs, take time to talk personally with those teachers so that you can agree on use of storage, which supplies will be shared, etc.

 **ONE**

Understand that teaching is ministry. Sharing eternal truths with the next generation is a privilege and a calling. What happens in a church classroom is the most important information in this world and the next. Pray for children and for wisdom in lesson preparation. Be aware that every part of the session—from greeting children to waiting for pickup—needs to be done with the goal of showing God's love in action.

 **TWO**

Show respect. Teachers earn respect by showing respect to their children. Talk *with* children, not *at* them or *down* to them. Get down to their eye level. Smile and speak kindly. Be interested in the children's lives and their priorities. Assist children with special abilities and accept their contributions to the class. Treat all children as equals and children of God.

 **THREE**

Lead gently. Give suggestions more often than commands. Give directions in a positive way. Treat children according to what they *can* do rather than what they *cannot* do. Be patient and understanding. Accept children's mistakes and help them to grow from their failures. Remember to *guide* a child into a relationship with God and not to *push*; you must live your relationship with Him out in front of that child.

 **FOUR**

Be a visionary. Accept challenges as opportunities. Love all the children that God sends: the most difficult, the most shy, the most confused, the most moody. Instead of trying to change the child, consider ways to change the activity to benefit the child.

 **FIVE**

Provide limits. Allow children freedom within boundaries. Set reasonable boundaries and stick to them. Keep learning fun, but also keep order in the classroom for effective learning. Expect children to honor your authority. Show the consequences for stepping outside of classroom boundaries. Expect the most from children and they will strive to give their best.

 **SIX**

Be a guide. Be ready when a child needs help. Guide informal conversation and lead meaningful discussions. Ask open-ended questions and encourage children to dig deep into the Bible. *Guide* children to discover Bible truths instead of *telling* them. Demonstrate how children can apply Bible truths to their daily lives. Lend a listening ear when a child needs to talk. Share age-appropriate examples of ways God's Word has helped you.

 **SEVEN**

Affirm children. Thank children often. Compliment children for positive things they say and do. Describe their right actions so that they can learn and repeat them. Thank them for their participation in the class and for the personality they bring to class.

 **EIGHT**

Know children. Know each child's name. Learn their interests. Study them to discover both their needs and their gifts. Be aware of the age-level characteristics of the children you teach so that your expectations are realistic. See each one as a person God has given to you to shepherd, love and lead to Christ.

 **NINE**

Use proven teaching methods. Prepare lessons well, with interesting activities that motivate children's participation. Make learning active (hands-on) rather than passive (listening). Provide a variety of age-appropriate activities. Be aware of the age-level characteristics of children. Read, study and attend workshops to improve teaching skills. Network with other teachers. Get needed help from a pastor, a children's ministry leader or your supervisor.

 **TEN**

Serve as a role model. A child's attitude toward Jesus Christ is largely based on what he or she sees adults say or do. If you model love, acceptance and enthusiasm, the class will follow. Show joy in your own spiritual journey and support the life of the church. Always give your best effort, no matter the size of the class. Three children deserve as much quality education as 20 children.

Learning Process

The Building Blocks of Learning

We may think of learning as a result—a "something" intellectual that was gained from a lesson, such as "Billy knows the alphabet." However, we need to recognize that learning is the process of building a series of neural networks and mental relationships that yield understanding and response. Learning may not always occur in a series of definable steps. Especially in children, the learning process is not always in a neat, sequential order. The steps may be simultaneous or in any order. In fact, the younger the child, the more likely it is that these steps will be taken in reverse order! Although learning can't be reduced to a formula, we need to be aware of the God-given ways in which we learn so that we are prepared to teach in ways that will make learning effective. Below are the major steps in the process of learning and ways each step fits into the process.

1. LISTEN: GIVE ATTENTION/RECEIVE INFORMATION

Learning is most efficient when a person realizes there is something to be learned. And that something must be of interest or value to the person for focused attention to be given!

Most commonly in Christian education, a teacher says something to gain the interest of the learners. But in no way is this first step limited to listening! Pique a learner's curiosity with a poster on the wall or a question on the chalkboard. Involve as many of a learner's senses (hearing, sight, smell, touch, taste) as possible to gain interest and attention.

While hearing and sight are the most common ways we present, far too many teachers approach the whole learning process as if this step were the only one! They feel they have succeeded if learners simply paid attention to what they had to say or show. (Never forget,

either, how often a learner may pretend to pay attention while not mentally engaged!) However, after a learner has listened or looked, he or she has taken only the *first* step in the learning journey.

2. EXPLORE: EXAMINE LIFE AND THE WORD

Having his or her interest piqued, the learner has received information that is valued. The next step is to investigate further. To learn effectively, humans need to actively pursue new or expanded insights. A teacher needs to relate the learner's experiences and insights to the new information.

A wise teacher guides this exploration in the direction of the current lesson. This way, learners examine their already-understood life situations in the light of the Word of God. Each week a teacher helps learners see commands, examples, principles and answers that apply to the child's life situations.

When a teacher actively involves learners in connecting God's Word to issues they care about, this increases the learner's understanding and retention of the passage being investigated. This approach also develops the vital ability of using the Bible themselves, instead of merely listening to someone else report about it. Even nonreaders can be guided to begin exploring Bible truths for themselves by posing a question before presenting a Bible verse or story and asking students to listen to the reading for the answer to that question.

3. DISCOVER: FIND THE TRUTH

The wise teacher plans for learners to make some discoveries for themselves. No matter how excited a teacher may be about discoveries he or she has made, it's more effective to let those same exciting discoveries be made by the learners themselves. Learners who are prepared through listening and exploring are ready to discover for themselves what the Bible says. Discoveries that learners make on their own will be remembered longer and have more impact than insights simply handed down from the teacher. The "light goes on" and the learner is filled with excitement when he or she has discovered a truth on his or her own. That truth now becomes "owned" by the learner!

4. APPLY: RESPOND TO THE TRUTH

Somewhere in the learning process, learners need to confront the personal implications of God's truth. The point of a lesson is not to discover interesting bits of historical or theological information but to recognize that the Bible is speaking directly to people. It is one thing to recognize that God is love; it is another to recognize that God loved the world; it is yet another to recognize that God loves *me*.

Taking Scripture personally does not happen automatically. Through prayer, questions and guided activity, the teacher is used by the Holy Spirit to cause students to see themselves as characters in the story, recipients of the epistle—the people to whom God is speaking.

Provide appropriate activities to stimulate learners' awareness and thinking about a topic to be considered. Children often think best when their bodies are in motion! When choosing activities, consider the life experiences of the children you are teaching: the younger the child or the more limited his or her life experience, the more he or she needs concrete, multi-sensory, firsthand experiences (experiments, construction, games, drama, art, etc.). Concrete activity can build understanding of seemingly simple concepts (sharing, being kind, helping, giving thanks, etc.) when a teacher who is aware of his or her goal guides conversation toward the lesson goals and points out ways children are applying Bible truth during these activities.

5. ASSUME RESPONSIBILITY: APPLY THE TRUTH

This step is the crown of the learning process, the point where God's truth not only makes changes in a person's heart but also works itself out in actions. God's truth has been given to produce growth and change in us. Learners take in information about what God said to understanding what that information means. They must then go on to understanding what it means to me personally and finally to ways I can *respond* to what I have learned, to what I understand and to what I have personalized.

Not every class session can end by carrying out a major new spiritual commitment, but each class can nudge learners to look beyond the class time and think of ways to put God's Word into action in the coming week.

Learning Styles

For the busy teacher at church, it's tempting to approach limited lesson preparation time with the notion of "one size fits all." That is, every child will get maximum learning out of every activity. However, as each person has different facial features, each person learns in different ways. Some children are more receptive to certain teaching techniques than others. Children use different senses to gather information. The challenge is to provide for a variety of learning styles to reach each child. Although most of the children in a classroom may be most comfortable with one learning style, the teacher must also be prepared to engage children who have other styles of learning.

LEARNING STYLES

Learning styles describe the way people use their senses to process information as they learn. Educators have classified three types of learning styles. Most people will fit somewhat into more than one category. Few people are completely of one style to the exclusion of others. Most children cannot describe how they learn best but do know which activities they like. Discovering the learning styles of children can help in lesson planning and in finding the most meaningful activities.

Auditory learners. These children best gather information with their ears. They prefer to hear oral instructions instead of following written directions. They like to hear a story read aloud rather than reading it silently on their own. They listen carefully during discussions and hear nuances in voice pitch, volume and tone. Working with music, using tape recorders and reading aloud from the Bible or a script will help these children learn effectively.

Visual learners. These children use their eyes to learn. They follow written instructions more easily than hearing a teacher give directions. They like lots of visual stimulation, such as posters, pictures, multimedia, graphs, maps and charts. They like to fill in worksheets and research written information from a book or the Internet. They like to sit close to you and near to visual aids, so they can see clearly. In a discussion they watch the speaker's face and hand gestures.

Tactile learners. These are hands-on, active, mobile learners. They prefer using their hands and bodies rather than their ears or eyes. They love games, art activities, motions, pantomime and any activity that gets them moving. These children delight in building models, making repairs and working with mechanical objects. They love to make discoveries and find things.

MULTIPLE INTELLIGENCES

Another view of the way in which people learn most effectively is called multiple intelligences. Seven types of intelligences have been identified by educator and author Howard Gardner. (Note: While additional types of intelligences have been identified, the first seven are the most commonly accepted by teachers.) These categories or types of intelligences identify talents and skills, and have nothing to do with I.Q. testing or whether or not a person is intelligent. Knowing a child's type of intelligence can help you identify and utilize a child's gifts. No one intelligence is better than the others, and every learner possesses a mixture of these categories. Each type possesses its own unique gifts and strengths. All skills are needed for the building of God's kingdom on Earth.

Visual intelligence. These children think in pictures. They like reading, writing, working puzzles, drawing, painting, watching videos, looking at pictures or creating a graph. Visual children do well with art activities and decorating the room.

Verbal intelligence. Such children are excellent speakers and prefer working with words instead of pictures. Their skills are speaking, listening, storytelling, writing and humor. Count on these children for leading a discussion, skits and public speaking.

Logical intelligence. These children are the so-called "computer whizzes" and "math brains." They excel with logic and numbers, and they love doing experiments. Such children enjoy learning for its own sake and ask many questions. These children are fascinated by nature and enjoy working with shapes and complicated puzzles.

Bodily intelligence. These children are great in sports and active games. They possess above-average physical coordination, strength and balance. They work well with their hands and like to keep active.

Musical intelligence. Obviously, these children are the singers, musicians and composers. Their minds process rhythm and sound better than verbal or visual information. They may prefer to memorize facts and Bible verses by singing the words instead of saying them. Get their attention with hand-clap patterns or a musical tone. Older children may be able to write a song for the class to sing.

Interpersonal intelligence. The person with interpersonal intelligence has great empathy and enjoys working with people. This person can understand other points of view and sense the moods and feelings of others. Such people like to bring about reconciliation and build bridges. These traits may not be well developed yet in children, who may not be aware of such gifts. However, these children understand people well enough to be manipulators to get what they want. They can be bossy because they are good group organizers. They may be the ones who automatically divide up the teams and give orders when it's time for games. These children are peacemakers and may be the ones who try to stop a classroom brawl. They're the group leaders for small-group activities.

Intrapersonal intelligence. This type is more abstract and mental than the others. These are the dreamers and philosophers who are self-aware and reflective. They analyze their feelings and relationships with others. It's possible that the great saints, visionaries and philosophers of Church history were this type. Young children do not think in abstract ways, but such tendencies can be seen in a child who perpetually daydreams or frequently asks why things are the way they are. Such children may be supercritical of themselves, since they spend much effort in self-analysis and evaluation without guidance. They may need a teacher to give them assurance and encouragement that they're OK.

THE VALUE OF LEARNING STYLES

God made each of us unique and He loves our uniqueness! Even in the way we learn new information, each of us is different. Consider the learning styles and strengths of the children in your group and then make sure to provide a variety of learning experiences so that each child is included and will have opportunity to explore God's Word in different ways.

Memorization

God's Word is too important not to commit it to memory! Memorization lays a strong foundation and provides a rich spiritual resource from which a child can draw throughout a lifetime. In times of doubt, stress or grief, an adult or teen will remember verses learned as a child. Telling about their faith to others is easier with the memorization of key Scriptures. When it's hard to put theological concepts into words, children can rely on Bible verses to express basic beliefs.

TIPS TO MEMORIZING WITH UNDERSTANDING

Learn with meaning. The goal is for children to understand what they memorize and not simply recite words. Memorization has little value unless the child can apply the Bible verse to life situations and use it for spiritual growth. Demonstrate and model for your children the principle of learning a verse and what it means before memorizing it. In class, explore the application of a Bible verse through discussion and learning activities. Explain any difficult or unusual words. Look at the verse in its context and help your children understand how it fits in with the rest of the paragraph or chapter.

Learn with purpose. Why should a child know this particular verse? Does it explain the way to salvation? Does it provide a promise of God? Does it make an important statement about Jesus? Avoid learning verses for the sake of learning or to win prizes. Select verses that children will find interesting and helpful to learn. Look for a curriculum that presents Bible memory verses that focus on life application of Bible truth—rather than on Bible facts.

Find it. Part of verse memorization is to become familiar with the Bible. Be sure each child has a Bible to use rather than sharing. Have extra Bibles in the room for children who do not bring one. Teach children how to use the table of contents to find a book and how to interpret the chapter and verse numbers in a verse reference. Help children locate the book and page where the verse is written. Accuracy is more important than speed. Always memorize the chapter and verse reference along with the words.

Provide a modern translation. In order to help children not only memorize but also understand God's Word, consider having a modern translation available that children can easily read. If a child brings a Bible from home that is different from the Bibles you provide in class, take advantage of this opportunity to enrich the child's understanding of the Bible. Help the child compare the words used in the different translations.

TIPS TO MEMORIZATION

Repeat and review. People memorize simply by hearing or saying something many times, such as saying multiplication facts every day at school. Repeat the verse together several times throughout the class session. Use various activities (games, music and discussion), so the children can hear, see, write and use the verse. Over time, children will find they have learned the verse without realizing it!

Don't forget to return to learned verses periodically. Apply the principle of "use it or lose it." Children will forget verses unless they are reviewed often.

Use music. Set the words of the verse to a familiar tune so that children can sing the verse. Many contemporary praise songs are taken word for word from the Psalms. Many children find that music helps them remember words. Long lists, such as the books of the Bible or the Ten Commandments, can also be learned easily when set to music.

Use artwork. Incorporate short verses into art projects. Children can write the words on bookmarks, boxes, scrolls and clay tablets or string together beads with letters. The class can write verses on posters or banners that are hung on the wall or in hallways for several weeks.

Use games. Incorporate the verse into noncompetitive games that are enjoyable and educational. Children like learning when they don't know they are being taught!

Use the games suggested in your curriculum. You may also be able to purchase board or card games that teach Bible verses. However, some of these games can be too expensive for a limited church budget. Before investing in a game, be sure that it can be reused many times, that it is suitable for several age groups and that the children will not grow tired of it.

Other game suggestions:

★ Matching game—write each word of the verse onto a separate card and lay the cards facedown on the table.

Children take turns flipping over one card at a time, trying to turn the cards over in the correct verse sequence. Correct cards are left faceup. If the card does not match the sequence, the card is placed facedown again.

★ Scavenger hunt—write each word of the verse on a separate card and hide the cards in the room. Children find cards and then put them in order.

★ Balloon game—write words of verses on separate narrow strips of papers and hide the strips inside balloons. Blow up the balloons. The children pop the balloons, read the words aloud and put them in verse order.

Use rewards. The goal of learning verses is not to get rewards, but children do like appreciation for their efforts. Plan cooperative memory contests in which children work together to reach a common goal of (20) verses memorized. When the goal is met, all children receive a prize (popcorn party, ice-cream treat, game day, etc.).

You may visualize the ideal Sunday School as each elementary grade meeting in its own large, well-equipped classroom full of children enjoying activities designed for their age group. However, in many churches the reality may be a group consisting of four or more grades gathered in one room. This happens when

★ there are not enough children in each age group for separate classes;

★ there are not enough teachers to staff all the classes;

★ attendance drops during holidays and summertime;

★ the church building lacks enough classroom space.

The major challenge of a mixed-age class is that children at either end of the spectrum of ages often find that their abilities and interests are not addressed. Therefore it is preferable for children to be grouped in classes with others the same age. But the class of mixed ages, if handled appropriately, can be a positive experience. Children build a sense of community as they watch each other grow up (literally!) and work together. Siblings study the same lessons that can be shared at home. There is a sense that everyone is part of the whole church and not just part of his or her class.

GUIDELINES FOR TEACHERS

It's important for the teachers of a mixed-age class to be well prepared! Such varied levels of development require that teachers plan a variety of activities so that each child learns best at his or her own level of development.

To a degree, younger children will enjoy being with the "big kids" and will be attracted to the activities in which older children are involved. Generally speaking, however, the younger the child, the more direct, first-hand activity he or she will need. So that all activities are not set at the level of the very youngest ones, divide the class into older and younger groups as time and helpers allow. If materials that older children enjoy are not suitable for use by younger children working independently, provide careful supervision at all times.

Facility. If the class must use one room, use the largest available room and invest in portable room dividers that help deaden sound and lessen visual distractions. Children can hang their artwork on fabric-covered dividers. Keep supplies in portable containers, one for each age group that can be easily moved to the appropriate section of the room.

Curriculum. Purchase a multiage curriculum or the age-level curriculum for which you have the most children and then adapt the activity ideas. It usually saves time to modify existing curriculum rather than spending valuable time to plan and write a complete curriculum.

Activity centers. Older children can usually work with one activity longer than the younger children. Older children want a "meatier" lesson while younger children need more variety and physical movement in their activities. In order to meet these divergent needs of children, provide several activities (games, art projects, storytelling, etc.) simultaneously. Set them up in separate rooms or areas within a single classroom. Children are separated by age and rotate from one activity to the next.

The advantage is that each activity leader handles only one age group at a time and focuses on the needs and interests of those specific children. The lesson is reinforced through repetition in each activity. Children anticipate moving to the next activity. This model can be used with only two or three activity centers.

In selecting activities, plan to use creative materials that let each child work at an individual level. Choose activities (collages, murals, etc.) that will provide each age level with successful participation, rather than worksheets or similar activities that require a specific skill level.

As you get to know children, you can observe their interaction. You will then be able to adjust activity ideas as needed.

Teaching assistants. Another option is to let older children serve as teaching assistants. (However, it is not safe to assume that an older student is ready to or wants to serve as an assistant.) Under adult supervision, older children can lead games, demonstrate art projects, lead song motions, act out stories and assist younger children with activity pages. Older children will learn by doing, develop leadership skills, become role models and take pride as the younger children look up to them. Take time during the week to contact the children and go over their teaching assignments, explaining the importance of being on time and prepared when they come to class. Remember to let the older children be *teachers* and not simply be *helpers*, doing only menial tasks such as setting out snacks or cleaning up.

A powerful way to implant in children God's Word and its principles is to sing with them. Songs learned early in life retain significance and can plant truth deeply in children's lives. The songs in your curriculum communicate God's love and His work in children's lives in words they understand.

The thought of presenting music in the classroom, however, can be scary for teachers who don't feel musically inclined. Some may feel they sing off pitch, can't remember lyrics or can't sing as well as a professional recording artist. However, remember that you are singing in front of a room of children, not music critics. Children will not judge a less-than-perfect singer because they, too, are developing their own musical abilities. Children love music and movement, so don't hesitate to integrate these elements into your class for effective learning.

WAYS TO USE MUSIC IN CLASS

Transition times. A transition "theme song" signals the class that it is time to move on to another activity. Depending on the age of your class, consider using songs during transitions as children arrive and depart, move to and from large group times, and clean up supplies. When the children hear and/or sing the song, they can prepare themselves for the next activity. Choose a favorite upbeat children's song from the curriculum you use or an instrumental recording of a lively classical song to use as a transition signal.

Mood. Using a variety of songs in group singing is a good way to offer a change of pace in your lesson. Some songs are more lively and will encourage participation. Other slower-paced songs can help to settle students and prepare them for prayer or a Bible story.

Movement. Children like activity and love fast, bouncy tunes. Use hand gestures or other motions (clapping

hands, stomping feet, etc.) while singing to illustrate the lyrics. Many songs tell a story, express emotions or describe actions. Let the children act out the words or create motions as they sing. Many children are familiar with American Sign Language and will enjoy signing the words to a song.

Some songs with motions attempt to express highly symbolic concepts that children often misunderstand. Just because a tune is catchy and the motions are fun does not mean children are learning the intended concept.

Instruments. Children can easily learn to play percussion instruments, such as drums, shakers, cymbals, triangles, chimes and bells. Older children may be skilled at piano or guitar. Find and use the talent in the class. However, avoid pressuring a child to be a regular class accompanist.

Music as ministry. Children can practice and sing songs during worship or for nursing home residents, homebound church members or church events.

Art and music. Let children create their own songbooks of favorite songs by writing out the words, decorating the pages and attaching the pages with brads or ribbons. Children will also enjoy drawing pictures for some of the lyrics. Invite children to contribute to worship services by providing materials for them to design and create banners that illustrate a phrase or two from a favorite song.

TEACHING MUSIC

A teacher need not be a musical expert to lead singing and teach new songs. The main key is preparation, not talent.

Knowledge of the song. When introducing new music, memorize the words and tune so that you can give attention to the children, not to looking at the sheet music. Practice singing at home to feel comfortable with the song.

Use of prerecorded music. Many children's audiocassettes, CDs and music videos are available with your curriculum and/or from church supply stores and music stores. Learn a new song by playing the CD several times and then play the CD in class to introduce the song to the children. Sing along with the CD and invite your students to sing along with you until the song is learned. Some music is available in karaoke version—only the instrumental track. If prerecorded music can't be found, have a musical friend sing or play the song into an audiocassette recorder, or invite your friend (or a choir member) to teach the song in person.

Learning new lyrics. Write the words to a new song on a large poster, chalkboard, white board or overhead transparency so that children can easily see them. Displaying words in this method helps children look up, so they can sing louder than if their faces are buried in song sheets. Another advantage of displaying words on a poster, board or overhead transparency is that children are not flipping through songbooks as they sing. For young children still learning to read, use pictures instead of words when appropriate.

Discussion. Talk with children about the songs you sing together. Ask questions such as What does this song help us learn about God? What does this song remind us to do? When would be a good time to remember and sing the words of this song? Explain any unfamiliar words. For effective learning and reinforcement of your lesson aims, use the songs that are provided with your curriculum and/or select songs that fit with the lesson's Bible truth and not simply because they sound nice or are useful as time filler. To be understood by children, songs should not use abstract words that express little specific action or feelings. Make sure it's clear what the words in the song are teaching children.

Repetition. When children like something, they want to experience it over and over. They may want to sing a song they like several times in one session. Repetition also helps the children memorize the lyrics. When teaching a new song, sing it for several classes in a row.

MAKING A JOYFUL NOISE

So what if a student (or you) sings sharp or flat? God sees the heart more than He hears the voice. Even shy children can be encouraged to participate in group singing as you model your enthusiasm and the purpose of your singing: to give praise and worship to God.

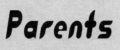

Parents

To be truly effective, a child's learning includes parental involvement. Children will attend regularly and be happy students when their parents actively support their classes at church. Developing good parental relationships, however, requires good communications.

Never assume that children will tell their parents necessary information. A child may forget or may pass on incorrect information. That's why it's important for you to get information directly to the parents. Also parents have positive feelings toward church when they establish a personal relationship with you and feel that you care enough to keep them informed.

GETTING THE WORD OUT

What do parents need to know? Parents are busy, and church news may be lost among the other information with which they deal. Clearly labeled parent letters and flyers need to be brief and to the point so that parents quickly see what they need to know.

Let parents know the topics and Scripture verses taught in class so that they can do follow-up learning at home. (Note: Your curriculum may provide take-home papers or handouts. Ask your supervisor or age-level coordinator for any handouts your church might provide.) Parents want to know about class projects, trips away from the church and their child's participation in church activities. Parents need to be told if their child became sick during class. If a child is continually disruptive in class, ask parents for suggestions to help the child get along better with others. Discipline and illness issues need to be kept confidential, told only to the parents involved.

Personal contact. Whenever possible, greet parents when they drop off and pick up their child. Relationships are built through continual contact and friendly greeting. However, this is not the time or place to talk about confidential information. If you have an issue to discuss or need further information from a parent, arrange an appointment for later in the week.

Just the facts. Prepare written information to distribute to children and their parents. Mail the information to the home, or create a "talk box." Set up a box by the classroom door with a hanging folder for each child. Written material is filed under the child's name. Parents are encouraged to check the folder when they pick up the child. If the folder is empty, then you will know that the parents received the information. If parents do not pick up their children from your classroom or do not attend for several weeks, mail or e-mail time-sensitive information.

Mass communication. Use the post office, e-mail and telephone to contact parents. Each method has its own advantages and drawbacks. Postage for letters can be expensive. E-mail is fast, but won't reach parents who don't have computer access. The phone can be time consuming if a large number of parents need to be called. Telephone trees are faster but can break down easily. Decide which method is most effective for your class.

DEALING WITH PARENTS

Get information. When parents bring a child to the class for the first time, make sure that you or other greeters get as much information as possible: address, phone numbers (including cell phones and pagers), names of siblings, the child's school and hobbies. It's important to know if parents are divorced and sharing custody. It's critical to know if the child has food allergies or health needs or is on prescribed medication. If the child is disabled, ask about the child's abilities. The more you know, the better the child's needs can be met.

Get the parents involved. The best way to keep parents excited about church classes is to involve the parents as active participants. They can provide snacks or art supplies. Parents can take turns helping as classroom assistants or event chaperones. Parents with special talents can share their skills with the class.

However, be conscious of possible burnout. Parents don't want to spend huge sums or feel that they are being overworked. Spread out the tasks so that no one person is providing all the supplies or doing all the work.

Inviting parents to participate. Offer the task as a ministry opportunity, not an obligation. When recruiting parents to teach, assure them that materials and training will be provided. When recruiting chaperones, tell the parents exactly what's expected of them (cleanup, transportation, etc.). When they come to help, don't expect the parents to do something other than what they were told.

Difficult parents. Occasionally, some parents present a challenge. They may feel their child is not getting enough attention or refuse to believe that their child has discipline problems. Always listen to a parent's comments and consider ways to make sure their needs and the needs of their child are addressed. If parents have ongoing complaints, ask your supervisor to set up a meeting with you and the parents. Let the parents describe their feelings. Make listening your main job. Some people feel better when they know someone has heard them. Sometimes the complaint is only a symptom of a larger problem out of your control. Stay calm and respond in a nondefensive manner. Try to work out a win-win solution for everyone, although occasionally individual parent requests cannot be met without negatively affecting the whole class.

Prayer

One of the most awesome responsibilities of the teacher at church is to give children the tools of prayer. Even young children can approach their heavenly Father with the confidence that He hears their prayers. It's never to soon for children to establish a habit of daily prayer.

WHAT TO TEACH ABOUT PRAYER

God listens. Children may feel that they are too young or insignificant for God's attention, or that God is only interested in grownups. Assure children that God cares and wants to hear from them at any time (see Matthew 7:7-8).

Some children may feel that when they pray, they must feel or express deep emotions. Let your children know that God hears, even if they don't feel like anything happened!

God provides. God is the source of everything on Earth. Children can give prayers of thanksgiving for food, shelter, clothing, friends, family and safety (see Psalm 103:1-5).

God is not a magician or Santa Claus. Prayer is often seen as something magical that grants instant requests. A child may feel sad or angry when a prayer did not "come true" right away. Sometimes prayers are answered after a long time. For example, a chemistry set is a great birthday present, but a very young child would not be able to use it. The child would need to get older and learn more before using it. Sometimes God waits for children (or adults) to mature before answering a prayer.

People commonly pray when they want something. Children often pray to get certain gifts for Christmas or that their team will win the championship. Sometimes God answers prayer not by giving us what we want but by giving the strength and wisdom to work for it. A child who works hard to earn an allowance can save money for a bike. A team can win a championship with practice and good sportsmanship.

Reassure children that God wants them to pray about all their needs and concerns, and that they can depend on God to always love and care for them (see Philippians 4:6).

God likes to hear prayers for others. Besides praying for their own needs, encourage children to think about and then pray for the needs of others. Children can pray for their parents (especially absent or divorced parents), siblings, friends, schoolmates, teachers and pets (see Matthew 5:44; Ephesians 6:18; James 5:16).

Why didn't God answer my prayer? In an imperfect world, bad things happen. A child can be caught in an ugly custody battle during a divorce. A child may be the victim of abuse or a criminal act. Natural disasters and accidents can destroy a family home. A family member or favorite pet dies. Children may wonder why a caring God would allow things to happen that they consider tragic.

Reassure children that God understands how they feel and that God can make something good come out of a bad situation (see Romans 8:28). For example, when a disaster happens, people in a church or community often help each other. God is still present and working through these people to see that needs are met.

HOW TO PRAY

Keep it simple. Children may feel that they need poetic language and "thees and thous" to pray. Children can talk to God in ordinary language.

Keep it honest. Children may feel that God will punish them if they are angry, upset or doubtful. It's okay to talk to God about unhappy feelings. God wants to hear how we feel.

Keep it short. Prayers don't need to be long or cover every subject. Young children can begin with short sentence prayers as they learn to pray.

Be a role model. Children will become comfortable with prayer when they see adults praying in ways that are appropriate and appealing. Make prayer a regular part of your class. Talk about personal answers to prayer during class.

Use a simple format. ACTS is a common acronym you can use to teach children how to pray.

Adoration: Praise and thank God for His love and power.

Confession: Admit actions and attitudes that do not show love for God and others, and say "I'm sorry" for sins.

Thanksgiving: Thank God for the good things He gives us.

Supplication: Ask God for things you need.

Keep a prayer journal. Older children can write down their petitions, thanksgivings and answers to prayer. They can record biblical prayers that they use in class. Lead children to make prayer journals by decorating a notebook or attaching sheets of paper together with a ribbon and cardboard cover. Prayer journals may be kept as personal, not to be read by other students.

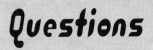

The art of a good discussion begins by asking effective questions. Most often, the best questions will not occur to you during a discussion but will result from good preparation. Take the time for thorough lesson preparation and for planning good questions. The best teachers continue to evaluate and refine their question-asking skills, even after years of service.

BASIC PREPARATION

Master the material. The teacher needs to know more about the lesson than what the child is expected to learn. Although the youngest children will have simple lessons, some teachers may find that their own Bible knowledge is less than that of their older children!

If possible, supplement your teacher's guide with a study Bible, concordance and a few basic Bible study tools such as an atlas of Bible maps and a Bible dictionary. Check the Internet or your church library for these resources. If a concept presented in your lesson material is confusing or difficult to understand, ask your supervisor, the pastor or another leader in your church for help. As you participate in adult Bible studies and personal Bible study, you will find that your knowledge and understanding will grow. In class, never be afraid to let a child know that you don't know the answer to a question. After class, look for the answer and share it with the child and others in the next class meeting.

Avoid yes and no questions. These kinds of questions provide little learning and little interest for the child and only reinforce what a child already knows. Yes and no questions do little to encourage discussion and, in fact, may inhibit discussion if children are worried about giving wrong answers.

Start where the children are starting. Try to gauge where the children are in their knowledge. Many children in church today come from unchurched families and are unfamiliar with the Bible and church traditions.

They may not know that the Bible is divided into the Old and New Testaments. In seeker classes, start with the basics and do not assume what the children know. Another challenge can be children with sporadic church attendance. They may be playing "continual catch-up" for the weeks missed. The challenge is to keep the interest of the more knowledgeable children while also meeting the needs of the beginners.

DEVELOPING QUESTIONS

Understanding the different types of questions can help a teacher ask the best questions for the lesson and the children.

Knowledge questions. These are questions that recall information and recite facts: What are the names of the 12 disciples? In what city was Jesus born? What cities did Paul travel to? Children are familiar with this type of question from weekday school. These questions may test what the child knows, but they do not stimulate discussion. If children give wrong information, never point it out, simply supply the correct facts. Remember that too many knowledge questions make children feel they are being grilled and may embarrass children who don't know the information. These questions also do not probe into the subject matter or help children understand how the subject matter relates to their lives.

Comprehension questions. These questions help children interpret their knowledge. Such questions ask the child to describe, explain, retell or identify. Some examples: What was different between the actions of the Samaritan and the actions of the Levite? What else could the father have chosen to do when he saw his son coming down the road? Why do you think Noah obeyed God's command to build an ark? These questions help the child move beyond just knowing the information to understanding it. Comprehension questions have no right or wrong answers, so a child can feel comfortable expressing his or her ideas.

Application questions. Bible knowledge reaches a new level when the child can apply it to his or her own life. Application questions help the child to make the lesson personal and to use the information in a new setting. These questions ask the child to apply, experiment, show, solve and describe. Questions such as What are some ways God provides for you? How can you follow Paul's example in telling others about Jesus? What are some ways we can be good stewards of the things we own? These questions move beyond "head knowledge" and into "heart knowledge."

Synthesis questions. These questions encourage children to use information in a creative and original way. Children are asked to design, create, construct, imagine and suppose: What do you think a disciple of Jesus is like? What do you think Noah and his family talked about on the ark? What would have happened if David had not trusted God when he challenged Goliath? Such questions stimulate children's natural creativity and curiosity.

Analysis questions. These questions challenge children to break apart information and examine its parts and relationships. Such questions require the child to connect, relate, arrange, analyze, compare and contrast. Some examples: Compare and contrast the actions of Saul and David. How did Joshua's actions make a difference in the lives of God's people? What factors contribute to our church's ability to worship God? These questions require abstract and analytical thinking that is most appropriate for preteens.

Evaluation questions. These questions motivate children to make informed judgments regarding the given information. The child is asked to judge, debate, decide and evaluate: Which Bible verse about honesty is the most helpful? Why? Which character in this Bible story is the best example of following God and why? Again, these questions are best handled by preteens who have developed skills in analytical thinking.

Imparting information is only part of what the effective teacher accomplishes in classes at church. Establishing an atmosphere of trust and love that makes the child want to return is just as important. Why do children gather at church instead of learning about God from a book or video? Because only in a communal setting can children and teachers build the Body of Christ and form friendships that last for years. Some adults who grew up in a church fondly remember the church teacher or camp counselor who made them feel valued.

TEACHER-CHILD RELATIONSHIPS

Trust. As the teacher, you have the opportunity to be someone whom children can count on to be present on more than an occasional basis. Children need to feel that they can talk to you in confidence and without ridicule or criticism. Children expect that what you present in class is accurate and useful.

Attitude. Children like teachers who are positive, upbeat, confident, cheerful, friendly and willing to help. Leave your personal problems at home and give children your undivided attention.

Fun. As responsibilities set in, adults tend to become serious and preoccupied. While the subject matter you present in class is serious in nature, the atmosphere of the class does not have to be dreary. This doesn't mean that you have to act silly or let chaos reign in the classroom. It means that you can enjoy games with your children, find joy in their discoveries and maintain a happy classroom environment.

Acceptance of feelings. Listen and empathize with the feelings of the children in your class. Children respond to situations with emotions rather than rational logic. Their reactions may seem childish because they have not learned how to control their feelings or how to think through situations. While you need not agree with everything a child says, you can be a sounding board and a sympathetic ear.

Acceptance of ideas. Adults are often self-critical and self-censoring. Children are freer to express wild and crazy ideas. Encourage children to think out loud and ask questions. Children are more involved in learning when they feel that their ideas are accepted. One way to encourage brainstorming is to ask open-ended questions about opinions instead of facts ("How did the lame man feel when he could walk again?" "How do you think David felt when he heard King Saul's threat to hurt him?") Questions with more than one right answer are less threatening to children because they don't feel that they will make mistakes in their answers.

Enabling questions. Allow children to make choices instead of telling the child what to do. Instead of saying "Put the paint back in the cabinet," ask, "Where do we put the paint?" Ask children what phrases or slogans best summarize the lesson's Bible truth. Children like to feel they have an important role in the classroom.

Praise and affirmation. Every child wants to feel like the most special child in the world. Compliment and encourage children frequently, mentioning specific actions you have observed. The more children feel valued, the more they want to participate in learning and feel that God accepts them.

Nonverbal signs. Use body language to show acceptance. Sit at the children's eye level and avoid hovering over them. Nod and lean forward when a child is speaking. Smile frequently!

Touching. Due to concerns over child abuse, touching can be a difficult issue in educational settings. While you don't wish to appear cool and aloof, neither do you want your well-meaning gestures to be misinterpreted. Children sometimes have crushes on a teacher of the opposite gender. Placing a hand for a few seconds on the child's upper arm, shoulder or upper back can be appropriate to express concern. Hold a child's hand when leading the child across a room, as part of a game, in a prayer circle or if the child is scared. Brief hugs are fine when you and the child have developed a trusting relationship over time. A child may be uncomfortable if you continue touching him or her for a long time or too frequently. It is always safer to have two adults present in a classroom at all times.

CHILD-CHILD RELATIONSHIPS

Trust and security. In many churches, children don't know each other. They go to different schools during the week and may live in distant parts of the city. The children won't automatically get to know each other, much less develop relationships of trust. Start by having children learn their peers' names (name games are fun) and something about each other (pets, hobbies, siblings, sports, favorite performers or TV shows). Maintain a safe place where children won't be hurt and their belongings won't be stolen.

Group activities. A good way to develop friendships is through group work. Children bond when they have a common goal or problem to solve. Have children work in pairs, trios and small groups using worksheets, skits, music, games, research projects and cooperative art projects. Be sure each person in the group has a task and is not left out. One person from each group can share the group's discovery or project with the rest of the class. Acknowledge the contributions of each child.

Sharing. Children learn about each other by sharing their heritage and interests. Invite children to demonstrate music, food or artwork from their home life. Children also enjoy bringing an item from home with spiritual importance in their family (heirloom Bible, gift cross, Scripture sampler, devotional book, etc.).

Prayer. During class prayer time, encourage children to pray for each other. This may be uncomfortable or threatening at first. Model sentence prayers for children to hear and imitate. As children feel comfortable in telling things for which they are thankful and/or their concerns, invite other children to pray for them. Children can say together, "Thank You, God," when someone describes something for which he or she is thankful.

Salvation

Many adult Christians look back to their elementary years as the time when they accepted Christ as Savior. Not only are children able to understand the difference between right and wrong and their own personal need of forgiveness, but they are also growing in their ability to understand Jesus' death and resurrection as the means by which God provides salvation. In addition, children at this age are capable of growing in their faith through prayer, Bible reading, worship and service.

However, children (particularly those in early elementary grades) can still be limited in their understanding and may be immature in following through on their intentions and commitments. They need thoughtful, patient guidance in coming to know Christ personally and continuing to grow in Him.

1. Pray.

Ask God to prepare the children in your class to receive the good news about Jesus and prepare you to effectively communicate with them.

2. Present the Good News.

Use words and phrases that children understand. Avoid symbolism that will confuse these literal-minded thinkers. *Discuss these points slowly* enough to allow time for thinking and comprehending.

a. "God wants you to become His child. Do you know why God wants you in His family?" (See 1 John 4:8.)

b. "You and all the people in the world have done wrong things. The Bible word for doing wrong is "sin." What do you think the Bible says should happen to us when we sin?" (See Romans 6:23.)

c. "God loves you so much, He sent His Son to die on the cross for your sin. Because Jesus never sinned, He is the only one who can take the punishment for your sin." (See 1 Corinthians 15:3; 1 John 4:14.) On the third day after Jesus died, God brought Him back to life.

d. "Are you sorry for your sin? Tell God that you are. Do you believe Jesus died to take the punishment for your sin and that He is alive today? If you tell God you are sorry for your sin and tell Him you do believe and accept Jesus' death to take away your sin—God forgives all your sin." (See John 1:12.)

e. "The Bible says that when you believe in Jesus, God's Son, you receive God's gift of eternal life. This gift makes you a child of God. (See John 3:16.) This means God is with you now and forever."

As you give children many opportunities to think about what it means to be a Christian, expose them to a variety of lessons and descriptions of the meaning of salvation to aid their understanding.

3. Talk personally with the child.

Talking about salvation one-on-one creates opportunity to ask and answer questions. Ask questions that move the child beyond simple yes or no answers or recitation of memorized information. Ask what-do-you-think? kinds of questions such as:

"Why do you think it's important to . . . ?"

"What are some things you really like about Jesus?"

"Why do you think that Jesus had to die because of wrong things you and I have done?"

"What difference do you think it makes for a person to be forgiven?"

Answers to these open-ended questions will help you discern how much the child does or does not understand.

4. Offer opportunities without pressure.

Children are vulnerable to being manipulated by adults. A good way to guard against coercing a child's response is to simply pause periodically and ask, "Would you like to hear more about this now or at another time?" Lovingly accepting the child, even when he or she is not fully interested in pursuing the matter, is crucial in building and maintaining relationship that will yield more opportunities to talk about becoming part of God's family.

5. Give time to think and pray.

There is great value in encouraging a child to think and pray about what you have said before making a response. Also allow moments for quiet thinking about questions you ask.

6. Respect the child's response.

Whether or not a child declares faith in Jesus Christ, adults need to accept the child's action. There is also a need to realize that a child's initial responses to Jesus are just the beginning of a lifelong process of growing in the faith.

7. Guide the child in further growth.

Here are three important parts in the nurturing process:

a. *Talk regularly about your relationship with God.* As you talk about your relationship, the child will begin to feel that it's OK to talk about such things. Then you can comfortably ask the child to share his or her thoughts and feelings, and encourage the child to ask questions of you.

b. *Prepare the child to deal with doubts.* Emphasize that certainty about salvation is not dependent on our feelings or doing enough good deeds. Show the child verses in God's Word that clearly declare that salvation comes by grace through faith (i.e., John 1:12; Ephesians 2:8-9; Hebrews 11:6; 1 John 5:11).

c. *Teach the child to confess all sin.* "Confess" means "to admit" or "to agree." Confessing sins means agreeing with God that we really have sinned. Assure the child that confession always results in forgiveness (see 1 John 1:9).

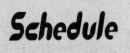

Schedule

WHAT IS THE MOST EFFECTIVE WAY TO LINK GOD'S WORD TO A CHILD'S LIFE?

Some of us confess to being fruitless gardeners: We buy seed with great enthusiasm but then don't have take time to prepare the soil. So we toss seeds willy-nilly over unprepared ground, maybe throwing a little mulch over them and watering once or twice. We don't mark the place where we tossed the seeds, so when weeds grow instead, we aren't inclined to pull them because surely some of our seeds are sprouted among them. Not much fruit results!

Many of us would have to admit we teach children in a similar fashion: Enthusiastic but poorly prepared, we scatter seed over unprepared children, seldom nurturing, cultivating or evaluating what takes place during a class session. Could this be part of the reason we see very little fruit?

An Intentional Plan

Effective Bible teaching requires us to pay attention to the lesson aims, to use class time wisely, to creatively involve students in the Bible learning process and to develop personal relationships with the children. Sound impossible? Such things don't just happen: They develop from an intentional teaching plan.

Here are some likely results of having an intentional teaching plan:

★ Children will come to class in anticipation, knowing that the schedule and activities are planned with them in mind;

★ Learning aims or goals will be more easily accomplished because the activities in a session are chosen so that they build on each other;

★ Activities and teacher-to-student ratios will aid

personal interaction, so teachers can share God's love and their faith with children!

Four Goals to Consider

Goal 1: Have specific lesson aims that deal not only with biblical knowledge but also with attitude and behavior. Meaningful aims take into account what children *know*, how they *feel* and what they are going to *do* about it. The more you pay attention to what results you want, the more likely you are to provide activities that achieve those results. Since the ultimate goal is shown by a change in behavior, effective aims are stated in terms of what students will do to show that they have learned. It is important to realize that while some children know and understand Scripture, and even feel good about it, they never *do* anything about it—their lives are not changed by the truth that they learn. Our goal is to teach so hearts and minds are changed; such change is shown through actions and choices! The world is not influenced by Christians whose actions and choices look just like those of unbelievers.

Goal 2: Plan for everything that occurs in the session to work toward accomplishing the aim. Church leaders agree on the value of teaching God's Word. Sunday School, midweek groups and Bible classes all place a high priority on communicating spiritual truths. However, these programs all face two similar obstacles: They only meet one to two hours a week and they often experience hit-or-miss attendance.

Then, in spite of the short time teachers and children spend together, other things (announcements, special music, taking attendance, birthdays, etc.) invade part of the learning time. Classes often start late due to tardiness of students or because teachers are busy with last-minute preparations. Early arrivals are forced to wait until class time "begins" when they could be involved in meaningful activity. The end result is that the valuable time for the real purpose of the class (Bible study, learning activities, relationship building) is cut to a minimum. Class becomes a "sit and listen" situation in which students have no opportunity to discover Bible truths for themselves or to interact with their teachers and with each other because "we've got to get through the material."

The most practical solution is to be sure all of the activities, songs, discussion times, study groups, etc., become avenues used to accomplish a single set of learning aims. Begin with activities that start a child thinking about the Bible truths to be studied. (These activities also allow for students to arrive at varying times.) Structure sessions so that students are involved in studying God's Word for themselves to discover Bible truths, balancing teacher input with child interaction. Challenge children to apply the Bible truths to their lives in ways they understand and take specific steps of action as a result of what God's Word teaches.

Encourage personal discovery and application of Bible truth.

Goal 3: Provide a variety of creative learning activities to help students discover Bible truths. The third aspect of an intentional teaching plan is to involve children in a variety of activities, because just as each child is different, so are the ways in which children learn. Each child needs to be motivated and challenged according to his or her unique abilities and interests. This can best be done by providing a variety of learning experiences and offering choices whenever possible. How many learning activities can you think of right now? There are *hundreds*! Yet some teachers stick to their old favorites (usually the way in which they were taught). Lecture, discussion and questions need to be interwoven with other activities that will make Bible study intriguing and help children understand truth in terms that have real meaning for them.

Goal 4: Create a balance of teacher input and student discovery. Strengthen relationships through teacher and student interaction. Two elements are necessary to make learning happen: *time* for teachers to guide learning in a direct fashion (leading a Bible study, telling a Bible story, guiding a discussion) and *initiative* by children to discover and apply Bible truths (reading and commenting on a Scripture passage, participating in a Bible learning game, drawing a picture in response). A key factor in an intentional teaching plan is to discover the right balance between the two.

Grouping elementary students into small groups of six to eight students will encourage personal discovery and application of Bible truth. Within small groups, teachers and students can relate on an individual basis and can ask and answer questions to connect Bible truths to children's lives. Teachers can share experiences from their own lives that relate to a Bible truth and can evaluate and clarify children's understanding of concepts and ideas.

ELEMENTARY SESSION SCHEDULE

The teacher of children in the elementary grades has the awesome responsibility of effectively communicating God's Word to children whose life circumstances are not only quite different from the teacher's but also may be quite different from other children's. A session schedule needs to allow for significant interaction among teachers and students as well as many opportunities to read and understand the Bible. This is foundational to helping children begin and grow in their relationship to Jesus Christ.

The following schedule allows teachers to teach children through meaningful learning experiences, each experience contributing to the session's learning aims.

Schedule at a Glance:

Prepare for the session by arriving 10-15 minutes early.

Step 1: Discover

5 to 15 minutes

Purpose: To help build relationships among students and start them thinking about the life focus and/or memory verse of the lesson.

Step 2: Bible Study

20 to 30 minutes

Purpose: To guide students to read, study and discuss the Bible for themselves.

Step 3: Apply

20 to 30 minutes

Purpose: To help students explore the relationship between the Bible truth they have been studying and their day-to-day experiences.

Before the Session

Teachers and helpers arrive 10 to 15 minutes early in order to prepare the classroom or to make a smooth transition between staff.

During the Session

Children arrive during the first 10 minutes of the session. A teacher or helper welcomes children at the door and supervises check-in procedures. (In large churches, check-in may take place elsewhere on your facility, but a teacher or helper still needs to be available to greet children as they enter the classroom.) As children enter the room, they are immediately involved in a discovery activity that introduces the life focus or memory verse for the lesson. Teachers and children can also be involved in relationship building as they interact and participate in activities together. Discovery activities accommodate varying arrival times and can be led by teachers with a small group of students or with all students together. Depending on the type of activity, the ratio of students to teachers and the space and materials available, more than one activity may be offered.

These brief activities at the beginning of the session help the child begin thinking about the concepts that will be developed during the session. When possible, offer a choice of activities not only to help meet the varied needs of students but also to allow each child involved to accept personal responsibility for participating and learning.

The second major time segment is Bible study. Students can be grouped in small groups or in one large group, depending on the number of teachers and students. To provide the most learning and interaction among students, it's best to group no more than 12 to 14 students for Bible study. During this time, the teacher introduces the Bible story, weaving in opportunities for students to find, read and discuss Bible verses. This segment becomes much more than listening to a story as children become active participants. Even beginning readers can find the books in the Bible or locate names of Bible characters. Some churches include worship activities such as songs and prayer, and video or DVD Bible story presentations.

During the third and last part of the session, the teacher guides a small group of children in discovering the relationship between the lesson's Bible truth and their day-to-day experiences by using a creative learning activity that encourages students to identify and discuss specific ways their behavior can be affected by the day's lesson. Over a period of weeks, a variety of learning activities are provided so that each child's interests and needs are met. (In large churches, each teacher may lead a different activity, allowing each child to choose the activity most appropriate to his or her learning style.) A key element of this time is the conversation that takes place between teacher and child. This time segment is a wonderful opportunity for teachers to nurture spiritual growth in children, not only by modeling and sharing their own spiritual growth, but also by guiding children to discover and plan steps of growth. (Note: This time segment may wrap up with one or more brief worship activities (song, prayer, group activity).

At the End of the Session

Depending on your church's schedule and safety policies, children either move into the next session, or they are dismissed or picked up by parents. Teachers briefly communicate with parents about their children and the activities they enjoyed.

After the Session

Teachers and helpers evaluate the session (whether aims were met, what challenges arose, what benefits were seen, etc.), clean up the classroom or work with incoming teaching staff to allow the start of a new program or class with a minimum of disruption.

Additional Sunday Morning Programs

In many churches some or all of the grade-school children may participate in an additional program that takes place either before or after the Sunday School session. Elementary-aged children need a change of pace to vary the program from Sunday School. The additional program needs to include new topics, different activities, a wide variety of learning approaches and a varied time schedule, all used with the intentional plan to accomplish the learning aim chosen for the session.

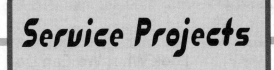

Service Projects

How many times does a child hear, "You're too young to do that" or "Wait until you're older." Too often, children feel that the church is just for grown-ups. But even young children can participate in service projects and feel they are a valued part of the Body of Christ. Service projects allow children to put their Bible lessons to practical use and live out God's love in action. A child who enjoys positive experiences serving others will build a lifelong habit of volunteering.

ORGANIZING SERVICE PROJECTS

What's useful? Nobody likes to waste time or energy on busy work. Children will be more excited about a project that has a purpose behind it. Rather than saying, "We better pick up the litter on the church grounds," say "Let's clean the church grounds before next week's all-church picnic" or "You and your friends will have a fun time playing when the playground is clean." Find projects that children can understand and give them a sense of accomplishment.

Personalize it. People are more likely to help those whom they know personally. Giving money to a large corporation or overseas missions means nothing to a child. Show photos and tell stories of children who live in mission countries. Let the children meet the families who receive aid from the church. Invite a returned missionary to the class to discuss his or her work abroad.

Put everyone to work. One shortcoming of service projects can be that a few children will accomplish all the work and the others will do nothing. The ones who are left out will be bored or disruptive and most likely uninterested in future projects. Plan and assign specific tasks ahead of time so that every child feels involved in important work. (Make sure there is enough work to go around!)

Be specific. Children need to know exactly what is expected of them. Avoid vague instructions or waiting for children to figure out what to do. Instead of saying, "Stock the food pantry," say "Girls, put the fresh food in the refrigerator. Boys, sort the cans of fruits and vegetables. Put the fruit cans on this shelf. Thank you." Rather than "Clean up the yard," say "Lily and Natalie, please rake the leaves. Dylan and Micah, please pick up the litter and put it in the dumpster."

Involve parents. When the parents see what their children are doing, they will likely encourage their children to participate. Invite the parents to provide supplies, donate cash to buy needed supplies or assist in other ways (deliver donated items, take pictures, etc.). Keep parents updated through letters, the church newsletter or the church website.

Reward the children. After completing a project, reward the children with snacks or a pizza party. Give out badges or ribbons. Post the children's names in the church newsletter or on the church bulletin board. Take photos or a video of the children during the project for display or viewing. Have a party to celebrate the completion of several projects.

Avoid guilt-producing motivation. The best way to encourage children to serve God is through love, not guilt. Help children develop a sense of cheerful Christian compassion toward others.

OFFSITE PROJECTS

If an offsite service project is planned, tell the parents exactly what the children will be doing, where they will be and what they need to bring (lunch, bottled water, gardening tools, a jacket, etc.).

Thorough planning. Be certain that parents know the time and place to drop off and pick up their children. Try to plan exactly when the project will end so that neither children nor parents are waiting a long time for pickup. Figure in travel time, traffic delays and cleanup time. End a project before the children become bored or exhausted. Never leave a child unattended to wait for a ride home.

Safety first. If the project is off the church grounds, signed permission slips from the parents are a must. Have all parents' phone numbers on hand as well as emergency numbers. Bring a first-aid kit and be sure that at least one adult leader knows first aid and CPR. Children must be dressed appropriately: sturdy shoes, work gloves and old clothes that can get dirty. Find out if any child will need to take medication and make arrangements for medical personnel or the child's parent to administer the medicine.

Discourage children from bringing large sums of cash to minimize the risk of loss or theft. The adults need to bring food or pay for meals so that children will not need money.

Provide plenty of adult supervision. Instruct the children to stay together and not to wander off. Use caution when working with tools, such as rakes, shovels, hammers and nails.

TYPES OF SERVICE PROJECTS

What children can do is limited only by their imagination and abilities! Let older children brainstorm service project ideas to increase motivation.

★ Collect and/or sort items for a food pantry or thrift store.

★ Perform songs or skits at a nursing home or retirement center.

★ Help church members who are unable to leave their homes. Bake and deliver cookies or healthy snacks, go Christmas caroling, make and deliver birthday cards or meals.

★ Adopt a child living overseas. Students write to the child and collect money to support the child. The church or denominational missions organization can provide names.

★ Make school packs for low-income children. Fill backpacks, shoeboxes or paper lunch sacks with school supplies, a toy and toiletry items.

★ Make and deliver holiday food baskets for needy families.

★ Each child buys, wraps and delivers a toy to a needy child his or her own age and gender (including the batteries!).

★ Participate in the worship service as greeters, ushers, handing out bulletins or readers.

★ Older children can organize a party for younger children or their unchurched friends.

★ Older children, with adult supervision, can provide child care during church events.

★ If a church campground is unused during the winter, schedule workdays before the summer camps begin to maintain the facility.

★ Help in the church office. Children can stuff bulletins or envelopes for a mass mailing. Computer whizzes can do data entry.

★ Write notes to be sent to elderly or infirm members of the church.

★ Make get-well cards to be used by pastoral care staff when making hospital visits.

★ Clean an area of the church building or grounds.

Special Needs

Society places a high value on both appearance and achievement. For this and many other reasons, including a child with a disability in class can cause some people to cringe inwardly, unsure of how to react or what to say. But a child with a disability is as loved by God as any other! Including a child with a disability in your class is a tremendous opportunity for the other members of the class to put God's love into action.

If you are unfamiliar with the condition of a child with a disability, you may be uncertain about how to best help him or her. Following this article are pages that give information and practical tips to help you deal with specific disabilities. But here are some general guidelines and strategies to help you become prayerfully prepared. Expect to be greatly blessed as you discover the gifts God sends through that child! With skills and understanding, you can minister effectively both to a child with a disability and to the other children in your class.

The foundation. Provide space on the children's ministry registration form for registering parents to indicate a child's special needs or medical concerns. If parents indicate that their child has a need, set up an interview with the child's parents to learn more about the child's situation and how best to meet the child's needs. Take complete notes and share the information only with those who need to know. If the child is enrolled in a public school, it might be appropriate to ask parents to share their child's IEP (individual education plan) developed by the school staff to outline ways they help the child learn best at school.

Also invite a parent to attend class with the child the first few times. The parent can demonstrate the most effective ways to help the child. Then your help will be understood by the child and consistent with help the parent gives at home.

The challenge. The biggest challenge when any child who is different enters a classroom is distraction. A child's disability or behavior may cause others to focus on that child to the exclusion of everything else. To prevent distraction, some churches train and then assign an aide to accompany each child with a disability. Each aide works with only one child during a class session so that the child can participate fully while keeping distraction to a minimum.

The structure. For many children with disabilities, a consistent routine provides structure that will help them function best. During the first few class sessions, establish a routine and follow it consistently. As you get to know the child, you can then adjust the routine to accommodate the child's strengths and learning styles. Use the learning center approach (centers well staffed with adults) to give all children the chance to work at their own levels of ability.

HEARING DISABILITIES

A child with a hearing disability is as intelligent and aware as a hearing child. Hearing disabilities can vary widely and include children who have partial hearing loss in one ear or a loss that can be corrected with a hearing aid. Some children are skilled at reading lips and others can only speak through American Sign Language (ASL). Talk to the child's parents to determine how much the child can hear and comprehend. Consider asking an adult helper to assist regularly with the child.

Methods of Communication

Speech. Interview the parents to determine the child's level of function with speech, too. If the child has some hearing capacity, you may be able to communicate through speaking. But remember to let the child choose the ways to communicate that best suits him or her. Avoid shouting at the child. This draws unwanted attention and distorts the words. Speak naturally and enunciate clearly. Do not talk too rapidly, but at the same time, avoid speaking too slowly or drawing out words. If you normally talk very softly or have a high voice, you may need to speak up a little. Exaggerated facial expressions or speech will not be understood. Look directly at the child and let him or her see your lips moving, especially if the child can read lips. Avoid turning away or covering your mouth when speaking. Keep your hands still, as unnecessary gestures are distracting. Do not use baby talk or talk down to the child. Use complete and grammatically correct sentences. Ask the child to repeat what he or she heard to ensure understanding.

The child may have hearing loss in only one ear. When speaking, face the child but stand toward the side from which the child hears best. The child may need to turn his or her ear toward the teacher instead of making eye contact.

Music. Even a deaf child is able to feel music by touching a stereo speaker or feeling the beat through the floor. A child may pantomime the words instead of singing. However, some children need or want the volume of music turned up very high. Music that is too loud will be uncomfortable for the rest of the class and surrounding classrooms. Ask the parents how much the child can hear and at what volume. If the child needs loud music, perhaps he or she can use a portable cassette/CD player with headphones.

Games. Children with hearing disabilities can play along with the rest of the class. If the child cannot hear a whistle, buzzer or bell, use a flashlight or hold up a stop sign as a signal. Explain the instructions clearly and demonstrate the game, so the child is not confused when the game starts. Written instructions may be useful, too. Make sure the players do not depend on only verbal cues to play the game. The other children may need to use hand signals to direct the child who cannot hear. Include hearing impaired children's ideas into the activities so that they feel they are contributing members of the group.

Love. Communicate to children who are hearing impaired that God loves them just the way they are. Don't oversimplify or trivialize their disabilities. Think of ways to encourage them that don't require listening. Nonverbal communication (a touch, a hug, a smile, etc.) is a great way to demonstrate God's love!

Tools for the Hearing Impaired

Imagination. Pretend you are in a foreign country where you don't speak the language. You would likely use your hands, your feet, facial expressions, draw and point as much as possible. Don't be afraid to use whatever communication method gets a positive response!

Sign Language. The child may use American Sign Language (ASL) as the principal form of communication. Learn some basic requests and words in ASL.

Training books are available, plus many schools offer ASL night classes for adults.

Teach some ASL words to the entire class. Better yet, have the hearing-impaired child teach the other children! Most children love to learn ASL. This will not only help the children to speak to the hearing-impaired child but also will make the hearing-impaired child feel included because the entire class is signing. The class can learn to sign simple prayers or short Bible verses.

ASL has a different grammatical structure than standard English for faster speech and fewer hand motions. A child who cannot hear regular speech may not be aware of how standard English is supposed to sound. Do not be surprised if his or her spoken or written sentences are grammatically incorrect. Accept the child's speech as his or her gift to the class. Instead of correcting the child, repeat the statement back with proper grammar.

Hearing Aids. A child with a partial hearing loss may be able to use a hearing aid. Today, such devices are incredibly small and effective. The other children may not be able to see the hearing aid. However, a hearing aid may not be able to fully restore all hearing loss. Even with a hearing aid, the child may not be able to listen to one voice if there is a lot of other noise in the room, such as other children talking or music playing. Continue speaking clearly and directly to a child with a hearing aid. If there is a lot of surrounding noise, stand directly in front of the child to speak.

Sometimes the child may need to stop and adjust the hearing aid if he or she is trying to hear someone speaking softly or the surrounding noise is too loud. If the child is working with the hearing aid, stop talking to the child and wait for him or her to finish.

At times, a hearing-impaired child may turn off the hearing aid or pretend not to hear. This may be due to sensory overload or problems with the hearing aid. Observe the child to determine if he or she simply does not want to be involved with the class. Talk with the parents to determine how they handle similar situations. Use positive reinforcement to increase the behavior you want to see. As you model appropriate behavior and establish trust, you can expect hearing-impaired children to behave as respectfully as other children.

PHYSICAL DISABILITIES

At one time or another you will likely encounter a child in your class who is physically disabled. Sometimes the disability is mild and the child can fully participate in all activities with minimal assistance. Other disabilities require more attention. Some disabilities are temporary, such as a broken leg, while other impairments are permanent. The most important thing is to focus on what the child can do instead of what the child cannot do. Get the child involved in classroom activities as much as possible instead of letting the child sit idly on the sidelines. If a particular activity is totally unsuitable, find an alternate activity that will allow the child to remain in the group and study the same material.

Types of Physical Disabilities

Allow all children with special physical needs to participate at their own level. Ask their permission, if possible, before helping them complete any project. Consider asking the parents of a child with a disability to come and tell about the disability and/or show appropriate visual aids or videos to help children understand the disability.

Arms and hands. Some children have limited use of their fingers on one or both hands, or they may have only one hand or arm. They may be able to write, color or paint if an adult puts the pen in their hands or bends their fingers. If they cannot operate scissors, precut materials for them. If they need assistance holding a book or turning pages, they can set a book on a small podium while they stand or you can tape pages together in one long strip.

Legs and feet. A child may need a cane or walker to move around, or he or she may be confined to a wheelchair. Recent federal legislation requires that all public buildings must be handicapped accessible. New churches are built to code with wheelchair ramps, elevators and accessible restrooms. However, some older church buildings were constructed with many stairs and narrow hallways and may be accessible in only a few areas. If a child cannot easily reach the classroom, move the class to an accessible room. Check to see that nearby restrooms are also accessible. If an elevator or stair climber must be used, be sure the child can safely operate the device or that an adult is present to assist.

Children in wheelchairs can still participate in games and may be quite mobile and quick. They may be able to move while carrying an object in a lap, one hand or a chair basket. Allow them to participate as much as they are willing and able. Make sure there is sufficient space in the playing area for wheelchairs to maneuver. Make clear rules that other students are not to grab, touch or push the wheelchair without permission. A wheelchair is a tool, not a toy. However, if the child is willing, others can learn a lot from having a turn using the chair.

Facial features. Some children were born with facial deformities and others have had their features changed through injury, disease or fire. Children with cancer may need to wear a medical mask or they may lose their hair as a result of chemotherapy. Other children may react by staring or by avoiding. Teach by modeling for your class that God loves each person no matter how we look. Treat the child with respect and dignity. Emphasize to the other children what abilities everyone in the class shares. Look into the child's eyes when speaking to him or her. The class will likely imitate your attitude.

Assisting the Child with a Disability

Plan appropriate activity. Find out the limits of the child's endurance. Most children have no problem with a typical one-hour class session. However, some children with special abilities tire easily. If the child is to be involved with an all-day event or an overnight camp, allow the child time out if needed. Have a quiet, private place where the child can rest. Do not make a big issue over rest time but allow the child to leave the group quietly. Some disabled children also require daily medications. Have a qualified medical professional or the child's parent present to safely administer all medicines.

Use an assistant. If the child suffered a recent injury, he or she may need help with simple daily tasks, such as holding a pencil or tying shoes. Recruit an adult assistant who can help the child while the teacher leads the class. However, children who have lived with a disability for a long time have learned ways to handle most tasks and compensate for their limitations. Allow the child to do as much as he or she can do without tiring or excessive strain. Be patient, as they may require more time to complete a task.

Solicit the parents' cooperation. Speak with the parents about the best ways to assist the child. Have the parents sit in on the class to gauge the activities where the child may need assistance. Get information about the disability from the child's therapist or school.

Speak to the class. The other children may have questions. They need to feel comfortable learning and playing with a classmate who has a disability. Allow the child to explain as much as he or she wishes, but the class does not need to know private details about the medical condition, what caused the disability or how the child handles personal functions.

Be loving and understanding. If the disability is from a recent accident, if it is permanent or if it is likely to be terminal, the child may be upset, depressed or angry. Show love and compassion consistently. Make your class an emotionally safe place for a child to ask hard questions and express his or her feelings. Allow the child time to deal with feelings. Give the child time and private space to talk about his or her feelings. The child may blame God or be upset with God, especially if a loved one was lost in an accident. Do not argue with the child. Assure the child that bad things happen in the world and God still loves him or her and is working something good out of the situation.

SPEECH DISABILITIES

A teacher may encounter a child in class who has difficulty speaking. Such children cannot pronounce words correctly, or perhaps they do not use proper grammar or sentence structure and their sentences are unintelligible. This can be frustrating if you feel that you are not able to understand what a child is trying so hard to communicate. Talk with family members to gain knowledge of the situation. Be patient with yourself and with the child to help establish communication.

Types of Speech Difficulties

Physical disabilities. Some children have problems with speech due to a birth defect, physical defect, injury or disease to the brain or neurological speech functions. Some examples include apraxia, cerebral palsy, cleft palate or mental retardation. In most cases, the speech difficulty cannot be cured but can be managed.

Learning disabilities. The speech of some children will develop slower than that of their peers.

Baby talk. Some older children may continue to speak below their age level, such as "Me want pencil" or "Go potty." This could be a learning disability but may also be an emotional problem. Be sure to consult with the family for more information. The child may feel that baby talk is a good way to get attention or special treatment. Encourage the child to speak properly by rephrasing the request. "Tiffany, do you want to use a pencil?" or "Do you need to use the restroom?" Invite the child to repeat the sentence correctly with you without turning it into a challenge.

Stuttering. A child may stutter only on certain words, because he or she is experiencing a growth spurt or because he or she is nervous. If the child stutters, be patient and loving. Avoid the temptation to finish a sentence for the child or show annoyance. Invite the child to choose a way to communicate that better suits him or her, such as writing or drawing. Respond by narrating what you see for immediate feedback ("I see. You meant the other dog. Now I understand!") If a child believes that you are not annoyed by his or her speech, the child will become comfortable speaking with you, even if it is difficult. Often, stuttering decreases as the child feels accepted.

Understanding. Some children may not understand what is said to them, such as English as a second language (ESL) students or students with cognitive disabilities. They may seem to disobey a request because the words make no sense to them. Always phrase directions positively, so the child hears exactly what he or she needs to do. Speak directly and calmly to the child. Repeat the request clearly. If necessary, pantomime or act out the request. If the child is learning English, learn basic words in the child's native language and use them until the child is more comfortable using English.

Tips for Communication

Get help. Enlist another adult who is aware of the situation to help the child.

Consult with the parents. Find out if the parents have any special techniques that they use to communicate with the child. Also consult the child's therapist or specialist who can share ideas on communication with the child. Keep updated on changes in the child's condition or treatment.

Preserve the child's dignity. Most children feel awkward that they are "different" and cannot speak as well as the other students. Avoid drawing attention to problems or treating the child as abnormal. Rather than saying, "Let's wait for Tom to write out a question," say "Hand me your question when you are ready, Tom." If the child feels he or she cannot participate in class discussion, allow the child to ask questions privately and encourage the child to say as much as he or she is comfortable saying. As you create a safe and accepting environment, some children will gain confidence to practice and improve their speech.

If another student makes fun of a child's disability, simply comment, "We show respect to everyone in our class." If the teasing continues, speak to the offender privately about the need to respect others. Teach a parable about tolerance to the entire class without pointing out the disabled child. Establish a safe and nurturing atmosphere so that the student is comfortable speaking without fear of ridicule.

Repeat for clarity. When the child has spoken, repeat the statement for confirmation. "Do you want a Bible?" "Are you saying that Daniel was brave when he was in the lions' den?" The child can confirm the statement with a nod. You have demonstrated that you understood the words. Don't pretend to understand unclear speech. If necessary, ask the child to show, draw or write what was meant. The child will only feel more frustrated if you give a vague answer in reply or do something other than what the child asked.

Be honest. If the child's speech is not intelligible, admit it. "Roy, I didn't quite understand. Could we try again?" If the statement is not clear, ask the child to point or act out what he or she wants. Invite the child to show, draw or write what was meant. If you still cannot understand, tell the child that you're sorry you can't understand and that you will ask the

child's parents for help in getting to know what the child is trying to say. The child knows that you are making an honest effort at communication.

Be patient. Children may become frustrated or angry at their limited speech ability. Assure the child that you are glad to have him or her in class and that what he or she says is important. You may also admit to feeling frustrated at the difficult communication! But continue to use every available avenue of communication. As you work with a child over time, you will grow accustomed to the child's speech and be able to discern the child's best communication style.

Visual aids. A child can indicate his or her needs by pointing to a picture. Keep flashcards on hand with pictures of items a child might need: a glass of water, a bathroom door, pencil or a question mark. An older child may be able to read and write without difficulty. Such a child may want to write out requests or point to words in a book that spell a question.

Sign Language. A child can communicate his or her wants through simple hand signals, point to an object, point to the bathroom door or make motions to indicate "drink" or "eat." If the child has extreme difficulty with speech, recruit another adult to be a child's regular aide during the class session. Spend time with the child, parents and the aide to learn better ways to communicate with the child.

VISUAL DISABILITIES

Visual disabilities comes in degrees of severity. A child may be totally blind or partially sighted. In the latter case, the child may be able to see somewhat if he or she wears glasses or holds items close. Speak with the parents to determine the extent of the child's abilities. Encourage a partially sighted child to use his or her vision as much as possible so that the child can develop independence and confidence.

A student may come to class with an undiagnosed vision problem. If a student insists that he or she cannot read the chalkboard from a distance, holds books close to the face for reading or is hesitant about walking into a crowded hallway or crossing a street, the child may have a vision problem. Mention your observation to the child's parents so that an optometrist can be consulted if needed.

Communicating with the Visually Impaired

Speak normally. Blind children are not deaf. Some people have a tendency to raise their voice when speaking to a blind person. Use a normal speaking tone, but enunciate words clearly since the child cannot see lips or facial expression.

Identify speakers. When greeting the child, say your name, even if the child recognizes the voice. Say the names of new children or those who are talking.

Explore the classroom. On the first day of class, give the child a guided tour of the room, so he or she will know the location of furniture, supplies, closets and restrooms. Older children may pace out the room to learn the layout. If possible, arrange for the child to arrive early, so he or she has plenty of time to explore. Keep furniture and supplies in the same place each week so the child can find them. Keep the floor clear of trash and objects so that the child does not stumble.

Use touch. A hand on the shoulder or a gentle hug is a good way to show love. When guiding the child, do not grab his or her arm. Tap his or her hand and let the child hold your fingers. Do not pull a child, but gently walk alongside the child at the child's pace.

Treat the child normally. There is no need to pamper or isolate a child with a disability. Such children have adapted and can deal with their abilities. The child will be happy to be included in all classroom activities. Allow the child to do as much as possible within his or her capacity. If necessary, let another child serve as a buddy if the child needs extra guidance. Always consult the parents for more ideas when you have difficulty.

The child can participate in many games if instructions are clear and easy to remember. Put raised bumps on objects so that the child knows what to pick up. Playing the game in pairs allows a child with a visual disability to participate.

A partially sighted child can make art projects and follow clear verbal directions if you describe the process step-by-step. Make an art project with him or her and let the child feel your hands as you create together. Describe the actions you see and the materials you use with words the child can understand. A child with a visual disability may enjoy art projects that he or she can feel, such as threading yarn through large holes or working with textured fabrics. Talk to the parents about the child's capabilities. With some imagination, alternative art projects can be designed if needed.

A child with a visual disability is expected to behave with the same courtesy as a sighted child. Expect cooperation and respect as you are cooperative and respectful—the same as for a sighted child.

What to say. A sighted person can still say "see" or "look" to a blind person. Some will say they are having a "look" when they feel an object.

Other students may have questions about the disability. Encourage the child to answer questions if he or she would like. If the child feels uncomfortable say, "Everyone sees differently. Julie doesn't see the way we do." The other children will grow comfortable around the child with a visual disability if you are confident and do not treat the child anxiously or differently. Encourage interaction so that the other children will become more comfortable and confident in dealing with the visually impaired child.

Tools to Help a Child Who Is Visually Impaired

Large print. A partially sighted child may be able to read large-print materials. If the child does not have a large-print Bible, perhaps the class or church can donate one to the child. The American Bible Society sells large-print New Testaments and Bibles in several versions. A photocopier can enlarge existing activity sheets, or retype activity sheets into a computer and print out sheets with large print.

Braille and audiocassettes. Some charitable organizations provide free Braille Bibles and Scripture portions to the visually impaired. The Bible is also available in audiocassettes, CD-ROMs and mp3 downloads.

Three-dimensional teaching aids. If the class is discussing an item such as a scroll, clay tablet, animals or well, make a sample from clay or play dough. The child can "see" the item through touch and learn more than by simply hearing a description. Sighted children will also enjoy touching and looking at the object!

Canes and guide dogs. A child who uses a cane and/or guide dog has been educated on how to use such aids, so you will not need to help the child with these items. Instruct your class that the cane is a tool, not a toy. Likewise, a guide dog is working and is not to be petted unless the child gives permission. Guide dogs are housebroken and trained to be calm around strangers, so you do not need to worry about the dog's behavior.

Storytelling

Everyone is a storyteller. Storytelling is how people communicate important, heartfelt information. Whether it is a promotion at work, moving into a new house, getting engaged or a child's hitting the winning Little League home run, we all love a good story—and when we are "full of" a good story, we're eager to tell it!

Storytelling is how the Bible was written. For centuries, stories of the patriarchs and matriarchs were handed down from parent to child. After the resurrection and ascension of Jesus Christ, His followers preached about Him through telling His stories until the New Testament Scriptures were completed. When a teacher tells a Bible story, he or she is continuing in the grand tradition of the ancient storytellers who passed on God's Word. It's a responsibility and a privilege.

TIPS FOR EFFECTIVE STORYTELLING

Know the material. Study the story. Understand the main theme, know the central characters, research the setting if needed and be able to answer questions about it. (Remember how important it is to be "full of your story!") As you read the story, focus on finding the answers to these questions: Who is the main character(s)? Where does the story take place? Does this setting need to be explained to the students? What elements of this story (characters, objects, feelings, actions, etc.) are similar to the experiences of your children? How does this story illustrate the lesson aims? What one Bible truth do you want children to remember and use during the week?

Additional questions to ask: What is the conflict in the story? Every good story has a conflict and a problem to be solved (Joseph is in jail, the soldiers are chasing the Israelites leaving Egypt, Paul is arrested, the lame man can't get into the pool, etc.). How is the problem solved? How is God involved with solving the problem? How are the characters' lives changed?

Use words familiar to the children. Rephrase Bible passages that children may not understand. Avoid talking down to children. Use modern language, not "thee" and "thou." Consult a children's Bible for easy-to-understand vocabulary if you have no curriculum resources.

No need to memorize. It is not essential to recite the story exactly as written in the Bible or your curriculum manual. While you should always have your Bible open to the story reference, storytelling is more interesting and spontaneous when the teacher doesn't read from a page. Telling rather than reading makes the presentation more natural and exciting. Reading the story from a book keeps your face buried in the pages and unable to look at the children. This is why preparation is essential: The better one knows the story, the less one needs notes. Know the plot points well enough to get back on track if the story digresses.

Practice, practice, practice! Many people feel uneasy about storytelling simply because they have little experience speaking to a group. Skills and confidence are built by repetition. Practice the story at home in front of a mirror. Tell it to your own family. Record the story on tape and listen back for improvements. One can always erase a bad tape!

Be bold. Bring the story to life through dramatic gestures, movement, and facial expressions. "Larger than life" and "over the top" are good rules when telling a story. Feel free to emphasize words, be expressive, even look silly. Vary your voice—loud in some spots and soft in others. Some people use different voices for various characters, although this is not essential.

Be confident. Have faith in the story. Bible stories are powerful because they contain God's Word for today's people. Be enthusiastic. Think about how excited people get when telling about their children or accomplishments. Carry that same energy into biblical storytelling. If you are "full of" and interested in the story, the children will be, too! Maintain eye contact with children.

Be relevant. Show why the story is important for today. The Bible is not a collection of 2,000-year-old fairy tales that are read for entertainment. Draw parallels between the story and children's lives. In the Joseph story from Genesis, discuss sibling rivalry and family relations in the children's homes. For Noah and the flood, ask how students might feel if they were teased for doing the right thing.

INVOLVE CHILDREN IN STORYTELLING

Children learn by doing! Incorporate the children into storytelling. This is particularly beneficial for children who already know the story and may feel bored by retelling.

Act it out. Have students pantomime or dramatize the story as it is told. Students may use puppets, hold up pictures or put felt figures on a flannel board. If a student already knows the story, let him or her tell the story for the class or assist you with the telling. Invite a student to retell the story in his or her own words. Play "What happened next?" with a child who is familiar with the story: "And Moses came down the mountain. What happened next, Jake? What did he see?"

Sound effects. Have children make appropriate sounds when they hear a cue word. They can make animal sounds when they hear an animal's name. They can gurgle for "river," stomp their feet for "walk" or "march" or say "grumble grumble" when characters are tired or hungry. Look through the story for repetitive words or ideas and think of sounds the children can make. This keeps children alert and listening so as not to miss a cue.

Use the Bible. Have students look up the story in the Bible. This familiarizes students with the books of the Bible and shows that the stories are not made up. Even young children can find chapters and verses with some help and even locate the name of a Bible story character.

Research. Older children look up unfamiliar words in a Bible dictionary, locate cities in a Bible atlas, and read more about characters in a Bible encyclopedia. Let the children find more information on the Internet or dramatize the story by making a home video.

Teacher's Role

Your role in children's ministry may well be a child's only or primary source of Christian education. The majority of adults who are active in church began as children in Sunday School. This is where children learn the Bible, and most important of all, it's the place where many children encounter God and make a personal commitment to Jesus Christ. Whether you teach in Sunday School, Saturday-night service or midweek program, you are following in the tradition of Jesus who taught the little children.

It's been said that the Church is only one generation away from extinction. The church will continue to survive and grow only when the children and youth receive a solid foundation in faith. Therefore, in this important ministry, do all you can to arrange a warm and open learning environment, present the gospel and show Christian love.

IN-CLASS RESPONSIBILITIES

Before class. Arrange with your supervisor for room repairs and replace furniture if needed. Decorate the room with appropriate posters, pictures and learning aids. Have the needed amount of student books, Bibles, name tags and learning supplies on hand. Contact your supervisor when more curriculum or supplies are needed.

Be punctual and dependable. Keep track of the schedule and know when it is time to teach. Arrive 10 to 15 minutes early so that learning materials are in place before the first child arrives. Arrange for a substitute (or follow the approved procedure in your church) as soon as possible if an absence is unavoidable.

Prepare the lesson with reading, study and prayer. Plan learning activities with other teachers and assistants. Try new teaching techniques and ideas.

Warmly greet the children as they arrive and learn their names. Assist them with coats, if needed. Show the restrooms to visitors. Start each child on a discovery activity as the class begins.

During class. Present engaging learning activities with enthusiasm. Give attention to students who may not be interested or who learn more slowly. Be sensitive to the needs of children with learning or physical disabilities or those who may feel uncomfortable in the group.

Use all the teaching tools provided with your curriculum to fulfill the lesson objectives. Plan to share personal examples to help connect the Bible story with the children's lives. Encourage teamwork, sharing and honesty among the children. Help children plan specific ways to apply the lesson's Bible truths to their daily lives, so they can grow in their Christian faith.

At the end of each lesson, evaluate student learning and progress. Use the lesson aims provided in your curriculum to help you know if lesson goals were accomplished. Adjust future learning plans to make better use of your class time and to better meet the needs of your students.

Love each child and listen to his or her joys and concerns. Model God's love and enthusiastically show your love for God and His Word.

OUT-OF-CLASS RESPONSIBILITIES

Follow up on visitors and absentees with e-mail, postcards and phone calls.

Engage in daily personal devotion time of prayer, Bible study and meditation. One who leads other to Jesus must first be walking with Christ. Regularly pray for each child and your coteachers. Pray also for guidance and wisdom in teaching. Participate in an adult class,

Bible study or prayer group for personal enrichment and regeneration.

Pray for other teachers and assistants and make suggestions of possible teachers to your supervisor. At least two adults should be present during any class session. This way, one adult can handle an emergency while the other adult continues the lesson.

Participate in teacher training events, workshops, seminars and retreats. Ask if the church will provide teachers with subscriptions to Christian education magazines or provide teacher resource books for the church library. As experience is gained, assist rookie teachers as they enter the ministry.

Get to know the children, their families and their school life. Find out their interests, sports, hobbies and needs. Identify unchurched families and encourage their participation in church life. Assist the church in promoting and publicizing the education ministry. Provide news updates and articles for the church newsletter and letters to parents.

Some teachers may feel overwhelmed at the many tasks asked of teachers. Take heart! Many of God's great heroes felt the same way. Moses, Gideon and others hesitated when God called them to do great things in His name. When God calls, God prepares. Jesus promised His disciples that when He left them, they would not be alone. God sends the Holy Spirit to all believers for guidance and support. God gives His grace to teachers who seek Him and who strive to accomplish His will among children.

In return for the teachers' hard work, the church in turn provides prayer, support, curriculum, teaching aids, learning supplies, problem solving, recruitment and acknowledgement for a ministry done well.

Teacher's Vision:
Why We Teach Kids

Adults send messages to kids all the time—by their behavior.

Sometimes these messages discourage kids,

demean their worth or diminish their hope.

But a teacher who arrives week after week

to faithfully love and look at, smile and listen to kids,

sends messages through behavior, too. Those messages say:

"You are important to me and to God. I choose to spend time with you."

"Your opinions and feelings matter to me because who you are matters to God."

"You are valuable—not someday, but now. You are not a problem to me.

You are God's gift. I am glad you are here!"

Where else in the world can a disheartened kid find such affirmation?

What better way could a lonely kid

find the welcome, acceptance and love that is in Christ?

This is how God's kingdom comes—week after week, building life upon life.

To become faithful givers of such cheerful loving and patient teaching,

we must surrender ourselves to the love of God in Jesus Christ.

Only He can empower us to love unselfishly, consistently and genuinely—

so that what we do sends the message that is truly from His heart.

Then our behavior will say that even without monetary compensation,

without applause or appreciation, we choose to love them

purely because we value them for who they are,

because we know Jesus loves them

and because we know

eternity would not be complete without their shining faces.

We humans first learn through what we experience. As children, we begin as concrete thinkers; that is, we understand what we see, touch, taste and experience. It is through living (not listening!) that we come to understand what life is about. As we gather more experiences, these experiences create a unique frame of reference by which we then process and understand new ideas.

We cannot see God. We cannot experience the kind of life people experienced in Bible times. So how then is it possible for children to learn about God or understand the Bible concepts of salvation, sin, prayer, love, faith and patience? Although those who study children say that until around 12 years of age children are not fully able to think in abstract terms, it is during this same "pre-abstract" time of life that most people report having begun a personal relationship with Christ! So the ability to absorb and act on abstract ideas is related to the work of the Holy Spirit, to a child's developing ability and to a teacher's ability to make those abstract concepts understood.

To teach an abstract idea most effectively, it is best to link it to a child's previous experiences and insights. The child then builds understanding of how the abstract information relates to his or her life. This process develops mental "hooks" upon which he or she may "hang" the new information. This means the information is more likely to be categorized, understood and remembered! Jesus taught this way through His parables: He began with experiences and items that were familiar to His hearers. Then He incorporated (new) abstract ideas in ways that His hearers could absorb and understand.

The biggest pitfall in teaching abstract concepts is our adult inclination to use words that we ourselves often don't understand! Terms like "the presence of Christ" or "communion of the saints" need to be put into words that can be understood by anyone. (This is often as big a difficulty for new adult believers as it is for children.) If we cannot put the idea into plain words, it is time to use the Bible, a children's dictionary and a children's Bible resource to find simple and direct words that will describe the idea. Using curriculum written for the age of child you are teaching will also help you gain language that is clear and direct. This method works with any term or concept you present. Think through what the words mean; use words that mean what they say. Avoid symbolic language, which often confuses rather than clarifies ideas; be simple, clear and direct. (You'll probably find yourself telling parables of your own to help children gain the hooks they need to hang onto new ideas!)

Because the ability to absorb abstract ideas is a unique developmental process, some younger elementary children will understand abstract ideas such as "being kind as Jesus was," especially when the teacher links the idea to children's life situations and gives examples that help them understand. When children indicate interest in becoming members of God's family, avoid using terms such as "Jesus in my heart" or "born again." Because many children do still think quite literally and concretely, it is better to talk about "joining God's family," helping a child begin with something familiar and understood—a family—to gain understanding of the abstract concept of salvation.

This ability to think in abstract terms develops at a unique pace all throughout childhood. While older elementary children will be far more able to talk about the overall concepts and principles of Bible stories and Bible verses, do remember that even at this age, they have a far more limited frame of reference than what their sophisticated exteriors may indicate!

Each of us moves through our path of intellectual development in as much of an individual way as we do in any other area. God is tirelessly at work to bring us into closer relationship with Himself and knows each of us intimately. Whatever the individual point of completely understanding the abstract, never forget that we present Jesus most effectively to children when our actions speak louder than our words: We teach God's love by showing it! As we listen, encourage and make each child feel loved and cared for, God's love is communicated in concrete, tangible ways through our joy, excitement and loving actions that create an *experience* of the *abstract* that teaches any child at any age!

Each generation faces its own unique challenges. Children today are growing up in a world different from the environment their parents knew. Yet children still process information and deal with life in predictably childlike ways. Understanding how a child sees the world today will help us meet the child's needs.

CHARACTERISTICS OF A CHILD'S WORLD TODAY

1. A child's world is sometimes scary. Children now live in a post-September 11 and post-Columbine world of fear and danger. Some children enter their school buildings through metal detectors and past police officers. Even at school, children are no longer safe from guns or drugs. A child may live in a neighborhood plagued by gang violence. Child abuse and abductions are common headlines. While most children will never experience such extreme tragedy, even small communities are not immune from calamity. The church should be a safe haven where a child feels protected.

2. A child's world is full of information. With cable TV, MTV, the Internet, magazines, videocassettes and DVDs, children are exposed to a wealth of information, including material too sophisticated for young minds. Fashion styles, fads and music change at lightning speed. What's in today is out tomorrow and impressionable children struggle to be cool and acceptable. With this media exposure, children are tempted to talk, dress and behave like adult or teenaged role models in ways inappropriate for their age. They mimic adults without understanding their actions. Although a child may try to act mature, his or her young mind is still that of a child. The church can minister to children by providing a sanctuary from the constant barrage of news and peer pressure that can overwhelm them.

3. A child's world is techno-savvy. DVDs, CDs, video game systems, cell phones, computers and other technology are a way of life for today's children. Even preschoolers can load and turn on a VCR. However, this high-tech lifestyle may often result in low-touch relationships, as children communicate more through instant messaging and cell phones rather than face-to-face encounters. The church is an "unplugged" place where cell phones are turned off and the focus is placed on children's experience of genuine, firsthand relationships.

4. A child's world is geocentric. "It's all about me." The younger the child, the more deeply the child is the center of his or her universe. Infants use this survival technique to command the parent's attention and get food or care. Even to children of elementary age, the most important time to a child is what is happening to him or her now. Children are unconcerned with long-ago events that occurred to other people, and they have little awareness of the future. A 2,000-year-old book about a faraway land with strange customs is meaningful only as far as it directly affects the child's life today. The church can be a place where adults model and teach how to move beyond self-centeredness to identify and respond to the needs of others, as well as to live out what the Bible teaches.

5. A child's world is full of imagination. Children love fantasy and make-believe! They relish hearing stories and playing creatively. Children are constantly active and have short attention spans. They are just beginning to develop their ability to reason logically and are unable to make sense of complex doctrinal arguments. The wise church helps children learn through activities that engage their bodies and all of their senses as well as their minds.

6. A child's world is diverse. No community is homogenous anymore. Children have friends and classmates of all races and ethnic backgrounds. They know schoolmates with physical and cognitive challenges. There is no longer a one-size-fits-all model of family life. Children may live with two parents, one parent, a stepparent, a relative, foster parents, parents of different races or same-gender parents. The church classroom is a place where children of all backgrounds can learn and play together because every child is valued and loved.

TIPS FOR COMMUNICATING BETWEEN THEIR WORLD AND OURS

1. Know the children. With such diversity among students, it's essential for teachers to know about the children's home lives, especially those who come from difficult situations and need extra care. Teachers may also want to pay attention to the music and media fads that interest students so that they know why a child dresses like the latest pop star or is fascinated by a particular sports figure.

2. Listen to children. Children love to talk about themselves and share their interests and concerns. A student with a troubled family life needs a caring adult role model. All students are more likely to remember the teacher who lent an empathetic ear more than the story the teacher told during class. The relationships built at church will last a lifetime and keep a child involved in the church family.

3. Praise the children. Sunday School is perhaps the only school children attend where they are not graded or given a test! The emphasis in Christian education is not in getting the right answer but in getting a right relationship with God in Jesus Christ. A child may not remember long Bible verses or make the prettiest art project, but he or she will remember the teacher as a loving adult. Look for the positive in each child. Effective teachers at church find ways to affirm and support their students.

Transition

Transition times are those moments when one activity ends and the next one begins. It can also be when students move from one room to another, when the class begins and when it ends. Transitions can be noisy and chaotic as children put away items, stand up, sit down, move around and shift from being active to quiet. Since an elementary class has many activities, transition times occur frequently. Your challenge is to smoothly move energetic children out of and into the activities with a minimal amount of noise and disruption.

Know the schedule. Be prepared for what's next on the schedule. If you don't know the next activity, your students will quickly become disruptive. If you begin the wrong activity by mistake, go ahead and finish it. Stopping in the middle and starting something new is even more disruptive.

Plan the schedule well. Children may find it hard to end a fast-moving game to suddenly be still for prayer time. Likewise, after a tiring game they may not have the energy to listen to a long story or do serious thinking. If possible, have a time for a "cool down" activity right after a hectic game to give children time to settle down.

Be prepared. Have all the necessary items (art supplies, Bibles, game equipment, etc.) stored in the classroom where they can be easily found. Be sure that supply cabinets and closets are unlocked or that the teacher has a key on hand. Children can get out of hand if the teacher has to stop and look for supplies or has to leave the room to get something.

Schedule adequate time. Children may not want to stop what they're doing because they haven't finished their art project or they are having too much fun at games. Set aside sufficient time for cleanup. If possible, make a sample art project at home to determine the needed time. If the children are enjoying a game, allow a few extra minutes to play it a second time. It's better to omit one or two activities than to cram in too much.

If one activity runs too long, readjust a new activity so that there is sufficient time to finish it.

However, children can get bored if too much time is spent waiting after a project is completed. If the children finish an art project quickly or lose interest in the game, move on to something new. It's better to end an activity while child interest is high.

Make it a game. If the children are slow getting started on the next activity, turn it into a fun challenge. Use a timer to test their speed and give a small reward when the class beats its best time. Mark the times on a chart so that children can see their improvement.

Give warnings. Children may not want to abruptly stop what they're doing. Give advanced notice a few minutes before it's time to move on. Younger children may not comprehend "five more minutes," so give concrete warnings they understand: "You can run the relay one more time." "We'll sing the song one more time."

Make use of signals. Use hand gestures, ring a bell, flick the lights on and off or sing a special song to indicate transition time. Use a different signal for crafts, cleanup, music, storytelling, games, end of class, etc. When the children see or hear the signal, they know what activity is coming up. Have children take turns giving the signal.

Give individual attention. Rather than shouting orders to the entire class, speak to individual students. This reduces the noise and children are more likely to hear and understand the directions.

Have special spaces. Mark off areas of the room for different activities. When it's story time, the children know to move to a certain area, perhaps a rug where they can sit. When it's art time, they walk to the art table. The teacher does not need to spend time with explanations.

Give directions, and then move. Children may have difficulty focusing on your directions when they're moving or walking. Give instructions while children are seated or standing quietly, and then allow them to move after everyone has understood and asked questions.

Plan how to line up. It's good to have an interesting plan for lining up so that students don't push and shove to get in front. Students can line up by age, by height, by the color of their clothes or by the schools they attend. However, vary the plan. Tall children and the oldest don't always want to be at the end of the line. If there's a large group, line up a few at a time by small groups, rows or tables.

Lead quiet treks. At times the class may need to move outside the classroom to the outdoors, the sanctuary or the kitchen. Children may want to talk and giggle while they walk or leave the group. This can disrupt other classes meeting in the building.

To keep children from talking, make it a game as well. "Let's see who can be the most quiet and tiptoe to the next room." Have children pretend they're walking through a jungle and they don't want to disturb the wild animals, or lead children in a game of Follow the Leader to keep their attention while moving from one place to another.

Avoid using punitive methods: "Anyone talking won't get a cookie!" This creates bad feelings and dampens student enthusiasm.

If children need to walk a long way and there is no need to be quiet (such as when walking outdoors or when nobody else is nearby), have the children sing or chant a verse as they walk. Lead children in a rhythmic pattern of clapping and finger snapping to help keep their hands busy and prevent pushing and shoving.

Be ready at the start. It's easier to begin class if students are immediately involved in a discovery activity when they enter the classroom. This puts their minds in learning mode. Create excitement for the class: "See how many of these hidden cards you can find." "Try out these experiments at the table."

Plan a routine ending. During class time, children not only need variety but also like to be part of routines. Have a standard dismissal practice: Sing a song, say a prayer, eat a snack. Use the same pattern each time so that students get a sense of closure. Think of a calm and orderly activity which will enable arriving parents to find their children easily.

An effective class builds strong bonds between its students; however, this bond may be so tight that a new child can feel unwelcome. Students and teachers used to seeing the same faces each week may give a new child the feeling that they consider him or her an intruder. Teachers need to be extra attentive to the needs of new children, for their presence gives the class the chance to practice what they have learned!

The new child is already feeling uncomfortable walking into the class. He or she may have just moved into the area or the parents may be looking for a church home. The child may also be from an unchurched family cautiously trying out the church or a one-time guest in town to visit relatives. Your challenge is to make the child feel at home and invite the other students to welcome the new child.

Good preparation and a warm welcome will help make a visitor comfortable and eager to return another time. For a child not raised in the church, the routines of Sunday School and other church programs can be strange. Love, attention and guidance will ease their fear and discomfort.

A GOOD BEGINNING

Warmly greet each visitor and introduce yourself as he or she enters the classroom. If parents bring the child, introduce yourself to the parents as well. Ask the parents if the child has any special medical needs. Tell the parents when the child's class will end and invite the parents to attend an adult class or worship service. (Note: Some churches provide a central check-in place where visiting children are registered.)

Visitors may feel self-conscious if they are the only ones with name tags, so avoid using name tags unless every child wears one. Invite parents to stay for a short time if the child is having difficulty leaving them.

Take a moment to introduce the visitor to one or two buddies of the same gender. Introduce these children as the ones who will help the new child find his or her way around the room and guide the visitor in the class routine. The new child will feel that he or she has at least one friend already!

DURING CLASS

Invite a visitor to participate in class activities, but don't overdo the attention. You may be tempted to gush over a new child, but keep in mind that visitors don't like to be pointed out or given undue attention.

Because a new child may feel uncomfortable sharing books with strangers, always have extra activity sheets, Bibles and other class supplies on hand.

Your students may be used to lining up in a certain way or sitting around the table in the same chairs. To make it easier for newcomers to fit in, have a "visitor's spot" always available. This is an empty chair reserved for guests and a place in the line where newcomers can stand. A new child won't want to compete with other students for a place in line or a chair.

Allow the visitor to participate in discussion as much as he or she wishes, but don't expect it. A new child won't know what has been taught in previous sessions and may know little about the Bible. Avoid calling on the visitor to answer a fact-based question; however, an open-ended question ("How do you feel . . .") can be appropriate. Call the new child by name, but avoid referring to him or her as "our guest" or "the visitor" after the initial class introduction. The child doesn't need a constant reminder that he or she is not one of the group.

Be attentive if the new child needs help; however, don't hover over him or her. If the guest needs assistance, move near the child and speak quietly so as not to draw attention. A new child may not be able to find verses in the Bible, so help the child and the child's buddy find passages.

An unchurched child may feel awkward during prayer time. Indicate that it's all right for children not to be an active participant: "Now it's time to pray. That's when we talk to God. Some of us might want to pray aloud. Others of us might pray silently. Some of us may want to listen to other people pray. Whatever you choose is fine."

AFTER CLASS

Be sure a visiting child leaves with all his or her belongings. Nobody wants to return to church to go to the lost and found office! If parents are late to pick up the child, stay with the child until they arrive. Never let a child wander through the building alone. Greet the parents as they arrive, and briefly mention an activity that the class enjoyed. Thank the parents for bringing their son or daughter to your class and let them know you look forward to seeing the child again. Inform parents about any routines related to children's programming at your church (children attend worship services for the first 10 minutes and then leave for age-level activities, children's choir or midweek club meeting, etc.). Within a day or two, send a postcard to the guest, thanking him or her for visiting your class.

Visual Aids

"Seeing is believing," the old saying goes. Exciting, colorful visual aids enhance classroom teaching and spark interest. When you carefully select and use visual aids, the Bible concepts you present will make an impact students will remember.

CHOOSING VISUAL AIDS

What's needed? Select from a variety of visual aids: pictures, posters, banners, graphs, maps, flags, flannelgraphs, pop-up books and sculptures. If available, use slides, overhead transparencies, PowerPoint programs, videos and DVDs. Look at what will be most appropriate and cost effective for your classroom. Perhaps several classrooms can share the more expensive equipment.

The purpose of a visual aid is to attract attention, stimulate interest, reinforce the lesson aim, illustrate a difficult concept or help students remember a point. Avoid visual aids that only repeat what you state verbally or are merely an outline of your presentation.

Update as needed. Some churches reuse old visual aids long past their expiration dates. Take a look at the visual aids provided to you. Do they look relevant to modern children? Are the figures dressed in outdated clothing? Do the aids depict a variety of ethnic types and people with disabilities? Are the aids worn out, dirty or torn? Talk with your supervisor about replacing unusable visuals aids as needed.

Consider what is age appropriate. For younger children, use visual aids with simple drawings and a limited amount of writing. A visual aid with too much visual clutter or extraneous detail will confuse, not illuminate. Older children will not enjoy pop-up books, flannelgraphs, pictures of children much younger than themselves or anything that seems too childish.

Keep it simple. A flashy visual aid can be appealing but may have little substance. A visual aid does not need to be elaborate or expensive to make an impact. A visual aid does little good if the children remember how great it looked rather than the message it taught.

Think three-dimensionally. Visual aids aren't limited to flat pictures. Artwork can include sculpture, fabric, stained glass, ceramic, clay or metal. Any object can be used in teaching, including a plant or animal. Be imaginative and creative.

Limit video and/or DVD viewing. Many children already spend a great deal of time passively watching television. At church, children need to be engaged in active learning that stimulates their minds. While the occasional use of a short video clip can be beneficial, avoid using videos frequently or running a video for the entire class session. Always follow up video viewing with a discussion that moves students from passivity to activity.

When using commercially produced videos or DVDs, first check on copyright laws. Some home videos cannot be shown outside the home unless a fee is paid to cover commercial use. Do not assume that it's OK to use a commercial product at a church.

USING VISUAL AIDS

Proper displays. When using a picture during story time, make sure it is at the proper height for smaller children to see. For a large group, let children in the front sit on the floor and students in the back can sit on chairs. Make sure that furniture or pillars do not block sight lines.

Don't make holding a visual aid cumbersome. Put large pictures or posters on an easel or the chalk tray of a chalkboard. This frees up your hands to gesture and point, and you don't need to worry about dropping the picture.

Use a pointer or penlight flashlight for emphasis. Pointers will draw in student attention and keep children focused.

When using flannelgraph figures, practice using them several times so that the figures can be easily moved and removed when needed. As much as possible, learn the story so that you do not need to consult notes while talking.

Avoid hiding behind a visual aid or letting it do the teaching. Visual aids are no substitute for a well-prepared, energetic, loving teacher. When using a visual aid, ask questions, maintain eye contact and interact with the students. Watch for signs of boredom or confusion.

Handmade visual aids. Children will enjoy making posters or banners for display. Banner kits are available with the materials ready to put together, or students may want to draw and cut out their own designs. A gifted artist in the class may be willing to make a drawing or painting for the class. Children are more engaged when the visual aid has a personal attachment.

High-tech pitfalls. While high-tech visual aids can be dazzling, the equipment can also break down or be difficult to use. Come in early to set up and check that the equipment is running properly. Learn how to use the equipment and prepare for emergencies. Keep spare projection bulbs on hand. Have overhead transparencies in order and right-side up. Keep equipment away from chalk dust, paint and dirt. Have videos and DVDs cued and in place. Practice a PowerPoint presentation so that the program can be presented without problems. When using an overhead projector or PowerPoint, be sure there is a screen or a large blank wall space where the images can be seen clearly. Turn off equipment when finished so that equipment noise or blank screens do not distract children. Have a plan B if the computer crashes or the electricity goes out. Allow only trained individuals to use the equipment.

Videos/DVDs. Carefully selected video clips can be useful supplements to your lessons. Use a video when no other visual aid can make the same impact. A video can show life in Bible times: people farming, fishing, baking. Videos can give students a virtual tour of the Holy Land and bring the Bible to life. Some videos depict heroes and heroines of Church history. Younger children can enjoy singing along with children's music videos.

Avoid "talking head" videos; that is, a video of someone giving a long speech or sermon. Such videos are dull for children to watch. Never use a video as a time filler, to settle rowdy children or as a reward for good behavior.

Miniposters

Photocopy these miniposters onto bright paper. Display them in classrooms, hallways, supply or resource storage areas and offices as reminders of key points about children's ministry.

The miniposters can also be made into transparencies for use in teacher training meetings.

THE BEST TEACHERS LISTEN MORE THAN THEY TALK.

238

The child who is hardest to love needs love the most.

Ready or not, the class begins when the first child arrives.

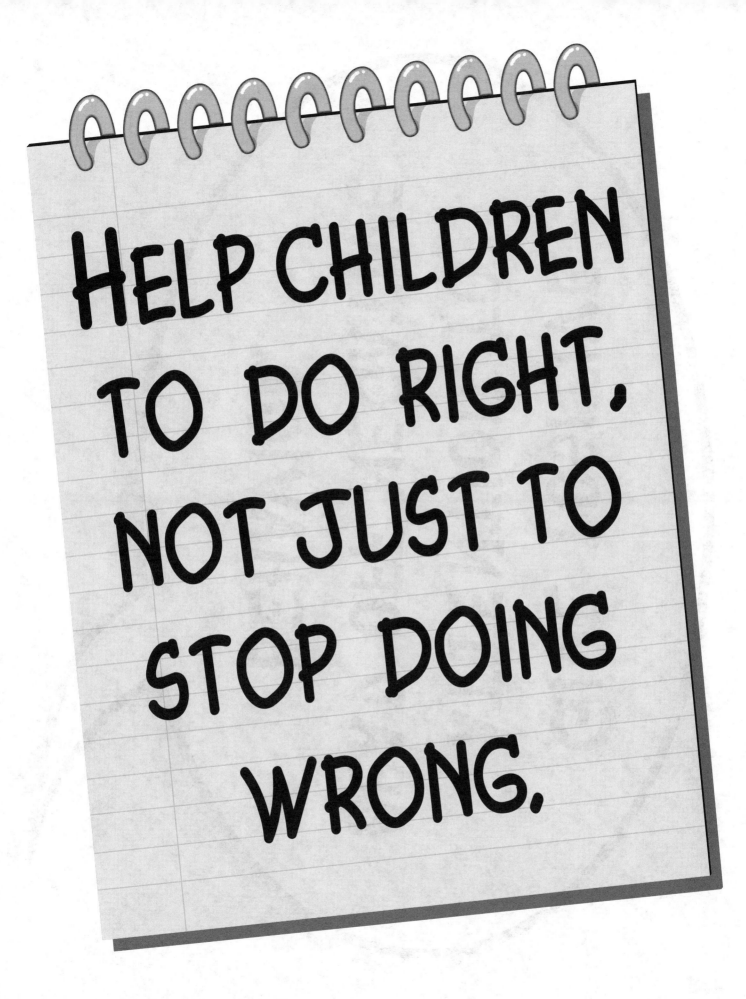

GIVE POSITIVE ATTENTION TO HEAD OFF NEGATIVE BEHAVIOR.

SET A FEW BASIC RULES PHRASED IN POSITIVE WORDS.

MODEL FOR CHILDREN THE KIND OF RESPECT YOU WANT THEM TO SHOW.

TALK ABOUT WAYS YOU SEE CHILDREN PUTTING GOD'S WORD INTO ACTION.

Welcome to our Resource Room.

If you borrow it, please return it.

If you spill it, please clean it up.

If you empty it, please leave a note.

If you need help, please ask.

5 BASIC GUIDELINES
FOR TEACHERS

 1 Always have two teachers in every classroom.

 2 Greet every child with a smile and a safe, loving touch.

 3 Place yourself at a childs eye level to talk with him or her.

 4 Use a child's name often to ensure attention.

 5 Use positive discipline (tell children what they may do, not just what they may not do).

Adapt this sample poster to your own church's needs and policies.
Post one in each classroom for easy reference.

Using the CD-ROM

Contained on the *Children's Ministry Smart Pages* CD-ROM are three file formats:

1. **JPG**—JPG files are clip-art images that **must be imported** into your word-processing or page-layout application.

2. **PDF**—PDF files are awards, certificates, etc. They can be printed as is via Adobe Acrobat Reader, or saved as EPS files and imported into most slide-show, word-processing and page-layout applications.

1. **RTF**—RTF files are modifiable text files (no images). These files can be opened within your word-processing or page-layout application. Use these text files to create and print customized versions of files.

JPG Instructions

Important Notes: You cannot open these files directly. These files may be too large for certain applications to be able to show you a preview.

Here's what to do:

1. Open the application you wish to use.

2. Open an existing document or create a new document.

3. Paste (import) the JPG into the document.

4. Enlarge or reduce the image according to your needs. (For specific instructions on how to use the image within your application, refer to your application manual.)

PDF Instructions

Important Notes: PDF files can be opened and printed by using Adobe Acrobat Reader software. PDF files on this CD-ROM cannot be modified via Adobe Acrobat Reader. You can download the most recent version of Acrobat Reader for free from the Adobe website, http://www.adobe.com/products/acrobat/readstep2.html.

Note: Pages can be printed individually by indicating so in the Print dialogue box.

RTF Instructions

Important Note: You should not open these files directly. It is better to open the files from within the application you will use to edit the files.

Rich Text Format (RTF) are modifiable text files. Most word-processing applications, including Microsoft Word and WordPerfect, are able to read and edit RTF documents. Use these text files to create and print customized versions of documents.

Here's what to do:

1. Open the application you wish to use.

2. From within the application, open the file you wish to modify.

3. You can now edit the document.

4. Save the document in the standard document format of the application that you are using.

Problems?

If you have any problems that you can't solve by reading the manual that came with your word-processing or page-layout application, please call the number for the technical support department printed in your software manual. (Sorry, but Gospel Light cannot provide software support.)

Index